Cookbook companion to the bestseller *The Great Cholesterol Myth*

Recipes & Meal Plans That Prevent Heart Disease— Naturally

THE GREAT CHOLESTEROL MYTH
COOKBOOK

Jonny Bowden, PH.D., C.N.S.
Stephen T. Sinatra, M.D., F.A.C.C., F.A.C.N., C.N.S.
RECIPES BY Deirdre Rawlings, N.D., PH.D.

FAIR WINDS
PRESS
BEVERLY, MASSACHUSETTS

© 2014 Fair Winds Press

Text © 2014 Jonny Bowden, Stephen T. Sinatra, and Deirdre Rawlings

First published in the USA in 2014 by
Fair Winds Press, a member of
Quayside Publishing Group
100 Cummings Center
Suite 406-L
Beverly, MA 01915-6101
www.fairwindspress.com
Visit www.QuarrySPOON.com and help us celebrate food and culture one spoonful at a time!

18 17 16 15 14   3 4 5

ISBN: 978-1-59233-590-9

Digital edition published in 2014
eISBN: 978-1-61058-883-6

Library of Congress Cataloging-in-Publication Data available

Cover and page design by Mattie Reposa Graphic Design & Illustration
Book layout by Claire MacMaster, Barefoot Art Graphic Design

Printed and bound in United States

The information in this book is for educational purposes only. It is not intended to replace the advice of a physician or medical practitioner. Please see your health care provider before beginning any new health program.

DEDICATION

Jonny Bowden:
For Jade and Zoe
And their Mom.
I love you.

Stephen Sinatra:
To Jan,
You have been a great inspiration in my life.
I love you.

Deirdre Rawlings:
For my mother Jeanne.
I love you.

CONTENTS

Introduction 5

Section 1: How to Live Free of Heart Disease

CHAPTER 1 **THE WRONGFUL DEMONIZATION OF SATURATED FAT** 10

CHAPTER 2 **HORMONES 101** 23

CHAPTER 3 **THE CASE AGAINST SUGAR** 34

CHAPTER 4 **THE TRUTH ABOUT GRAINS** 42

CHAPTER 5 **FOODS FOR A HEALTHY HEART** 52

CHAPTER 6 **SUPPLEMENTS FOR A HEALTHY HEART** 63

Section 2: How to Eat Well for a Long and Healthy Life

CHAPTER SEVEN **100 DELICIOUS AND NUTRITIOUS RECIPES YOUR HEART WILL LOVE** .. 76

A MONTH OF MENU PLANS FOR HEART HEALTH 179

ENDNOTES 182

ACKNOWLEDGMENTS 185

ABOUT THE AUTHORS 187

INDEX 188

INTRODUCTION

What is the great cholesterol myth, anyway? How this book can help you live a heart-healthy life

When our book *The Great Cholesterol Myth* reached best-seller status, people approached us at conferences, in airports, and at numerous events understandably asking us to define, in a nutshell, "the great cholesterol myth."

Definitely a fair question, so here's the short answer:

The great cholesterol myth is the persistent idea that cholesterol is an important—if not the *most* important—measure of risk for heart disease; that we should be spending billions of dollars educating people on how to lower it; and that the drugs given to lower it are by and large safe and effective in multiple populations.

The devil, as they say, is in the details.

Although that makes a great fifteen-second elevator speech, the truth is that numerous doctors and other experts continually perpetuate that myth. After all, what's the number-one reason you've been told to keep your saturated fat intake as low as possible? Because saturated fat has been associated with higher cholesterol levels. (We'll talk more about what that really means in a moment.)

So—and stay with us for a minute now—

if cholesterol is *not* the major risk factor for heart disease,

and *if* the relationship between animal fats and cholesterol was far more complex than we had been taught,

and *if* the effect of animal fats on cholesterol, when accurately measured, was actually *positive*, then dietary recommendations over the past thirty years crumble like a house of cards.

Evidence clearly shows that all of the above are true, as we explained in detail in *The Great Cholesterol Myth*. Cholesterol is not a major risk factor for heart disease, certainly not the most important, and certainly not the one that deserves a four-decade (and counting) pharmaceutical war against it while the real culprits in heart disease get comparatively little attention.

Consider a tsunami. Water is *involved* in tsunamis—you can't have a tsunami without it—but water doesn't *cause* tsunamis, and trying to prevent tsunamis by draining the ocean is a fool's errand. Yet that's kind of the approach we've been taking for forty years when it comes to cholesterol and heart disease. Rather than focusing on the conditions under which cholesterol becomes a problem, we've focused all our attention on the molecule itself. As Dr. Sinatra is fond of saying, "Cholesterol is found at the scene of the crime—but it is *not* the perpetrator."

Which leads us to the obvious question—if cholesterol doesn't cause heart disease, then what does?

THE FOUR RISK FACTORS FOR HEART DISEASE

It's a great question; and the answer is undoubtedly multifactorial and complex, and we are very far from having all the answers. Surely there's some genetic component, not to mention dietary, environmental, hormonal, and lifestyle factors. That said, we believe that four of the major promoters of heart disease are

- Inflammation

- Oxidative damage

- Stress

- Dietary sugar

We also believe that these four factors are far more important than overall cholesterol levels, and that there is a great deal we can do about each one of them. This book is an attempt to tell you how to do just that.

For instance, you can lower stress, cut out sugar, and eat an anti-inflammatory diet. The recipes in this book may not help you lower stress, but they will certainly address the dietary components of heart disease. The foods and recipes in this book are low in sugar, low in inflammatory omega-6 fatty acids, and high in natural anti-inflammatories and antioxidants. (Three out of four ain't bad!) As far as reducing the fourth promoter of heart disease—stress—well, that's beyond the scope of this book, but fortunately, there are many resources in the field of stress management that address that component brilliantly. (We strongly suggest you investigate them.)

The recipes in this book will certainly address the dietary components of heart disease.

ARE WE ANTI-STATIN DRUGS?

Now when we say these things, people often accuse us of being anti-pharmaceutical or anti-drug, or at least anti-statin drugs. What we really oppose is statin *over-use*, and there's a ton of that happening. We oppose using statins in populations in which they have not been tested and could reasonably be expected to do serious harm, such as children.

Drug companies need us to believe that fighting cholesterol is essential to our own personal "homeland security." Why not? Reports show that cholesterol-lowering statin drugs bring manufacturers about $30 billion a year. That success is fueled by the myth that statin drugs save large numbers of lives. Little wonder drug companies fund countless studies, which researchers then write up to highlight a small benefit while hiding some real liabilities.

The use of a legal (but misleading) type of statistic called a *relative statistic* allows drug companies to easily exaggerate benefits. (Unfortunately, relative statistics have now become the *lingua franca* of research reports in general. That doesn't make them any less misleading.)

Here's an example. If you have a 4 in 1,000 chance of getting a disease, and you take a drug that reduces that to a 2 in 1,000 chance, drug manufacturers can tell you this drug cuts your risk by 50 percent! Technically, it does, because 2 is 50 percent of 0.4. But what *really* happened is your chance went down 2/1,000ths (1/500th), from 4/1,000 to 2/1,000.

If you told the average person he'd have a copay of $50 a month to take a drug that decreased his chances of a heart attack by 1/500th but increased his chances for diabetes, muscle pain, loss of libido, memory loss, and nonmalignant skin cancer, how many do you think would say "sign me up!"?

I wouldn't expect to see too many hands going up.

Don't get us wrong: We are not wholly against statin drugs. Dr. Sinatra himself occasionally prescribes them in his practice, largely, if not exclusively, to middle-aged men with existing cardiovascular disease or who've already had a heart attack. This group, which is called a *secondary prevention* cohort, because we're trying to *prevent* a *second* heart attack, is a group in which statins show modest benefit. (They have not shown consistent benefit for *primary* prevention, which means in people who have not had a heart attack and are generally healthy.)

Furthermore, we, like many of our colleagues, believe that whatever modest benefits statin drugs have are *not* because they lower cholesterol (which they do quite well) but because they do two *other* things that are really important: They lower inflammation and they thin the blood.

So what's the big deal? Even if they do just those two things, why don't we just put 'em in the water supply? Because they *also* do a lot of *nasty* things. We can't predict exactly who those nasty things will happen to, but we can tell you that they happen all the time. (Our friend, the renowned Australian cardiologist Ross Walker, M.D., believes that between 20 and 70 percent of people taking statins experience side effects from them.) These side effects range from the mild to the serious and include loss of sex drive, memory impairment, muscle pain, joint pain, and loss of energy.

The coup de grâce is that you can do the two good things statins do—lower inflammation and thin the blood—with far more gentle substances. Fish oil and

> You can lower inflammation quite well with omega-3 fatty acids, which have basically no side effects unless you count improved blood pressure, triglycerides, mood, and appearance as "side effects."

omega-3 fatty acids, curcumin, resveratrol, gamma-tocopherol, and garlic all make gentle but effective blood thinners. You can lower inflammation quite well with omega-3s, which have basically no side effects unless you count improved blood pressure, triglycerides, mood, and appearance as "side effects."

A Personal Note to Our Readers

We want this book to be accessible, practical, and user-friendly. So we've avoided a lot of references to studies and journals. Our purpose here is to be breezy and conversational and to venture into technical terrain as infrequently as we can (unless it's absolutely essential). We want you to use this book not as a reference textbook but as a practical guide to finding answers. About, say, how to protect your heart (and those of the people you love). How to live a long time and stay healthy. Which foods to eat and even which supplements to take. These and other simple habits we discuss will create large, long-term dividends.

In the first section of the book we'll discuss the truth about saturated fat, probably the most demonized food subgroup in food history. You'll also learn something about omega fatty acids, both omega-3s (e.g., fish oil) and omega-6s (e.g., corn oil), and why balancing the two can make a significant difference to your health. We'll also talk about cooking oils—the good, the bad, and the truly ugly (I'm not mentioning names, canola oil).

To really understand what comes afterward—the chapters on sugar and grains—we'll need a short (and, we promise, not-too-eye-glazing) tour into hormone land, with a sharp focus on the crucial hormone *insulin*. When you understand how insulin contributes to the big picture, you can better understand how sugar and grains affect your body.

Warning: It's not a pretty story.

Sugar and grains are the "meat" of the matter (sorry, bad pun). We'll explain their impact in layman's terms—for instance, how sugar breaks down into glucose and fructose—and hopefully you'll understand why sugar creates far more damage to your heart than fat. We'll discuss grains, what they *do*, what they *don't* do, and what to do *about* them.

We think this is important because it will help you to understand our choices of recipe ingredients. If we didn't cover this material in section 1, you might well look at the recipes and ask yourself questions like:

- "Why didn't they use agave nectar? That's healthy, right?"

- "How come so few grains?"
- "I wonder why they use butter and other foods that have saturated fat?"

We'd like you to know the answers to those and other questions you're likely to have, which is the reason for the first part of the book. When you understand the effect various foods have on your system—your hormones, your metabolism, and, yes, your heart—you'll be much more able to appreciate the choices we've made in the recipe section of this book. At least we hope you will!

And speaking of recipes—may we brag a moment, and say they're extraordinary? Put together by master chef Deirdre Rawlings, N.D., Ph.D., who is a traditional naturopath with an advanced degree in nutrition and the author of several books on food—the recipes are not only incredibly heart-healthy, they're also mouth-wateringly delicious. Seriously.

Before we get to the recipes, we'll conclude this section of the book with a discussion of our favorite heart-friendly foods and supplements.

We hope you'll find the information in this book—and in its companion, *The Great Cholesterol Myth*—empowering. Empowering in that it will help you take practical and positive steps to protect your heart and to live a long, healthy life, which is exactly what we want for you—and for ourselves, our families, and our loved ones. Both Dr. Sinatra and I have been fortunate enough to live incredibly rich, productive lives in amazing health, well into our seventh decades and counting. We've done it in large measure by following our own advice, which we present in this book.

And we hope you'll share this advice with your doctors. Not, mind you, in a necessarily adversarial way, but in a collaborative way. Show them *The Great Cholesterol Myth*. Arm yourself with good information. If you have a trusted doctor, then engage him or her in the issues in these books. We think if your doctor looks a little more closely at some myths about cholesterol that we have *all* been sold—doctors *included*—he or she might take a new look at the case against cholesterol.

1 THE WRONGFUL DEMONIZATION OF SATURATED FAT

Why you shouldn't skip the butter, the importance of balancing omega fatty acids, and a guide to cooking oils

The great writer H. L. Mencken once said, "For every complex question, there is a simple answer. And it is always wrong."

If you ask the average doctor why you should avoid saturated fat, he or she will probably tell you this: It raises cholesterol and causes heart disease. Saturated fat has become so demonized that it's next to impossible to find it mentioned in a newspaper or magazine article without being accompanied by the description "artery-clogging."

But what most people—including, probably, your doctor—don't know is that studies have *never* convincingly demonstrated the relationship between saturated fat in the diet and heart disease. (We discussed this subject at length in *The Great Cholesterol Myth*, so we'll keep it brief here.) Two major research review papers—papers that look at the combined findings of many high-quality studies in an attempt to see the big picture—found that the relationship between saturated fat and heart disease was nonexistent: There was no statistically significant relationship between the two. One of these reviews, published in the *American Journal of Clinical Nutrition*, wryly noted in its summary, "Results and conclusions about saturated fat intake in relation to cardiovascular disease

[CVD], from leading advisory committees, do not reflect the available scientific literature." The other, published in the *Journal of Nutrition*, went even further: "There is no significant evidence for concluding that dietary saturated fat is associated with an increased risk of [coronary heart disease] or CVD."

In other words, despite its demonization by health authorities and despite the massive efforts by Big Food to sell you junky, sugar-filled, no-fat products, no evidence exists to support a direct relationship between saturated fat and heart disease. None.

Research *does* show, however, that replacing saturated fat with *carbohydrates* actually *increases* the risk for heart disease. That counterintuitive finding—from a Harvard study, no less—will become much easier to understand when we examine the role of sugar in the diet and in heart disease later on.

WHAT IS SATURATED FAT, ANYWAY?

Fats come in three "flavors": saturated, monounsaturated, and polyunsaturated.

Fats—or more properly, *fatty acids*—are just chains of carbon atoms that are bonded together. The carbons themselves can either "hold hands" with hydrogen atoms or with each other (what chemists call a "double bond"). To avoid some complex biochemistry, I'll describe saturated fat as holding hands with all the hydrogen atoms it possibly can—it is "saturated" with hydrogen atoms and has no double bonds at all. (*Mono*unsaturated fats have *one* double bond; *poly*unsaturated fats have two or more.)

Now, you've probably heard terms like "omega-9," "omega-3," and "omega-6," and wondered what the heck an "omega" is. It's actually simple.

Chemists like to describe fats in terms of real estate—location, location, location. For instance, monounsaturated fats have one double bond, and it's on the ninth carbon—hence, it's known as an omega-9. Easy, right? Polyunsaturated fats have two or more double bonds. If the first double bond is on the third carbon, it's called an omega-3, and if it's on the sixth carbon, it's called an omega-6. There. Now you know.

Far more important than their biochemical makeup, however, is how these fats—these different arrangements of double bonds—function in the body. And, of course, where they're found in the diet.

Monounsaturated fat is predominant in olive oil (as well as in nuts and nut oils, such as macadamia nut oil). Its health benefits have been well documented and aren't at all controversial, which is why we're not going to spend any time on them here.

Monounsaturated fat is the primary fat consumed in the highly touted Mediterranean diet. It's also anti-inflammatory, which is precisely one of the reasons it *is* so healthy. We use it in many of the recipes in this book.

We will, however, later more fully discuss omega-6 and omega-3 fatty acids—the two classes of polyunsaturated fat—because they are major players in our story. For right now, though, let's stay focused on saturated fat.

Saturated fats are primarily found in animal foods, such as meat, cheese, butter, and eggs. A few plant foods such as coconut and palm oil also contain saturated fats. If you've kept coconut oil in your pantry (and I hope you do!), you know how saturated fat behaves. At room temperature, coconut oil becomes solid and hard. During hot weather or when you heat it, however, it softens considerably and even turns into a thick liquid.

Although we certainly don't recommend eating french fries, the lard that restaurants once used to cook these sliced potatoes in, which is predominantly saturated fat, was a far better choice than the cheap, unstable, inflammatory vegetable oils that replaced it.

The molecular nature of fats accounts for their ability to stand up to heat. Much as metals have melting points, fatty acids have "damage points," meaning the point at which they begin to deteriorate or fall apart. When that happens, they turn into something that's far more difficult for the body to use. Some of these damaged molecules become inflammatory. It's not a great situation.

The very nature of polyunsaturated fats such as omega-6s and omega-3s makes them more susceptible to damage, i.e., oxidation from free radicals. When we say fat has gone rancid, that's exactly what we mean— it's become *oxidized,* like if you burned the bottom of your cast-iron skillet and turned it rust-colored.

Saturated fats, however, stand up to heat the best. They don't mutate, or become damaged, as easily as unsaturated fats. In fact, the stability of saturated fat in high heat is one of the reasons that swapping real lard for vegetable oil was a big mistake. Although we certainly don't recommend eating french fries, the lard that restaurants once used to cook these sliced potatoes in, which is predominantly saturated fat, was a far better choice than the cheap, unstable, proinflammatory vegetable oils that replaced it.

So polyunsaturated fats—both omega-3s and omega-6s—such as vegetable oil are far less stable in high heat and become oxidized, i.e., damaged by free radicals. And because oxidative damage is a major promoter of heart disease, oxidation of fats is hardly of minor concern.

Omega-3 fats are the most delicate fats of all, which is why you should never cook with them and why you should store foods that contain them, such as flaxseed and walnuts, in the fridge to prevent oxidation. (Oxidation of fats is one reason fish smells horrible when it goes bad.) Omega-6 fats are sturdier than omega-3s, and you can certainly cook with them. But they have a whole other set of problems. I'll discuss vegetable oil—the main source of omega-6s—in a bit. Right now let's take a closer look at saturated fat and why it got such an awful—and undeserved—rep.

The Paradox of the Ultra-Low-Fat Diet

I bet you have a friend who successfully maintained a low-fat diet. Maybe his doc put him on it to lower his cholesterol levels, and maybe your friend even lost a nice bit of weight. Doesn't happen all that often, but it *does* happen.

I have a theory about your friend. I think the true benefit of his low-fat diet is that it's lower in omega-6 fat. You see, when your friend reduced his dietary fat intake, he cut out everything with oil in it. That means he also substantially reduced his intake of proinflammatory omega-6s, which are the dominant fats found in the Western diet.

A very-low-fat diet automatically lowers the pro-inflammatory omega-6 to anti-inflammatory omega-3 ratio, even if you don't eat a drop more omega-3 fat than you did before. (The fact that you eat less saturated fat is actually incidental.) And some of the most famous, clinically studied low-fat diets—such as those of Dean Ornish or Caldwell Esselstyn at the Cleveland Clinic—are not only low in fat, but very low in processed foods and sugar of any kind.

People may believe they're benefiting because they're cutting out cholesterol and saturated fat, but we believe something else is going on. We believe the reason some people benefit from those diets is because they've cut out sugar *and*—because they're now eating less fat overall—they've significantly lowered their omega-6 intake. They've also upped their intake of fiber, vegetables, and fruit. Those dietary principles are dear to our hearts as well—we just don't think you need to cut out animal products and saturated fat to achieve them.

We believe you could get those same benefits (and probably more) by simply reducing sugar and processed carbohydrates, eliminating trans fats, increasing omega-3s, and decreasing omega-6s.

Reducing saturated fat and dietary cholesterol intakes has virtually nothing to do with it.

STUDIES VINDICATE SATURATED FAT

Everyone knows saturated fat raises cholesterol and leads to heart disease, right? Not so fast.

A Harvard study in the *American Journal of Clinical Nutrition* concluded that "greater saturated fat intake is associated with *less* progression of coronary atherosclerosis, whereas carbohydrate intake is associated with a *greater* progression."

Did you get that? To prevent atherosclerosis, skip the bread and other high-carb foods, *not* the healthy saturated fats from whole foods such as coconut, palm oil, and grass-fed beef. In fact, in the famous Framingham, Massachusetts, heart study, the more saturated fat one ate, the more cholesterol one ate, the more calories one ate, the lower the person's serum cholesterol. Sound incredible? It's right there in the data. Researchers found that "people who ate the most cholesterol, ate the most saturated fat, [and] ate the most calories *weighed the least* and were *the most physically active* [italics ours]."

There's more. In a 2008 study in the journal *Progress in Lipid Research*, William Lands, Ph.D., wrote: "Advice to replace saturated fat with unsaturated fat stimulated my early experiments in lipid research. It made me ask by what mechanisms could saturated fats be 'bad' and unsaturated fats 'good' . . . Fifty years later, I still cannot cite a definite mechanism or mediator by which saturated fat is shown to kill people. . . ."

But what about those studies that *do* connect saturated fat with heart disease? Closer examination reveals a somewhat different story. Most often, the studies that condemned saturated fat looked at its effect on *cholesterol*. They did not look at its effect on *heart disease*.

> Most often, the studies that condemned saturated fat looked at its effect on *cholesterol*. They did not look at its effect on *heart disease*.

There's a big difference.

See, it's a lot easier to measure and quantify cholesterol than it is to wait thirty years and watch to see how many people die of heart disease. So over the years, an awful lot of studies used cholesterol as a stand-in, kind of like a body double in a movie (it's way cheaper to have an actor stand in for Brad Pitt while the director lights the scene than it is to have the real Brad!). So scientists frequently use cholesterol in the same way, as a stand-in for heart disease. Researchers measure diet, look at its effect on cholesterol, and infer—from the cholesterol measurements—the risk of heart disease. They essentially use cholesterol as a surrogate for what we *really* want to know about, which is heart disease.

Studies that measure the effect of saturated fat *directly* on heart disease and mortality—rather than *indirectly* by measuring its effect on cholesterol—are few and far between. And those that do measure it reveal a much different story.

Saturated fat in the diet often does make your cholesterol go up. It *doesn't* make your risk for heart disease go up, however. And if you see cholesterol as equivalent to heart disease, that would be a very bad thing.

But it isn't.

Not only that, but the particular way that saturated fat raises cholesterol is actually a good thing.

Let me explain.

The Need to Look Under the Hood

Once upon a time experts saw cholesterol as one simple number. You went to a health fair, had your skin pricked, and the nice lady told you, "Mr. Jones, your cholesterol is 239." Or 190. Or 260. That number was your "total" cholesterol, and for a while, back in the '50s and '60s, it was all we had.

Later, we started to pay attention to the fact that cholesterol travels in the bloodstream in two distinct types of "packages"–LDL (low-density lipoprotein) and HDL (high-density lipoprotein). Because they function somewhat differently in the body, doctors began referring to HDL as "good" and LDL as "bad" cholesterol.

It was a huge oversimplification, but it was the best we could do at the time. Now it's obsolete. And the *reason* it's obsolete is very relevant to saturated fat.

(Particle) Size Matters

We now know that there are several different kinds (or subtypes) of both HDL and LDL. For instance, HDL-2 particles are large and buoyant, anti-inflammatory, and anti-atherogenic, making them very healthy indeed. But HDL-3 particles, on the other hand, are smaller,

denser, and possibly inflammatory. So all HDL is not created equal. You obviously want more protective HDL-2 hanging out than HDL-3. But the differences among HDL subtypes are relatively minor compared to the differences between LDL subtypes, particularly between LDL-A and LDL-B.

LDL-A is a larger, fluffier particle and not as invasive as the smaller LDL-B.

LDL-B, on the other hand, is a whole different story. It's a small, hard, dense molecule that becomes easily oxidized and promotes inflammation. Because it's small, it's easy for it to penetrate the artery wall. You want your LDL-A numbers to be higher and your LDL-B numbers to be as low as possible. If your doctor is treating you for high cholesterol without knowing what *type* of LDL you have, she is throwing a dart at a dart board with a blindfold on. She is treating a *number*, not a patient.

As important as particle size is, it's even more important to know your particle *number*. (When you have a very high number of particles, this usually means it's because they're small–i.e., LDL-B, the kind you *don't* want to have.) Standard cholesterol tests–the old-fashioned kind–won't tell you this.

And here's where saturated fat comes in.

You see, saturated fat makes *more* of those big, fluffy, less invasive particles and much *less* of the small, dense, inflammatory particles (such as LDL-B and HDL-3).

So if you eat a lot of saturated fat, your total cholesterol–even your total LDL–may indeed rise, and if that's all your doctor looks at, you can be sure you'll be looking at the business end of a prescription pad. But your cholesterol will rise because your body is *increasing* the number of big, fluffy, buoyant (and less harmless) cholesterol particles, and *reducing* the number of small, nasty atherogenic particles. Sure, your overall number rises, but overall, your cholesterol particle size has been modified to the lesser of two potential threats. Remember, when any cholesterol particle becomes oxidized, it becomes inflammatory, and pattern B is more aggressive than pattern A.

Because we're now beginning to understand the much more subtle effect saturated fat has on cholesterol, we're also beginning to understand that saturated fat is very far from the unhealthy molecule we've been taught it was.

Unfortunately, though, too many people—including, sadly, doctors—haven't gotten the memo.

A TYPICAL SCENARIO AT YOUR DOCTOR'S OFFICE

Let's say you follow your doctor's low-fat diet for lowering cholesterol. You've got to replace that fat with something, and nine times out of ten you replace it with carbs. Why not? We've been taught that carbohydrates are the perfect food. They give you energy. They have no fat. They're "healthy." But if you're like most people, you're not swapping fat for carbohydrates such as vegetables and fruits. Most likely, you're swapping it for breads, cereals, and grains, winding up with a diet high in processed carbohydrates, convenience foods, pastas, potatoes, and rice. You've dumped the saturated fat alright, but are you any better off?

Actually, as you'll soon see, you're *worse* off.

Meanwhile, back at the doctor's office, everyone is all smiles. You've lowered your cholesterol levels! See?

Saturated fat was indeed the villain!

So what's the problem?

Plenty. If your doctor is only looking at the old-fashioned cholesterol test, he may indeed be happy as a clam because your numbers have gone down. But the devil is in the details.

If your LDL cholesterol is, let's say, 150, most doctors in America will call for Lipitor faster than you call "Check, please" at the end of a bad date. Conversely, if it's lower than 100, most docs will be thrilled. But look at what those numbers conceal. If that 150 LDL is mostly big, fluffy cholesterol particles (i.e., pattern A), you are less vulnerable to inflammatory response. On the other hand, if you have a "healthy" number lower than 120, but most of your cholesterol consists of small, nasty, inflammatory molecules, you're in trouble. You need to know what's under the hood—exactly what *kind* of LDL are we talking about? Without knowing that, you're just guessing about what's going on. You may end up taking potentially damaging drugs to solve a "problem" that may not even be a problem in the first place.

Cutting out saturated fat will probably lower your overall LDL number, but most of that reduction will come from lowering the number of big, fluffy particles (which are less inflammatory). Meanwhile, the proportion of your LDL population shifts in favor of the nasty, angry, atherogenic, BB gun pellet-type particles.

So when you reduced saturated fat on your doc's prescribed low-fat diet, your LDL went down. Only problem is, your risk for heart disease just went up.

Hardly a good bargain.

A low-carb diet, on the other hand—especially one

Cutting out saturated fat will probably lower your overall LDL number, but most of that reduction will come from lowering the number of big, fluffy particles (which are less inflammatory).

with some healthy saturated fat and plenty of omega-3s and -9s—will have the opposite effect. You'll see a significant shift to more of those big, fluffy LDL particles and away from those small, dense, angry LDL particles.

As a nice bonus, you'll also shed fat. You'll feel better. You'll have fewer cravings, and probably, less inflammation. You'll feel fuller on less food. And, once you get accustomed to dumping junk food, you'll probably enjoy eating a whole lot more.

The Most Dangerous Fat That I Hope Isn't in Your Food

I told you earlier that fat comes in three flavors. Actually, I lied. There's a fourth kind, but it's a type of fat you want to stay far, far away from.

Remember a few decades ago when "heart-healthy" margarine trumped butter and people were spreading that stuff everywhere? Request butter at a restaurant or serve it at your dinner party, and people gasped that you would put such an artery-clogging food into your body.

In the immortal words of Richard Nixon, let me say this about that: The butter swap-out was one of the most supremely stupid nutrition faux pas in history. And for two reasons. Number one, margarine was sold to us as a healthy alternative on the sole basis of having less saturated fat (which was never the problem in the first place). And number two, the stuff they replaced saturated fat with was a zillion times worse than saturated fat ever could have been. I'm talking about trans-fatty acids.

Trans Fats and the "Zero Trans Fat" Scam

Manufacturers create trans fat by using a kind of turkey baster to inject hydrogen atoms into a liquid (unsaturated) fat, creating a cheap, solid fat with a shelf life of basically forever (Twinkies, anyone?).

Whenever you buy processed foods at your grocery store (which we hope will happen somewhere between "infrequently" and "never"), look for the term "partially hydrogenated oil" or "hydrogenated oil" in the ingredients list. If you see it, put the product down and step away from the grocery shelf. Those words are synonyms for trans fats—in fact, they're the definition of them. And their presence on the ingredients list should serve as a big red flag to *put it back*.

Trans fats are great for shelf life. For *your* life—not so much. But for Big Food's bottom line, they're absolutely essential. Big Food needs them because you can't make junk food without trans fats (or without

We strongly believe that saturated fat got blamed for a lot of the damage done by trans fats.

something equally horrendous). So a hit to trans fats is a hit to their bottom line, and—in case you hadn't noticed—Big Food doesn't take hits like that lying down. Enormous lobbying efforts on the part of the food industry led to a tiny loophole that lets manufacturers use trans fats while legally claiming "no trans fats!" on their packaging.

Here's how it works: As long as a processed food contains *less than half a gram of trans fat per serving*, manufacturers can claim "no trans fats" on the label. So they got "zero" defined as .4 grams or less per serving. Now all that was left was to make the serving size ridiculously, unrealistically low. Bingo. Check the label on your next snack food. You're probably consuming two to four servings in what you—and I, and the rest of the world—believe is a single portion.

By making serving sizes so small, and by keeping trans fats to just under half a gram per serving, they were able to technically comply with the rules. A typical pat of butter substitute could easily contain three servings, according to the manufacturer, and if each had the legal limit of 0.4 grams per serving, you'd be consuming 1.2 grams of the stuff just from that nice pat of fake butter. And that's just one tiny example.

Let's remember that the ideal amount of artificial trans fats in the human diet is zero. Yet for decades, trans fats flew under the radar, only recently distinguished in the public's mind from saturated fat (with which they're frequently lumped). We strongly believe

that saturated fat got blamed for a lot of the damage done by trans fats. Evidence in the last decade has clearly shown a relationship between trans fat consumption and cardiovascular disease, but not between cardiovascular disease and saturated fat.

So far, we've looked at saturated fat and trans fat and found some significant differences between them. Now we're going to look at the polyunsaturated fats and note some significant differences between them as well.

And those differences have a huge implication for the health of your heart.

THE OMEGAS: THE GOOD AND THE NOT-SO-GOOD

You may remember that the category of fats known as polyunsaturated has two star players: omega-6 and omega-3 fatty acids.

Omega-3s are primarily found in fish such as wild salmon, tuna, and sardines. Plant sources of omega-3s include flaxseed, chia seeds, walnuts, and algae. Much argument exists about which sources are best, but for our purposes, we'll treat them as a single group because they all share one primary characteristic that is hugely significant in preventing heart disease: Omega-3s are anti-inflammatory.

Omega-6s, however, are a different story.

Your body builds anti-inflammatory compounds out of omega-3s, but it builds *inflammatory* compounds

One Trans Fat That's Actually Good for You

There is a naturally occurring trans-fatty acid that's actually good for you, but it's the exception to the rule. (We mention this not to confuse you, but simply for accuracy's sake.) It's called conjugated linoleic acid, or CLA, and it's found in dairy fat, but only dairy fat from grass-fed, pasture-raised cows. CLA has been shown to have some anticancer as well as antiobesity activity.

CLA is not what we're talking about when we encourage you to cut out man-made (artificial) trans fats. Virtually 95 percent or more of the trans fats we consume come from processed food, and those are the fats we should be eliminating from our diet, not CLA or saturated fats.

out of omega-6s. We actually need both kinds of compounds for human health because the inflammation response is an important part of the healing process.

So the problem isn't that we consume omega-6s. It's that we consume them like a twelve-cylinder Ferrari consumes gasoline. The primary source of omega-6s in our diet is vegetable oil, and you can't swing a rope in a supermarket without hitting dozens of products that are made with processed vegetable oil. For a fuller discussion of many of the oils we used in the recipes and a chart showing their smoke point and other information, see "Making Sense of Cooking Oils" (page 20) and "The Best Fats for the Job" (page 22). Almost every food that you buy in a package has vegetable oil in it (read the label). Same with most foods that are cooked in restaurants. Reliable studies consistently show that we consume between sixteen and twenty times as much omega-6 fat as we do omega-3 fat!

And that's bad news for the health of our hearts.

The average ratio of omega-6 to omega-3 consumption in the Paleolithic diet was just about 1:1, or even a little less (meaning slightly more omega-3s than omega-6s). Experts believe this is the best balance to keep inflammation in check and everything running smoothly. That's precisely the ratio we should be eating today.

Most of us aren't.

Why does this matter?

Because inflammation is at the root of heart disease. And our high-vegetable-oil diet is fanning the flames of that very inflammation. In fact, it's throwing gasoline on it. If you think of the inflammatory and anti-inflammatory hormones as two armies that work together to create balance in the body, that means we're overfunding the inflammation army by 1,500 to 2,000 percent!

We believe that a major promoter—*the* major promoter—of heart disease is inflammation. That's one of the take-home points of *The Great Cholesterol Myth*. And it's the main reason you'll see much less vegetable oil used in the recipes in this book and much *more* omega-3s and monounsaturated and saturated fats.

Trying to balance our intake of omega-6s and omega-3s should be one of our primary dietary and health goals—far more important, in our opinion, than lowering cholesterol.

Making Sense of Cooking Oils

I hope you see now how authorities have unfairly demonized saturated fat, when the real fat culprits have been trans fats and excessive intake of omega-6s.

With that in mind, we've provided a chart listing which oils to use and what not to use them for (see page 22). There are a few predominantly omega-6 cooking oils on this list (peanut oil, for example), but I want you to use them carefully and sparingly. And I'm sure it won't surprise you that there are saturated fats on this list as well.

But worry not. By the end of this section you'll know a lot about cooking oils, and you'll know exactly what to look for when choosing one. You may even change your mind about a couple of oils you thought were healthy and a couple you thought were not.

In the chart, I've emphasized healthy, anti-inflammatory monounsaturated fats and some saturated ones. Because, as mentioned, omega-3s are delicate and can't stand up to heat, I recommend that you get those fats from food (such as fish and flaxseed), supplements, and cold-pressed oils, which can be used in salad dressings but should never be used for cooking.

Other oils, such as almond and avocado, remain quite stable even at very high temperatures. They are the best ones to use for any type of high-heat cooking, such as searing or broiling.

What's Your Smoke Point?

Earlier, we talked about how oils have damage points. Another way to conceptualize damage points is to think of them as smoke points. The smoke point is the temperature at which an oil begins to break down, so you want to keep each oil below its smoke point at all times. If you do overheat an oil and it begins to smoke in the pan, simply empty and wash the pan and start again with a fresh batch at a lower temperature. There is some disagreement as to the precise smoke points for different oils, so in this chart I offer you smoke points erring on the lower, rather than the higher, side for safety.

If you're looking for an oil and don't see it on the chart, then it just didn't make the cut, and you may be surprised at some that didn't. Canola oil, for instance, has been widely advocated as a healthy choice, but contrary to popular belief, canola oil is NOT a preferred choice. It's an overhyped and unhealthy oil that has undeservingly reaped the benefits of great marketing by the oil industry.

As an esteemed lipid biochemist and author of the textbook *Know Your Fats*, Mary Enig,

Ph.D., points out, "Like all modern vegetable oils, canola oil goes through the process of caustic refining, bleaching, and degumming—all of which involve high temperatures of questionable safety." The wonderful omega-3s in canola oil easily become rancid when subjected to the high temperature needed to extract the canola oil. Therefore, they have to be deodorized. This deodorizing process turns a large number of the omega-3s into trans fats.

And canola oil used in foods is even worse, as it hydrogenates beautifully, making it ideal for shelf life but not for *your* life, as the hydrogenation just increases the trans fat content. "I would never use this oil," says Fred Pescatore, M.D., author of *The Hamptons Diet* and a well-respected expert on fats and cooking oils.

So if you're looking for canola, safflower, grapeseed, corn, soybean, or other oils on this list and don't see them, there was a reason for it. Remember, this list wasn't created to be the end-all, be-all, but rather to serve as a general guide. And if I left off your absolute favorite oil that you just discovered, don't get mad—that's what sequels are for! No matter which oil you reach for, remember these basic guidelines:

1. **Store oils properly.** Oils should be stored in opaque or dark containers and away from heat. Keeping them in the fridge is a good option and will guarantee protection against any free-radical formation.

2. **Take a multivitamin with your oils.** Because oils consist of delicate carbon chains, they can go rancid pretty easily, and another name for rancidity is free radicals, which destroy cells. A good antioxidant will help to stem the progression of free radicals, so remember to take a multivitamin if you are not eating an antioxidant-rich meal that contains foods such as dark greens or colorful fruits and berries.

3. **Look for cold-pressed.** Cold-pressed means that the oil was not subjected to commercial heating and processing, which offers greater protection against free-radical formation.

The Best Fats for the Job*

OIL	HEAT	PRIMARY TYPE OF FAT	SMOKE POINT	FLAVOR	IDEAL FOR	HEALTH BENEFITS
Almond	High	Monounsaturated	430°F (221°C)	Nutty	Sautéing, stir-frying, searing, baking	High in omega-3 essential fatty acids
Avocado	High	Monounsaturated	510°F (226°C)	Mild, Neutral	Any type of cooking	High in vitamins A, B₁, B₂, D, and E
Butter	Low-medium	Saturated	300°F (148°C)	Buttery	Cooking and baking	Contains vitamin A, selenium, iodine
Clarified butter (ghee)	Medium-high	Saturated	350°F (180°C)	Slightly nutty flavor	Any type of cooking	Enhances digestion
Coconut	Medium-high	90 percent saturated	350°F (180°C)	Mild, distinct odor	Baking	Antiviral, antibacterial properties
Flaxseed	Low/no	Polyunsaturated	225°F (107°C)	Nutty	Drizzle on salads or vegetables	Highest plant source of omega-3s
Hempseed	Medium	Polyunsaturated	330°F (165°C)	Mild, nutty	Salads, protein shakes, and vegetable juices	Rich in essential fatty acids
Macadamia nut	Medium-high	Monounsaturated	390°F (195°C)	Mellow, nutty flavor	Salads	High in antioxidants and vitamin D
Olive	Medium	Monounsaturated	Unrefined extra-virgin 320°F (160°C)	Neutral	Salads, cooking	High in antioxidants
Peanut	High	Monounsaturated, some polyunsaturated, and saturated	Refined, 450°F (230°C) Unrefined, 320°F (160°C)	Peanut	Stir-frying, sautéing	Resistant to rancidity
Sesame	High	Monounsaturated and polyunsaturated	Refined, 410°F (210°C) Unrefined, 350°F (180°C)	Sesame	Stir-frying, Asian salads	High in vitamin E, detoxifying properties
Walnut	Medium	Polyunsaturated	320°F (160°C)	Walnut	Drizzle on salads and vegetables	High in omega-3 fatty acids

* adapted from *The Most Effective Ways to Live Longer Cookbook*.

2 HORMONES 101

How your major fat-storage and stress hormones affect your heart and what you can do about them

To better understand how sugar, not fat or cholesterol, contributes to heart disease, I'll need to briefly discuss a few hormones. I promise the journey will be nothing like your high school biochemistry class.

The main player in our hormonal story is insulin. Insulin is an anabolic hormone. And if the first thing you think of when you hear the word *anabolic* is "steroids," I don't blame you. Anabolic means "building up," while its opposite—catabolic—means "breaking down." Steroids are indeed "anabolic," and so is insulin.

So insulin is known as an anabolic hormone, meaning it helps build things up. For example, insulin delivers sugar (as glucose) to your cells, where it can be used for energy, or it takes it to your liver to be stored as glycogen, which can be thought of as the storage form of carbohydrate.

Insulin's sister hormone, glucagon, is catabolic: It's responsible for breaking things down. So whereas insulin stores glucose in the cells, glucagon opens up those cell doors and releases it.

Put another way, insulin is responsible for *saving*; glucagon is responsible for *spending*. Together, they work to maintain blood sugar levels within a tightly regulated range so that your metabolic machinery runs smoothly.

So far, so good. The muscles need glucose for energy, and insulin shovels it right in. And when we need extra, glucagon opens up those cells and releases the stored fuel. It's kind of like saving for a rainy day; you put money (glucose) in the cellular bank for when it's needed, and you open up that savings account when money runs short.

So insulin, despite its reputation as a bad guy, is absolutely necessary. Without insulin, your blood sugar would skyrocket, leading to coma and death. Prior to insulin's discovery in 1921, this happened to virtually every person with type 1 diabetes. (Type 1 diabetics simply don't make insulin.) Similarly, bad things would also happen if you didn't have glucagon. Glucagon senses when blood sugar is going too low and opens up the cellular piggy bank, saving the day. Without glucagon to come to the rescue, you'd be looking at plummeting blood sugar that can result in brain dysfunction, coma, and death.

> Insulin, despite its reputation as a bad guy, is absolutely necessary. Without insulin, your blood sugar would skyrocket, leading to coma and death.

So these two sister hormones, when things are working right, harmoniously maintain blood sugar levels, keeping them from soaring too high (insulin) and preventing them from dropping too low (glucagon). Insulin is so powerful, in fact, that your body has four other hormones in addition to glucagon to balance its effects.

Note that I said, "When things are working right."

Which, unfortunately, they rarely are.

WHEN INSULIN WORKS WELL

To understand how insulin *should* work, let's look at what happens when you have normally functioning levels of this important hormone.

Let's say you live on a farm that only grows organic produce. Your cows graze on grass and the chickens roam around pecking at worms. You breathe in fresh air, you get eight hours' sleep every night, you have a supportive, loving family, and you maintain relatively stable stress levels. You don't even need an alarm clock to wake you in the morning. (I know, far-fetched, but stay with us here for a moment.)

So in this wonderful fantasy world, your metabolism is perfect and you are healthy, energetic, and full of vitality every single day.

Now let's say you eat an apple. Your blood sugar goes up slightly (as it would with just about any food), and your pancreas responds with a little squirt of insulin. Insulin takes that extra sugar in your bloodstream directly to your cells, which are happy to use it efficiently. If there's any left over, insulin hands it to your liver and muscles to store as glycogen.

Everything works correctly because in our perfect little hypothetical world, there is no such thing as impaired carbohydrate metabolism, insulin resistance, diabetes, or heart disease.

Broken Machinery: How Insulin *Actually* Works in Most People

But wait: This is not your life. (For the record: This is also not the life of anyone we know, either.) And this ideal metabolism that accompanies this fantasy life is not *your* metabolism.

No, your metabolic diary goes something like this: You go to bed stressed after a ridiculously busy day. The alarm clock blasts you awake after a poor night's sleep. Sleep-deprived and cranky, you fight freeway traffic and then grab a gargantuan cup of coffee and one of those "healthy" low-fat muffins before you step into your office. Your main stress hormone, cortisol, is already dancing on the ceiling while you mentally prepare to confront your boss- or client-from-hell about that overdue third-quarter sales report where you didn't meet your quota.

Then you sit in your office for eight or nine hours. As you mindlessly devour your muffin while your coworker babbles on about last night's episode of *Celebrity Apprentice*, your blood sugar skyrockets in response to the muffin. Your pancreas responds by screaming "Code Blue" and opening the insulin spigots in a desperate attempt to bail out all that sugar from your bloodstream and get it to the muscle cells *pronto*! But there's just one problem. The muscle cells aren't having it.

"What do we need all this sugar for?" they ask. "This guy's just going to sit around all day pushing a computer mouse, and when he goes home, he's going to sit on the couch and play with the remote."

Your muscle cells begin to *resist* the actions of insulin. "We're good," they say, "go somewhere else." Insulin now has no choice but to take its sugar payload to another location. Care to guess where that might be?

Yup. Your fat cells, which at first are only too happy to welcome that sugar in. "Come on in," they say, "the water's fine. We're happy to have you. The more the merrier!"

Now if this was just one 900-calorie "healthy" low-fat muffin, it probably wouldn't be a big deal. But add to that a sandwich for lunch; a bread basket, pasta or potatoes, and dessert for dinner; maybe some "healthy" low-fat cereal for a late night snack, and pretty soon you're in deep metabolic trouble. Keep eating this way—typical of what's called the "standard American diet"—and your blood sugar begins to be elevated all the time, putting greater and greater demands on your pancreas.

Elevated levels of insulin are not without serious consequences, for your weight, your metabolism, your health, and your heart.

For a while, your poor pancreas may be able to keep up with the added demand for more and more insulin, which is needed to clear this unnaturally high amount of sugar from your bloodstream. And between the wildly elevated levels of insulin, and your muscle cells absorbing a trickle of the stuff, you might be lucky enough to keep your blood sugar just under the level where you become officially diabetic.

At least in the beginning.

But those elevated levels of insulin are not without serious consequences, for your weight, your metabolism, your health, and your heart. After a while, under the constant assault of more and more sugar and insulin, even the fat cells start to say, "Enough, already!" Like the muscle cells before them, they become *resistant* to the effects of insulin.

Now your blood sugar is really high (after all, it's out of options and has nowhere left to go!). On top of that, your insulin is constantly high as well. Next stop? Full-blown diabetes.

How Insulin Resistance Develops

To understand how insulin levels get out of whack and the condition of insulin resistance develops, let's return to a typical, stressed-out, sleep-deprived office worker—or maybe even you.

You eat that low-fat muffin—or any other high-carb breakfast—raising your blood sugar and causing a surge of insulin to be released into your bloodstream. (Remember, insulin's main job in this scenario is to get that sugar out of your bloodstream either by taking it to the muscle cells or, alternatively, the fat cells.)

But all that insulin floating around in the blood-stream has dire consequences. Eventually it pulls your blood sugar down *too* low, leaving you lethargic, foggy, irritable, or worse. Now you're ready to kill someone if you don't get a bagel. You crave something sweet or starchy, and guess what—there's no shortage of foods to satisfy that craving.

So you wander into the break room, where a co-worker's homemade chocolate chip cookies await. You eat one—and then another. Your blood sugar jumps back up like an L.A. Laker doing a slam dunk, the pancreas releases another surge of insulin to pull it back down, and the cycle begins again.

We call that roller coaster "blood sugar hell"—and it's an all-too-common scenario, repeating itself throughout the day as you eat lunch, have a midafternoon snack, and finally eat dinner. Blood sugar rises, insulin jumps into the fray, blood sugar crashes, cravings follow, rinse, and repeat.

When Your Cells Stop Paying Attention

After a while, the cells just stop listening to insulin. Like the residents of a big metropolitan city, they learn to live with the "noise" of insulin pounding on their doors, eventually becoming—for all intents and purposes—immune to it. This is what we call *insulin resistance*—first the muscle cells resist the effect of insulin, then, ultimately, the fat cells do, too. The cells literally ignore insulin's call and keep their doors locked.

Though there's no one perfect test to determine insulin resistance, it tends to cluster with other symptoms that also increase the risk for heart disease. You can have insulin resistance without being diabetic, but you can't be diabetic without having insulin resistance. The cluster of symptoms that center on insulin resistance—such as high blood pressure, low HDL cholesterol, abdominal obesity, and high triglycerides—is collectively known as *metabolic syndrome* (or prediabetes), and it's an enormous risk factor for heart disease.

It's been estimated that at least one in four people in the United States has full-blown insulin resistance, but the American Association of Clinical Endocrinologists suggests it's even higher (one in three). And it gets worse as you age. One study indicated that more than 40 percent of people 60 years and older have metabolic syndrome. Any way you look at the statistics, we're talking about 70 to 80 million Americans with a condition that many (correctly) characterize as a "disease" of carbohydrate metabolism.

What does this have to do with heart disease?

Everything.

INSULIN RESISTANCE'S FAR-REACHING DAMAGE

Not only does insulin load up your cells with sugar, making you fatter, it locks the doors to the fat cells, making it fiendishly difficult to lose weight. One reason being overweight significantly increases the risk of heart disease is that all those fat cells don't just sit there, annoying you to death—they're actually little hormone factories, and the chemicals they spit out contribute mightily to inflammation, a major risk factor for heart disease (more on this later).

After a while, the cells just stop listening to insulin. Like the residents of a big metropolitan city, they learn to live with the "noise" of insulin pounding on their doors, eventually becoming immune to it. This is what we call *insulin resistance*.

Insulin resistance left unchecked puts you on the fast track to full-blown diabetes, which is itself a fast track to heart disease. (And diabetes, even *without* heart disease, is hardly a picnic. The numerous complications of diabetes include glaucoma, neuropathy, hearing loss, and depression.) People with diabetes are two to four times more likely to have heart disease, and heart disease is present in 75 percent of diabetes-related deaths.

"[H]aving chronically elevated insulin levels has harmful effects of its own—heart disease for one," writes science and health author Gary Taubes in the *New York Times*. In fact, high insulin levels raise triglycerides, the main type of fat found in the tissues and bloodstream, and blood pressure and lower HDL cholesterol: a triple whammy for your heart, a trifecta for heart disease. Insulin resistance creates a conglomerate of diseases with the appropriate acronym CHAOS: coronary disease, hypertension, adult-onset diabetes, obesity, and stroke.

Insulin Resistance and Triglycerides

We've argued that cholesterol is an overrated risk factor for heart disease, but the same can't be said of triglycerides. High triglycerides in the blood are an independent risk factor for heart disease, and guess what raises them? Insulin! (Incidentally, triglycerides drop like a rock on a low-carbohydrate diet, largely because low-carb diets don't raise insulin nearly as much as high-carb diets do.) The sweetener fructose, which I'll discuss later, doesn't raise blood sugar so much, but don't break out the kazoos just yet—it's a particularly menacing triglyceride raiser, not to mention a major cause of insulin resistance.

> Calculating your ratio of triglycerides to HDL cholesterol provides a much better way to predict heart disease than assessing cholesterol levels.

Calculating your ratio of triglycerides to HDL cholesterol provides a much better way to predict heart disease than assessing cholesterol levels. Lowering triglycerides automatically improves that all-important ratio of triglycerides to HDL, even if HDL stays the same. Think about it. If your triglycerides were 150 mg/dl and your HDL was 50 mg/dl, you'd have a ratio of 3, but if you brought your triglycerides down to 100 mg/dl, the ratio would automatically drop to a very desirable 2, or 100:50.

The triglyceride-to-HDL ratio—something integrative physicians and health professionals have been talking about for years—has received a big boost in public awareness in recent years. Just as we were writing this chapter, the *Wall Street Journal* published a full-page article ("Children on Track for a Heart Attack") on a study from the Cincinnati Children's Hospital Medical Center that looked at nearly 900 children and young adults. The study, originally published in the journal *Pediatrics*, found that the higher the ratio of triglycerides to HDL, the greater the likelihood that a child would have stiff and damaged arteries. "Stiff vessels make your heart work harder," said Elaine Urbina, head of preventive cardiology at Cincinnati Children's and lead author of the study. Stiff vessels are not something you want to have.

Indeed. The triglycerides-to-HDL ratio is also a great indicator of insulin resistance. In one study, a ratio of 3 or greater predicted insulin resistance with great reliability, while in a classic study from Harvard researchers, those with a high ratio were sixteen times more likely to develop heart disease than those with a low ratio.

But the triglycerides-to-HDL ratio is also a great stand-in for another number you should be aware of— LDL particle size. As you may recall from the previous chapter, when it comes to LDL cholesterol measurement, the metrics that matter are *not* total cholesterol or even total LDL, but the *number* and *size* of your LDL particles. (The particle test, now given by at least four major laboratories in the United States alone, will tell you exactly what kind of LDL you have, which is essential information if you are going to "treat" high LDL cholesterol.)

The triglyceride-to-HDL ratio is an excellent stand-in for the particle-size test. Those with high ratios of triglycerides to HDL tend to have much more of the atherogenic LDL-B particles, while those with low ratios tend to have less invasive LDL-A particles. We would certainly not recommend treatment of high cholesterol with a statin drug just based on total LDL, and especially not for a person with a very low (2 or under) triglyceride-to-HDL ratio.

INSULIN RESISTANCE AND HYPERTENSION

Unlike total LDL cholesterol, blood pressure is a serious risk factor for heart disease and should be taken very seriously. Once again, insulin plays a role here because elevated insulin raises blood pressure in a number of ways. Insulin can narrow the artery walls. Narrower walls translate into higher blood pressure, because a harder pumping action is required to get the blood through the narrower passageways.

But there's an even more insidious way in which insulin raises blood pressure: It talks to the kidneys.

Insulin's message to the kidneys is this: Hold on to salt. Insulin makes the kidneys do this even if the kidneys would much prefer not to. Because the body controls sodium within a tight range—just as it does with sugar—the kidneys figure, "Listen, if we have to hold on to all this salt, we'd better bring on more water to dilute it so that it stays in the safe range." And that's exactly what they do. Increased sodium retention results in increased water retention.

More water means more blood volume, and more blood volume means higher blood pressure. According to Mark Houston, M.D., M.S., head of the Hypertension Institute in Nashville and author of *What Your Doctor May Not Tell You about Hypertension*, fully 70 percent of people with hypertension (high blood pressure) have insulin resistance.

THE INSULIN-CHOLESTEROL CONNECTION

High insulin levels have a profound effect on cholesterol as well. Insulin turns up the cholesterol-making machinery by turbocharging the activity of the enzyme that actually controls the cholesterol-manufacturing machinery in your body. This enzyme, with the unwieldy name of HMG-CoA reductase, is the very same enzyme that's shut down by cholesterol-lowering drugs!

You could probably lower your cholesterol–if you still care about that–by simply lowering your insulin levels. Doing so would have none of the side effects of cholesterol-lowering medication, unless you call a longer life span and better health "side effects"!

If this all sounds grim, there's light at the end of the tunnel: Insulin resistance is almost completely reversible. When you remove sugar and processed foods from your diet, you normalize blood sugar levels, optimize insulin levels, and greatly reduce your risk for diabetes, heart disease, and other complications.

How Do I Know If I'm Insulin Resistant?

Good question. We can recommend blood measures to determine this, such as fasting insulin and a glucose tolerance test, but there's also a nice, simple, low-tech way to find out, and it won't cost you a penny. You won't even need to get a doctor's prescription for a lab test!

Here's how to do it. Stand in front of a wall and walk toward it. If your belly touches the wall before the rest of your body, there's an excellent chance that you're insulin resistant. Men with waist sizes of 40 inches or more are almost certainly insulin resistant, as are women with waist sizes of 35 inches or more. Sure, there are people with insulin resistance who are rail-thin, but the vast majority of people with insulin resistance are not.

Insulin Resistance, Heart Disease, and the Four Horsemen of Aging

In my book *The Most Effective Ways to Live Longer*, I talked about something I called "the four horsemen of aging." These "horsemen" are behind the scenes of every age-related disease on the planet. The four horsemen are oxidative damage, inflammation, glycation, and stress.

No surprise: All four horsemen contribute mightily to heart disease.

Here are the CliffsNotes: Stress hormones can overwhelm a vulnerable physiology and, in some cases, precipitate a heart attack even in cases where the arteries are completely clear. Glycation (explained at length in *The Great Cholesterol Myth*) is basically the result of too much sugar in the diet. And if you've ever seen rust on metal, or browning apple slices, you understand oxidation (a.k.a. "oxidative damage"). But the most important reason to mention oxidation here is that it initiates *inflammation*, which ultimately leads to plaque formation and heart disease. Inflammation is the real story in heart disease (cholesterol, on the other hand, is a minor player).

Insulin Resistance and Inflammation

Inflammation comes in two "flavors," acute and chronic, and they're quite different. Most of us are very familiar with acute inflammation. It occurs whenever you stub your toe or get a splinter in your finger, or have an aching back, an abscessed tooth, or an eruption of acne. Acute inflammation is visible, uncomfortable, and usually painful as heck.

But acute inflammation—painful and annoying though it may be—isn't always bad. It's actually part of the body's healing response to injury. The swelling, soreness, and pain that occur actually protect against infection and help heal the wounded area.

Chronic inflammation, on the other hand, is a whole different ball game. As our friend Barry Sears, Ph.D., said, "Acute inflammation hurts, but *chronic* inflammation kills."

You see, chronic inflammation flies beneath the pain radar and provides no obvious symptoms. (No wonder *Time* magazine called it the "silent killer.") Yet it's a significant component of virtually every single degenerative condition, including Alzheimer's, diabetes, obesity, arthritis, cancer, neurodegenerative diseases, and yes, heart disease.

Chronic inflammation left unchecked in your cardiovascular system spells big trouble for your heart. Inflammation, in fact, is a major player in the development of plaque, and a far more important risk factor for heart disease than cholesterol is.

> Inflammation, in fact, is a major player in the development of plaque, and a far more important risk factor for heart disease than cholesterol is.

As you probably imagined, insulin resistance triggers inflammation. Whereas for healthy people insulin can be *anti-inflammatory*, if you're insulin resistant it has the opposite effect.

"Normally, insulin has some fairly positive effects on the body, such as being anti-inflammatory," says Jeff Volek, Ph.D., R.D., of the University of Connecticut, and one of the top researchers in the field of diet and health. "But if you're insulin resistant, chronically high insulin levels have the opposite effect. They actually promote inflammation and cardiovascular problems."

Being overweight or obese only adds fuel to the inflammatory fire, fuel that can be traced back to insulin. Here's the drill. Excess insulin causes fat gain. Excess fat creates more inflammation. And it's a vicious and unending cycle, because your fat cells are *not* going to release fat to burn as long as insulin levels are high.

How do you break the cycle? By now, the strategy should be crystal clear: You lower your levels of insulin and your levels of inflammation. And the best strategy for both is to lower the sugar, processed carbs, and other inflammatory foods in your diet, while increasing anti-inflammatory foods and anti-inflammatory supplements like omega-3 fatty acids. That's what we've done in this book, and that's why you'll see so little sugar and relatively low amounts of grains in our recipes. It's also why you won't see low-fat recipes here, because fat is *not* what's causing insulin to rise. We'll discuss some top anti-inflammatory foods in chapter 5.

When Sugar Goes Rogue: Glycation

So far, we've been talking about the effect of sugar—and foods that convert to sugar quickly, such as starchy carbohydrates—on insulin and insulin resistance. But there are other ways that sugar negatively affects our health. It's directly responsible for one of the most damaging processes in the body, *glycation*.

Here's how it works. Sugar is sticky (think cotton candy and maple syrup). Proteins, on the other hand, are smooth and slippery (think oysters, which are pure protein). The slippery nature of proteins lets them slide around easily in the cells and bloodstream and do their jobs effectively.

But when you've got a lot of excess sugar in your system, it keeps bumping into proteins, ultimately getting stuck onto the protein molecules. These sticky proteins are now known as *glycated* proteins.

Those glycated proteins are too big and sticky to get through small blood vessels and capillaries, including those in the kidneys, eyes, and feet. Now you know why so many diabetics are at risk for kidney disease, vision problems, and toe, feet, and even leg amputations. The sugar-coated proteins become toxic and make the cell machinery run less efficiently. They damage the body and exhaust the immune system. (Not surprisingly, studies show glycation also contributes to insulin resistance.)

These sticky proteins eventually "find" one another and stick together, making even more damaging compounds to which scientists have given the acronym AGES, or *advanced glycation end products*; the acronym is both ironic and fitting because these proteins are so deeply involved in aging the body.

GLYCATION, DAMAGED CHOLESTEROL, AND HEART DISEASE

So glycation "gums up" your proteins, making them much less efficient at doing their jobs. But what does this glycation thing have to do with cholesterol and heart disease? Actually, quite a bit.

Let's remember that cholesterol is never a problem until it becomes damaged. And that happens in two ways. One is free-radical-induced *oxidative damage* (very much the same process that browns the sliced apple when left to bake in the sun). The second way is—you guessed it—*glycation*.

"High blood sugar causes the lining cells of the arteries to be inflamed, changes LDL cholesterol, and causes sugar to be attached to a variety of proteins, which changes their normal function," says Dwight Lundell, M.D., author of *The Cure for Heart Disease*.

Scientists are still uncovering glycation's far-reaching damage to your heart and other organs. New research funded by the British Heart Foundation has uncovered still another subtype of LDL cholesterol called the *MGmin-low-density lipoprotein*, which is more common in people with type 2 diabetes and the elderly. It's "stickier" than normal LDL, which makes it much more likely to attach to the walls of the arteries.

What creates this superbad type of LDL cholesterol? You guessed it again! *Glycation*. Which brings us to the real culprit in the American diet, the subject of our next chapter: sugar.

3 THE CASE AGAINST SUGAR

*The airtight case against fructose and an easy-to-understand explanation
of sucrose, glucose, and high-fructose corn syrup*

Now that you understand how insulin works—and just as
importantly, how it can malfunction—we can discuss the
number-one culprit that knocks insulin out of whack and creates
so many of the problems discussed in chapter 2.

It's not fat, which hardly gets a hello from insulin. Protein will raise insulin a little bit, but nothing to write home about. And in any case, protein also raises glucagon, your fat-*releasing* hormone, which counters some of insulin's effects.

So what does that leave?

Carbohydrates.

Now before we go any further, let's clarify something. The term *carbohydrates* is a big tent. It includes Froot Loops and cauliflower, white pasta and broccoli. And although it's true that carbohydrates in general have a much more significant effect on blood sugar than protein or fat, it's the simple sugars such as glucose and fructose that cause the most damage. Glucose raises blood sugar almost instantly, and fructose does all kinds of other metabolic damage. (Sucrose, or table sugar, is a combination of the two.) When we talk about the dangers of carbohydrates, we're speaking specifically of these sugars.

We're also speaking about a class of starchy, processed carbohydrates (e.g., cereals, breads, crackers, pasta) and even some starchy carbohydrates that aren't processed (e.g., potatoes). Although these foods may not *be* sugar, they convert to sugar in the body in the blink of an eye. Do not kid yourself. The moment that mouthful of Cap'n Crunch hits your gullet, the pancreas alerts the troops just as quickly as if you swallowed a Ding Dong.

So for the purposes of this discussion let's be clear that we're not talking about vegetables, which are, after all, carbohydrates. No, when we talk about the dangers of carbs, we're talking about the dangers of sugar and foods that convert to sugar in a hummingbird's heartbeat. And let's not mince words—we consider sugar the number-one dietary foe of heart health.

Sugar, in fact, is *way* more of a threat to heart health than almost anything else in the diet, with the possible exception of trans fats. It's certainly more of a threat to your health than saturated fat or cholesterol.

From hypertension to dental cavities, nothing good comes from sugar. Occasionally indulging in a piece of birthday cake won't do much metabolic damage for most people, but when it comes to sugar, many people make every minor victory or defeat an occasion to have something sweet, and that paves the road for long-term problems, especially for the estimated 70 to 80 million people in the United States who have difficulty with carbohydrate metabolism.

Remember, we're not just talking about an occasional indulgence here. When it comes to sugar, the U.S. Department of Agriculture estimates that as of 2011, the average American consumes up to 156 pounds a year of the stuff. That's nearly *half a pound* every day! And that's not counting the natural sugars found in fruits and vegetables. We're talking about added sugar here, much of which comes from sweetened drinks loaded with high-fructose corn syrup (HFCS) and from processed foods in general.

> # Sugar is *way* more of a threat to heart health than almost anything else in the diet, with the possible exception of trans fats.

IS HIGH-FRUCTOSE CORN SYRUP REALLY THE ENEMY?

Over the past few years, HFCS has gotten a bad rap. So bad, in fact, that the Corn Refiners Association launched a major campaign (www.sweetsurprise.com) to defend this increasingly maligned sweetener. After all, it comes from corn, so how bad can it be?

High-fructose corn syrup was first invented in Japan in the 1960s and made it into the American food supply around the mid-1970s. Almost from its introduction it was a major hit with Big Food because, from their point of view, it had two major advantages over regular sugar. One, it was sweeter, so theoretically you could use less of it. And two, it was much cheaper than sugar. What's not to like?

The gist of the marketing campaign by the Corn Refiners Association can be summed up succinctly:

This stuff is no worse than sugar. It pains us to side with the Corn Refiners Association here, but they're right: High-fructose corn syrup *is* no worse than table sugar. Regular old table sugar—known as sucrose—is 50 percent glucose and 50 percent fructose. High-fructose corn syrup is 45 percent glucose and 55 percent fructose, essentially a wash. But to try to rehabilitate HFCS's reputation by saying it's "no worse" than sugar is like saying Montezuma's revenge is "no worse" than explosive diarrhea. They're both terrible, and we don't want either of them.

High-fructose corn syrup is no worse than table sugar.

Because HFCS was so cheap, it began to be added to products that never had added sweeteners before. Manufacturers quickly noted that they could make just about anything taste decent, including fat-free and low-fat foods, if they sweetened it enough, and before you knew it, HFCS was in everything. And we do mean *everything*. It's in processed meats, hamburger buns, orange juice, bagels, "multigrain breads," more breakfast cereals than we can count, ketchup, biscuits, crackers, and just about anything with a bar code. (Please don't take our word for it—go on a field trip to your local supermarket and start reading labels.)

We collectively began to expect a sweet taste from darn near anything we ate, and our palates changed accordingly. Did we mention that the average American now consumes an incredible 156 pounds of added sugars a year? (We know we did. Just wanted to see if you were listening!) And by the next edition of this book, that figure will probably be obsolete, as it is expected to go up even further in the next decade.

The ironic part is that because HFCS has received so much heat in the press, some food manufacturers now proudly boast that their products contain none of it and are instead sweetened with "natural" sugar (meaning ordinary sucrose). No wonder the public is utterly confused.

By Any Other Name . . . Sugar's Many Disguises

Manufacturers have become savvy about adding sugar to foods. They know you're reading labels more closely these days and paying attention to what stuff your kids snack on after school. So they've stepped up their game by using ingredients you're less likely to recognize as sugar (e.g., maltodextrin, maltose), or using sugars that have healthy-sounding names (e.g., grape sugar, rice syrup).

Visit your health food store and you'll find some of these disguises. Organic cane syrup sure sounds healthier, doesn't it? So do brown sugar, organic sugar, raw sugar, turbinado sugar, and brown rice syrup. Well, guess what: Your pancreas doesn't know the difference between any of them. As far as your pancreas is concerned, they're all a Ding Dong, and they all require insulin.

Occasionally someone will ask us whether coconut sugar or honey, which provide trace amounts of minerals and other nutrients, are better options than sugar. Although their ratios of glucose and fructose differ, these sweeteners are still sugar. Especially in large doses, they can create metabolic and hormonal havoc.

Making Sense of Sugar: Some Definitions

Carbohydrates is the general name for a large group of compounds that includes starch, sugar, and fiber.

Starch consists of a large number of glucose molecules joined together by chemical bonds. It's found in starchy vegetables such as potatoes and corn and in legumes such as beans and peas.

Sugar is the general name for a group of related, sweet-tasting substances. Simple sugars (consisting of only *one* type of molecule, such as glucose) are known as *monosaccharides* (mono = one). When two monosaccharides are joined together, they're known as a *disaccharide* (di = two). Note that high-fructose corn syrup is a man-made disaccharide.

Glucose is a simple sugar (monosaccharide) that's found in plants and absorbed directly into the bloodstream. When your doctor measures your blood sugar, she's measuring blood glucose.

Fructose is also a simple sugar found in plants (especially fruits). It is metabolized differently than glucose. It goes directly to the liver via the portal vein and triggers *lipogenesis*, which is the production of new fats such as triglycerides. Fructose is sweeter than glucose. Because it's metabolized differently, it doesn't raise blood sugar like glucose (or sucrose) does. But it causes insulin resistance through other pathways.

Sucrose is table sugar and the best known of the disaccharides. It's a 50-50 combination of the two simple sugars glucose and fructose, connected by a chemical bond.

High-fructose corn syrup is very similar to sugar in its chemical makeup. HFCS is 55 percent fructose and 45 percent glucose, but without the chemical bond between them that sucrose has. Some experts feel that the absence of the chemical bond—meaning no digestion (breakdown) is required—means it is more rapidly absorbed into the system.

Visit your health food store and count how many products contain "healthy" sweeteners. You might be surprised (or disgusted).

Agave syrup is basically high-fructose corn syrup masquerading as a health food.

Agave: The "Healthy" Sugar Impostor

One particular sugar "substitute" deserves special attention because it's been so aggressively and successfully marketed as a "healthy" alternative: agave. But the truth is, agave syrup (nectar) is basically HFCS masquerading as a health food.

It's easy to understand how agave syrup got its great reputation. After all, agave comes from the Greek word for *noble*. And agave plant extracts have been shown to have anti-inflammatory and antioxidant properties. Unfortunately, there's zero evidence that any of those compounds are present in the commercially made syrup.

Agave nectar is an amber-colored liquid that pours more easily than honey and is considerably sweeter than sugar. The health-food crowd loves it because it's gluten-free and suitable for vegan diets, and, most especially, because it's low glycemic. (I talk more about the glycemic index on page 50.)

Agave nectar has a low glycemic index for one reason only: It's largely made of fructose, which doesn't have the same effect on blood sugar that other simple sugars do (more on this below). Despite this, fructose is probably the single most damaging form of sugar when used as a sweetener. With the exception of pure liquid fructose, agave nectar has the highest fructose content of any commercial sweetener. (High-fructose corn syrup, you may remember, is 55 percent fructose, but agave syrup is typically 92 percent fructose, which makes it a kind of "super" high-fructose corn syrup.)

Agave nectar syrup is a triumph of marketing over science. In the added-sugar sweepstakes, it's the clear winner when it comes to creating metabolic damage.

Fructose: The Real Culprit

We've mentioned how damaging fructose can be in table sugar, HFCS, and especially agave. But what specifically is it about fructose that makes it so much worse for your health than other sugars?

Glad you asked.

To understand how fructose is essentially metabolic poison, you need to understand how your body processes it. Your body breaks down most sweeteners into the simple sugars *glucose* and *fructose*. Glucose goes right into the bloodstream and then into the cells to use or to your liver to store. Because it goes right into the bloodstream it has a high "glycemic index," meaning it raises blood sugar quickly. But because fructose is processed in an entirely different way, it does not.

Fructose bypasses the bloodstream and goes right to the liver via the portal vein. Unlike glucose, fructose does not trigger insulin secretion, and for a long while experts thought it was an ideal sweetener for people with diabetes.

Turns out they were very, *very* wrong.

Ironically, even though it does not trigger insulin, fructose causes insulin resistance. (More on that in a minute.) And more than any other sugar, fructose significantly raises triglycerides, which, as we mentioned earlier, are an independent risk factor for heart disease.

Fructose also makes you fat. Your body metabolizes fructose like fat, and it turns into fat (triglycerides) almost immediately. "When you consume fructose, you're not consuming carbs," says Robert Lustig, M.D., professor of pediatrics at the University of California, San Francisco. "You're consuming fat." Or might as well be.

Fructose-triggered inflammation especially damages your liver. In fact, fructose is now recognized as a major cause of nonalcoholic fatty liver disease, one of the most prevalent conditions in America. Rats given high-fructose diets developed a number of undesirable metabolic abnormalities including elevated triglycerides, weight gain, and extra abdominal fat.

But wait, there's more.

Remember earlier I discussed those artery-damaging AGES (advanced glycation end products)? (No? Here are the CliffsNotes: AGES are created when proteins—made sticky by excess sugar—start to clump together and make nasty little supersticky clumps, which clog up narrow blood vessels and cause inflammation in the arteries.) Well, fructose is *seven* times as likely to create them. And that's hardly good news for your heart.

Fructose and glucose behave very differently in the brain as well. The result is that glucose decreases food intake while fructose increases it. If your appetite increases, you eat more, thus making obesity, and an increased risk for heart disease, far more likely. "Take a kid to McDonald's and give him a Coke," Lustig says. "Does he eat less? Or does he eat more?"

One reason for this constant overeating of high-fructose foods and beverages is that fructose interferes with a hormone called *leptin*, which tells your brain to stop eating. Obese people have more than enough leptin, but it isn't getting to the target sites in the brain, creating a kind of "leptin resistance" similar to what happens with insulin.

Fructose is a major culprit in creating leptin resistance. When you eat foods high in sugar, whether "regular" sugar or HFCS, the glucose part raises insulin, which ultimately makes you hungry again, while the fructose part essentially acts like an out-of-control spam filter, keeping the leptin message from reaching the brain so you don't realize you've had enough to eat. That's an oversimplification, but close enough to make the point. Sugar, especially the fructose component, deregulates appetite and creates metabolic havoc, with disastrous results for both your waistline and your heart. Your body also absorbs fructose far more rapidly than glucose.

M. Daniel Lane, Ph.D., of the Johns Hopkins University School of Medicine, states, "We feel that [the findings on fructose and appetite] may have particular relevance to the massive increase in the use of high-fructose sweeteners (both high-fructose corn syrup and table sugar) in virtually all sweetened foods, most notably soft drinks."

> Getting fructose from whole foods is entirely different from getting it from a concentrated syrup extracted from the fruit and then inserted into practically every food you find in the supermarket.

CREATING INSULIN RESISTANCE ONE SODA AT A TIME

Fructose is the major cause of fat accumulation in the liver, a condition known technically as *hepatic steatosis* but which is more commonly known as *fatty liver*. And there is a direct link between fatty liver and our old friend, insulin resistance.

Varman Samuel, M.D., of the Yale School of Medicine, a top researcher in the field of insulin resistance, told the *New York Times* that the correlation between fat in the liver (fatty liver) and insulin resistance is remarkably strong. "When you deposit fat in the liver, that's when you become insulin resistant," he said.

And guess what causes fat to accumulate in the liver? Fructose.

If you want to watch a bunch of lab animals become insulin resistant, all you have to do is feed them fructose. Feed them enough and, sure enough, the liver converts it to fat, which then accumulates in the liver—with insulin resistance right behind it. This can occur in as little as a week if the animals are fed enough fructose, whereas it might take a few months at the levels we humans normally consume.

Studies conducted by Luc Tappy, M.D., reveal that feeding human subjects a daily dose of fructose equal to the amount found in eight to ten cans of soda produced insulin resistance and elevated triglycerides within a few days.

WHERE YOU GET FRUCTOSE MAKES ALL THE DIFFERENCE

But wait a minute, you say. An apple has fructose, and apples are healthy. So what's the deal?

It's actually simple. Getting fructose from whole foods is entirely different from getting it from a concentrated syrup extracted from the fruit and then inserted into practically every food you find in the supermarket, from hamburger buns to fat-free cookies.

Sure, your apple contains some fructose, but it also comes wrapped in a high-volume package containing a ton of antioxidants, fiber, and other nutrients. It's got a lot of water and takes a bit of time to chew and digest, so the glucose doesn't hit your bloodstream all at once. Extracting the small amount of fructose in an apple, putting it on steroids, creating a liquid out of it, and adding massive amounts to the food supply—that's a whole different ball game.

The result of this "sweetening of America" is that our fructose consumption has skyrocketed. Twenty-five percent of adolescents today consume 15 percent of their calories from fructose alone!

As Lustig points out in a brilliant lecture, "Sugar: The Bitter Truth" (available on YouTube), the percentage of calories from fat in the American diet has gone down at the same time that fructose consumption has skyrocketed, along with heart disease, diabetes, obesity, and hypertension. Coincidence? Lustig doesn't think so, and neither do we.

Rodents consuming large amounts of fructose rapidly develop metabolic syndrome. In humans, a high-fructose diet raises triglycerides almost instantly; a triple whammy because (1) triglycerides increase the risk for heart disease, (2) high triglycerides increase the all-important triglyceride-to-HDL ratio that we spoke about earlier, and (3) triglycerides further interfere with leptin signaling. The rest of the symptoms associated with metabolic syndrome take a little longer to develop in humans than they do in rats, but develop they do.

Fructose also raises uric acid levels in the bloodstream. Excess uric acid is well known as the defining feature of gout, but did you know that it also predicts future obesity and high blood pressure? Those with gout have long been told to stay away from red meat and foods with purines (substances in food that break down to uric acid), but it's become increasingly clear that fructose may be the main villain here, albeit one whose damaging effects are just starting to be appreciated.

So the real culprit for heart disease? No contest: Sugar, particularly the fructose component of it. It's certainly *not* fat or cholesterol. In fact, every single bad thing that fructose does to increase our risk for heart disease—and it does a lot—has virtually nothing to do with elevated cholesterol.

But that's never stopped the diet establishment from continuing to stick to its story that fat and cholesterol are what we ought to be worried about.

As the old journalistic adage goes, "Never let the facts get in the way of a good story."

4 THE TRUTH ABOUT GRAINS

Which grains to eat and which to avoid; what "whole grains" really means; the glycemic index and glycemic load, explained

Next time you're at the grocery store, pay a visit to the bread and cereal aisles. Not because we want you to become a carb addict, we just want you to pay attention to how manufacturers have hijacked the term "whole grains," hoping its patina of "healthiness" will now glaze over decidedly unhealthy high-carb foods from cookies to cereals to granola bars all the way down to Pepperidge Farm Goldfish.

Don't buy it for a minute.

Many of these foods (including breads) come loaded with high-fructose corn syrup (HFCS) and other sweeteners, preservatives, and even trans fat. But the deceptive term "made from whole grains," usually prominently displayed on the wrapper, creates what marketing executives call a *halo effect*. You've been told how healthy whole grains are, and this food contains whole grains; hence you believe you're eating something healthy, although in reality, nothing could be further from the truth.

The truth is that you'd be *way* better off putting this junk down and stepping away from the aisle that contains it. Here's why.

WHAT ARE WHOLE GRAINS, ANYWAY?

You hear the term "whole grains" tossed around frequently by dietitians and other "experts." You know the spiel: Eat a diet rich in vegetables, fruits, and whole grains. These three food groups are spoken about in the same sentence so often that we tend to think of them as equivalent, which they most certainly are not.

The healthiness of this holy trio—fruits, vegetables, and whole grains—becomes embedded in our consciousness, making differentiating between them a challenge. You already know what a vegetable is, and you certainly know what a fruit is. But have you actually thought about the definition of "whole grains"?

Probably not.

So let's get that out of the way first. A grain has three basic parts—the bran, the endosperm, and the germ. The bran is the outer coating and the endosperm is everything else except the germ, which is a little oval-shaped area inside the endosperm. So to qualify as a whole grain, 100 percent of the original kernel—all of the bran, germ, and endosperm—must be present. A refined, or processed, grain contains only the endosperm.

Examples of whole grains include amaranth, barley, buckwheat, whole cornmeal, millet, oats, quinoa, brown rice, rye, sorghum, triticale, wheat, and wild rice.

Sounds really healthy and nutritious, right?

Here's the problem.

You can't eat a whole grain out of the ground. No one plucks a stalk of wheat and starts chowing down on it. So to make this stuff edible, some processing is necessary. Often, though, once it's been processed and pounded and pulverized into oblivion, not to mention mixed with HFCS and a zillion other chemicals, very little of the original ingredient remains.

And that's just the beginning of the deception. Aware that you're more likely to associate color with health, many manufacturers add molasses or caramel color to give breads and other "healthy" foods a whole grain *look* even if they contain little or no whole grains at all.

You can buy doughnuts that contain whole grains and chips that contain whole grains, but guess what? They're still doughnuts and chips.

The only way to really know whether a food is whole grain is by reading its ingredients. If you see "whole" in the first ingredient—whole wheat, for instance—you're buying a whole grain food, or at least (and this is critical) one that *contains* some whole grain. So what? You can buy doughnuts that contain whole grains and chips that contain whole grains, but guess what? They're still doughnuts and chips.

Finding a cereal or bread with more than 2 grams of fiber per serving is as rare as an August cold wave in Vegas.

Though whole grains may have marginally more nutrients than the processed variety, the truth is they're not the healthiest food in the world even in their purest form. For example, on the glycemic index–a measure of how quickly a food raises blood sugar (see page 50)–white and whole wheat breads are only a point apart, with "white wheat bread" scoring a whopping 75 out of 100, whole wheat bread scoring 74, and a whole grain baguette scoring 73. (Wonder white bread–the poster child for junk food bread–scores between 71 and 77. For comparison, beans are around 30; peanuts are 7.)

Then there's the "standards" problem. When exactly can a product be labeled "whole grain"? The answer is fairly simple when you're dealing with 100 percent whole grains such as a dish of brown rice or oatmeal. But the answer is anything but simple when the ingredients in a product include *both* whole grains and refined or enriched grains. As the Whole Grains Council points out on its website, whether such a product is considered whole grain "depends on which government agency or program, in which country, has a say in the answer." In the United States, for example, the Food and Drug Administration allows a "whole grain health claim" when at least 51 percent of the total weight is whole grains. The other 49 percent can be whatever junk the manufacturer wants to put in there as long as there's a limit on fat and cholesterol–a pitch-perfect example of government idiocy.

If you think this seems confusing, you're not alone. Researchers at Harvard School of Public Health recently criticized manufacturers' obfuscating claims and demanded "a consistent, evidence-based standard for labeling whole-grain foods." They found, for instance, that some foods with the whole grain stamp contained more sugar than foods without the stamp!

The truth is, none of these terms–*whole grain*, *multigrain*, whatever–really mean anything; they simply allow manufacturers to sell more products under the guise that they're healthy.

With few exceptions, they're not. Whole grains don't really have much more going for them, nor are they necessarily any richer in fiber or nutrients. I'm often amused–and saddened–when I hear the conventional claptrap about how we need whole grains for fiber. You want to talk fiber heavyweights? Look at beans (11 to 17 grams per serving), avocados (about 8 grams per 1/2 fruit), edamame (8 grams per cup), canned pumpkin (7 grams per cup), or even the lowly apple (4.4 grams). Finding a cereal or bread with more than 2 grams of fiber per serving is as rare as an August cold wave in Vegas.

Why Most Whole Grains Are Basically Processed Carbs

Processed carbs include almost any carbohydrate food that comes in a package: cereals, pasta, bread, minute rice, you name it. As mentioned earlier, whole grains, despite their name, have some degree of processing, often way more than you might think. And did we also mention that these foods are almost always high glycemic, meaning they quickly and dramatically raise your blood sugar?

According to our friend, William Davis, M.D., cardiologist, whose book *Wheat Belly* should be required reading for anyone interested in health, "The degree of processing, from a blood sugar perspective, makes little difference. Wheat is wheat, with various forms of processing or lack of processing, simple or complex, high-fiber or low-fiber." Not surprisingly, he cites several studies in which wheat bread raises blood sugar just as much as white bread.

In Davis's view, wheat—more than any other grain—deserves special attention for myriad reasons, not the least of which is that the wheat we're eating today bears little resemblance to the wheat our grandmothers knew. The high-yielding wheat of today is a whole different animal. "Such enormous strides in yield have required drastic changes in genetic code, including reducing the proud 'amber waves of grain' of yesteryear to the rigid, 18-inch-tall high-production 'dwarf' wheat of today," says Davis.

To turn those amber waves of grain into tiny little bamboo poles takes quite a bit of genetic tinkering. Such fundamental changes to the wheat seed have come with a huge price tag. "Small changes in wheat protein structure can spell the difference between a devastating immune response to wheat protein versus no immune response at all," he says. In other words, tinkering sometimes has unforeseen—and unpredictable—consequences.

And remember, "contains whole grain," or whatever claim manufacturers slap onto labels, doesn't make a whit of difference to your pancreas. Eating these so-called healthy grain-based foods throughout the day keeps your blood sugar elevated, increasing your risk for insulin resistance, diabetes, and heart disease. A 2010 study in the *Archives of Internal Medicine* demonstrated that women who ate the highest amount of carbohydrates had a significantly greater risk of coronary heart disease than those who ate the lowest amount, and that consumption of high-glycemic carbs was particularly associated with significantly greater risk for heart disease.

So whole grains aren't really so "whole," and they can often raise blood sugar levels as much as or more than other heavily processed carbs.

And then we must consider the gluten issue.

> A 2010 study demonstrated that women who ate the highest amount of carbohydrates had a significantly greater risk of coronary heart disease than those who ate the lowest amount.

GLUTEN: WHAT'S ALL THE HYPE ABOUT?

A few years ago, if someone mentioned being on a gluten-free diet, you might well have had a puzzled look on your face. But that was then and this is now. Now virtually every supermarket in America has a gluten-free section, and many restaurants routinely offer gluten-free options.

So what's the deal with gluten and why does it get such a bad rep?

Gluten is simply a protein found in barley, rye, and all varieties of wheat. Although *you* may not have heard much about gluten, one group of people has heard about it: those with a condition called celiac disease. For someone with this genetic condition, even the tiniest bit of gluten can set off an immune reaction, inflammation, and numerous symptoms that can range from miserable to debilitating.

One of the reasons for those nasty reactions is a situation in the body called "leaky gut syndrome." Leaky gut syndrome refers to the state in which the tight junctions of the cells that line the digestive tract start to loosen and become less of a barrier to the bloodstream. When this happens, partly undigested particles of food as well as toxins and microbes and all sorts of riffraff can slip through and enter the bloodstream, triggering an immune reaction that can involve headaches to cell bloating to aches and pains. For someone with leaky gut, gluten can be an especially annoying problem, even though it may not reach celiac-diagnosis land.

Though full-blown celiac disease was originally thought to be a rare childhood syndrome, we now know that it's a much more common genetic disorder, affecting more than 2 million people in the United States alone, or about 1 in 133 people. And among those who have a parent, sibling, or child diagnosed with celiac, it's even more common, with as many as 1 in 22 first-degree relatives having the disease.

Celiac disease is the most dramatic manifestation of gluten intolerance. But we're finding out that gluten sensitivity exists on a continuum, and just because you don't have full-blown celiac disease does *not* mean gluten isn't a problem for you. Many people—far more than you can imagine—have what's called "gluten sensitivity," meaning that their bodies just do not handle gluten very well.

The late great nutritionist, Shari Lieberman, Ph.D., wrote eloquently of this in her wonderful book, *The Gluten Connection*. She points out that misdiagnosis of gluten sensitivity is rampant because the symptoms look so much like those of other diseases and disorders. "Not only are people who are misdiagnosed relegated to 'living with' a disease (when they may be able to be free of it), but living with this condition can lead to severe consequences—such as the irreversible crippling of rheumatoid arthritis, bone loss and breakage, infection, or even death," she writes.

Misdiagnosis of gluten sensitivity is rampant because the symptoms look so much like those of other diseases and disorders.

Oats: One of Our Favorite Grains

We use oatmeal in this book, so a word about oats. Oats are naturally gluten free, but it's worth mentioning that they're often processed in facilities that also process gluten-containing grains, thus creating potential cross-contamination. For people who are not extremely gluten sensitive this shouldn't be much of a problem, but for people who are, it most definitely is.

Lieberman believes that conditions as diverse as psoriasis, eczema, headaches, autoimmune diseases, chronic fatigue, fibromyalgia, and digestive disorders such as irritable bowel, Crohn's disease, and ulcerative colitis may all be related in some way to gluten sensitivity. Many of these conditions—not all, mind you, but many—improve on a gluten-free diet.

Even if you don't have gluten sensitivities (and keep in mind most people *do* to some degree), other substances in gluten-containing grains can be a problem. For example, the protein *zonulin* can damage the tight junctions that protect your gut lining, so that stuff not intended to get through your gut suddenly begins to slip through, triggering an immune reaction.

There are also proteins in gluten called *lectins* that bind to insulin receptors, which can interfere with insulin doing its job of escorting sugar into the cells. Put this together with how high-grain products frequently raise blood sugar and bam! You've got a double whammy for insulin resistance.

Even worse, those lectins can create *leptin resistance*. (You may remember from chapter 3 that leptin is a hormone that signals your brain to stop eating. Leptin resistance is a huge topic in medicine right now, as we're finding that it's almost always present in obesity.) When leptin receptors become resistant, your brain doesn't get the message that you're full, and you're more likely to reach for seconds. And thirds. And fourths. And if that weren't bad enough, compounds in gluten-containing foods contain something called *phytates* (also found in soy), which block the absorption of minerals, one of which is chromium—known to help regulate insulin sensitivity.

Beginning to get the picture?

Gluten can also increase inflammation. And as we wrote in *The Great Cholesterol Myth*, we consider inflammation one of the four major promoters of heart disease, possibly the most important one. A study that involved almost 30,000 people over nearly 40 years published in the *Journal of the American Medical Association* found people with celiac disease or gluten intolerance had a higher risk of dying in any given year than those without it. Heart disease or cancer triggered most of those deaths.

Those in the study with full-blown celiac disease had a 39 percent increased risk, but those with gluten intolerances weren't far behind, with a 35 percent increased risk of death. But here's the study's most interesting finding: People with *gluten-related gut inflammation* had a whopping *72* percent increased risk of dying earlier than those without the condition.

Whole Grains and Inflammation

We described earlier how gluten could damage your gut wall, creating leaky gut and triggering an immune response that is nearly always accompanied by inflammation. Having leaky gut makes it much easier for proteins to slip (leak) through your gut wall and take up residence within certain tissues or joints. You're likely to suffer localized chronic inflammation because your body overreacts to what it sees as a foreign invader. Joint pain is a classic symptom of gluten intolerance.

OK, you say. Good reason to go gluten free. But what about gluten-free grains?

Here's the bad news. It's not just the gluten in the grains that causes problems. Whole grains and other high-glycemic carbohydrates are inflammatory, *period*. According to research from Harvard Medical School and the Harvard School of Public Health, quickly digested and absorbed carbs (i.e., those with a high glycemic load) are associated with an increased risk of heart disease.

In the *American Journal of Clinical Nutrition* these same researchers examined the diets of 244 apparently healthy women to evaluate the association between glycemic load and blood levels of C-reactive protein (CRP), a systemic measure of inflammation. They found "a strong and statistically significant positive association between dietary glycemic load and [blood levels of] CRP."

That's putting it mildly. Women whose diets were highest in glycemic load had almost *twice* the amount of CRP in their blood as did women whose diets were *lowest* in glycemic load.

The difference in inflammation levels was even more pronounced for overweight women. Among women with a body mass index (BMI) greater than 25 mg/L, those whose diets were lowest in glycemic load had an average CRP reading of 1.6, but those whose diets were highest in glycemic load had a CRP reading more than three times that amount (average measurement: 5.0 mg/L).

Bottom line: Whether they're "made from whole grains" or not, processed carbohydrates can create and exacerbate inflammation.

THE GLUTEN-FREE SCAM

Aware that you know gluten isn't good for you, manufacturers have leapt onto the gluten-free bandwagon. Witness the ever-widening array of gluten-free doughnuts, chips, and other junk foods. To further create a healthy illusion, manufacturers add agave as a sweetener, even though agave contains more metabolism-damaging fructose than high-fructose corn syrup!

Yes, we know it's disappointing news, but just because your Whole Foods or local health food store sells it, does *not* make it healthy.

Nature packaged its own gluten-free diet, which conveniently also happens to be the perfect anti-inflammatory diet, and guess what? It didn't come with a bar code or labels. Here it is, and it's real simple: Healthy protein, good fats such as avocado, coconut, and the healthy saturated fat in grass-fed meat, tons of vegetables, low-glycemic fruits, and a whole bunch of nuts and seeds. There's no need to scrutinize labels or ingredients with a stalk of broccoli or an apple.

Nature packaged its own gluten-free diet, which conveniently also happens to be the perfect anti-inflammatory diet, and guess what? It didn't come with a bar code or labels.

If You Do Eat Grains . . .

We don't buy into the whole grain promise, or at least we don't buy it completely, and here's why: (1) because most commercial products made with whole grains don't contain all that much of them; (2) because whole grains raise blood sugar almost as much as (and sometimes *more* than) processed grains do; (3) because gluten, whether in whole grain products or refined grain products, creates additional problems for a wide swath of the population.

Despite what bread manufacturers and some establishment health "experts" will have you believe, you can live a healthy, vibrant life without ever touching another grain. And if you have blood sugar imbalances or insulin issues (and most of us do to some degree), you might find you're better off completely eliminating grains from your diet, at least for a trial period.

That said, there are some whole grain "finds" on the market, starting with oatmeal. Brown rice isn't so bad on occasion, and products such as Ezekiel 4:9 breads are light-years better for you than their processed counterparts.

But when it comes to grains, it's important to be mindful. Grains aren't good for everybody, nor are they *necessary* for everybody. That doesn't mean you should never eat them. But it *does* mean that you should be an educated consumer.

Just because a label says "gluten-free," or "wheat" instead of "white," or "made with whole grains," don't automatically assume that product is good for *you*.

Do I Need to Pay Attention to the Glycemic Index?

The glycemic index is a measure of how quickly and how high your blood sugar rises after eating food. It's not nearly as important as a less famous measure called the glycemic load. And the glycemic load *is* something worth knowing about.

As you know, when you eat any food, especially carbohydrate and to some extent protein, your blood sugar goes up. (It hardly goes up at all when you eat fat.) In response to the rise in blood sugar, your pancreas secretes insulin, whose job is to act as a traffic cop and escort the excess sugar out of the bloodstream and into the cells where, in an ideal world, it can be used for fuel. Blood sugar and insulin both gradually go back down to pre-eating levels, and in a few hours you repeat the whole process.

Problem is, this is anything but a perfect world. Let's recap:

We eat too many high-sugar carbohydrates, which quickly drives our blood sugar up into the stratosphere.

The pancreas sends out a ton of insulin in an attempt to lower blood sugar.

Insulin escorts the sugar to the muscle cells.

The muscle cells are pretty much on vacation because they're not being used very much. So when insulin comes knocking, they *resist* opening their doors.

Sugar winds up going to the fat cells.

Meanwhile both blood sugar and insulin have been raised, setting you up for hypertension, fat storage, hunger, cravings, and mood crashes when your sugar eventually does fall.

To measure the effect of food on blood sugar, scientists came up with the idea of the glycemic index. Using pure glucose as a standard (with an index of 100), they tested 50-gram portions of digestible carbohydrates and measured how quickly and how high blood sugar rose in reaction to eating them. By eating low-glycemic-index foods you presumably could avoid the blood sugar roller coaster.

But there are two big problems with using the glycemic index as a guide to eating. One, it only applies to a food eaten alone—in other words, a banana, not a banana with peanut butter. Two, and more important—the glycemic index doesn't take into account portion size.

The glycemic index of 50 grams of spaghetti is moderate, but no one eats 50 grams of spaghetti, at least they don't at the Olive Garden, or at any home-cooked Italian meal I've ever been to! (A 50-gram portion of pasta is the size of a small appetizer—about 2 ounces.) And the glycemic index of 50 grams of carrots is high, but no one eats 50 grams of carrots (there's 3 grams of carbohydrate in a carrot, so you'd have to eat a bushel to get the required 50 grams).

The glycemic load is much more accurate because it takes into account portion size. Carrots, which have a high glycemic *index*, actually have a very low glycemic *load*. Spaghetti, which has a *moderate* index, has a very *high* glycemic load. (You can find a definitive table of glycemic index *and* glycemic load of foods at www.mendosa.com/gilists.htm).

Glycemic load is all you need to pay attention to, because it tells you what's going to happen to your blood sugar in the real world. (Even then, it still refers to food eaten alone. Add some fat to your carbs, peanut butter on an apple, for example, and you've just lowered the glycemic load.)

Bottom line: Eat as little sugar as possible and go easy on the foods that turn into sugar quickly, such as cereals, breads, pastas, and anything white (except chicken, cauliflower, and mushrooms!).

When it comes to sugar one thing is very clear: Less is more, and zero is better.

5 FOODS FOR A HEALTHY HEART

Which foods—including a few surprising ones—are critical to heart health and why; how to decipher nutrition labels

"Food may be the most powerful drug you will ever encounter because it causes dramatic changes in your hormones that are hundreds of times more powerful than any pharmaceutical."

—Barry Sears, Ph.D.

In the past few chapters we've told you to skip sugar, processed foods, and trans fat, and to cut way back on vegetable oils, all of which can wreak havoc on your health. Considering those items constitute a big portion of the calories in the standard American diet, it could easily leave you wondering, "What's left to eat?"

Plenty, actually.

We covered many of the best foods for heart health in *The Great Cholesterol Myth* along with copious studies to support their benefits. (And, shameless plug, if you'd like more, please refer to Dr. Jonny's best-selling book, *The 150 Healthiest Foods on Earth*.) For the purposes of this book, though, we're going to keep references to studies at a minimum. We don't want this to be a textbook on food composition—we want it to be a hands-on primer about designing meals that benefit cardiovascular health while also helping you burn fat, build muscle, and look and feel your best.

We consider this the most effective heart-healthy eating plan in the world.

What all—OK, most—of these foods have in common is that they're whole, unprocessed foods. (Not all of them, because a dark chocolate bar is certainly processed to some extent, but we wouldn't want to leave that off our list!) If you're looking for labels, you might call this a kind of neo-Paleolithic eating plan, which is fine with us. That just means the foods on the list are very close to what your ancestors would have eaten, with perhaps a few adaptations for modern life. The basic diet is lower in carbs and definitely low glycemic, a one-two punch for optimal health. Whatever label you want to put on it (or even if you don't want to label it at all), we consider this the most effective heart-healthy eating plan in the world, one that has a great deal of overlap with what's eaten in the Mediterranean regions as well as what's traditionally eaten by healthy, vital indigenous groups all over the globe.

The foods listed in this chapter also happen to be quite tasty! And you'll see exactly what I mean when you taste the amazing dishes Deirdre Rawlings has come up with, incorporating them, and others, of course, into 100 mouthwatering recipes.

You see, deprivation is not in our vocabulary. We enjoy healthy, satisfying foods, and we want you to as well. So although every food here points to heart health, we haven't forgotten that food should be enjoyed. As our good friend the late, great nutritionist Robert Crayhon used to say, "Pleasure is a nutrient."

We couldn't agree more.

BANISH THE ENEMIES

First let's recap. Here are the things that have got to go in your diet, at least if you want to keep your heart in tip-top shape:

Sugar. Sugar is the number-one dietary enemy of heart health. As we've pointed out, sugar hides in ingredient labels under numerous disguises, including many with healthy-sounding names. Honey, agave, brown rice syrup, organic cane syrup: Whatever you want to call it, sugar is sugar is sugar. The less you eat, the better off you'll be.

Processed foods. Most of the foods in the center aisles of your grocery store are processed foods. And this includes foods that have labels proclaiming "whole wheat goodness." It also includes a large number of low-fat chemical concoctions passing as real food these days. Don't be fooled. Your heart and your health deserve better than these Frankenfoods.

Trans fat. Never mind that the label boasts "zero trans fat." Read the actual ingredients. If you see the words "partially hydrogenated," that food has trans fat, period. Put it back.

Processed meats. Bologna, sausage, and sliced luncheon meats come loaded with gluten, preservatives, sodium, nitrates, and a lot of other crap you don't want. When it comes to meat—or should we say, meat "products"—these are the worst of the worst (followed closely by feedlot-farmed meat, which is high in antibiotics, steroids, hormones, and inflammatory omega-6s). Processed meats bear no resemblance to the grass-fed meat we talk about below, which is a true health food.

When in doubt, just remember that when it comes to selecting foods, the emphasis should be on whole, unprocessed, nutrient-rich foods. Stuff your great-grandparents would recognize as food. Stuff that Dr. Jonny has been referring to for years as members of the "Jonny Bowden Four Food Groups"—food you could hunt, fish, gather, or pluck. Most of this comes without a bar code and spoils relatively quickly, because it's actually alive (or recently was). (Compare that with a Twinkie, which has a sell-by date of nearly forever.)

The following list isn't inclusive, and you'll find many more foods in *The Great Cholesterol Myth*. What we've chosen here are a basic selection of the healthiest options for fantastic heart and overall health.

Grass-Fed Beef: Health-Food Meat from Happy Cows

In 2013, Dr. Jonny participated in a Huffington Post Live event, on a panel with two organic butchers in Los Angeles and a small organic farmer in Iowa. The subject? Meat. Here's the main take-home message: The feedlot-farmed meat you buy in the supermarket and grass-fed beef are as different as West Virginia and West Hollywood.

Cows eat grass. That's what they thrive on. Grain should not be a part of their diet.

You might have read something about the horrific conditions feedlot animals are subjected to. It's even worse than you imagined. The animals are pumped with hormones and steroids and injected with antibiotics because they invariably get sick from their unnatural (for them) grain-based diet and from their horrendously crowded living conditions. Cows that produce conventional meat are fed grain (usually corn) to fatten them up prematurely for slaughter, yielding beef with a disproportionate amount of pro-inflammatory omega-6 fatty acids and a paucity of omega-3s.

Let's be real. Cows eat grass. That's what they thrive on. Grain should not be a part of their diet. Grass-fed beef contains less inflammatory omega-6s and more anti-inflammatory omega-3s, creating a better omega balance. And their meat contains no hormones, steroids, or antibiotics.

That's not all. Pasture-raised, grass-fed beef is higher in many nutrients, including vitamin E and beta-carotene. It's also rich in a cancer-fighting, fat-burning fatty acid called *conjugated linoleic acid* (CLA).

Not surprisingly, grass-fed beef is usually more expensive, though bargains can be had. (In Southern California, the wonderful Novy Ranches—run by a very conscientious veterinarian named Lowell Novy—produce remarkable grass-fed beef for about $5 a pound, but you have to live in Southern California to get it.) But more stores are now carrying it as the word spreads about the health properties of grass-fed (pasture-raised) meat. Our answer to the price problem? Get the good stuff, but eat less of it. We'd rather have one or two great grass-fed buffalo burgers a week than seven burgers from the fast-food emporium. If you're on a budget, focus on more plant-based foods but definitely include grass-fed beef or other high-quality protein in your diet.

We like to visit our farmers' market for grass-fed beef, eggs, and organic produce. We talk to the vendors, learn what they feed their animals, and how they treat their animals. Conscientious farmers who raise their cattle humanely and healthily are usually passionate about this stuff and will talk to you for as long as you'll listen. Talk to them sometime—it's an education.

Wild-Caught Fish: A Whole Different "Animal" from Farm-Raised!

Farm-raised fish sounds good. After all, you can feed the fish whatever you want and you don't have the mercury problem cold-water fish have.

Unfortunately, fish farmers now raise salmon under the marine equivalent of the abysmal feedlot conditions under which cows are raised. They feed them grain and actually use dye to produce an appealing color. (We're not kidding. Wild salmon get their beautiful pink color from eating krill and shrimp high in the reddish antioxidant *astaxanthin*, the benefits of which are passed on to you when you eat wild-caught fish. Grain-fed fish come out a dullish gray color, so fish farmers dye them a more appealing pinkish hue.) The issues with hormones and antibiotics also plague farm-raised fish.

This is too bad, because fish is an excellent source of protein, nutrients, and the two important omega 3-fatty acids *eicosapentaenoic acid* (EPA) and *docosahexaenoic acid* (DHA). We'll cover their benefits more in chapter 6, but for now let's just say these essential fatty acids pack a serious anti-inflammatory, heart-healthy wallop.

Unfortunately, fish farmers now raise salmon under the marine equivalent of the abysmal feedlot conditions under which cows are raised.

What about mercury, you might ask? Well, that's definitely a problem with wild-caught fish, though most studies that have evaluated the pros and cons of fish have found that the enormous nutritious gains of eating cold-water fish outweigh the potential hazards of mercury, at least in the amounts in which it's commonly found. Meanwhile, the trace mineral selenium helps chelate (bind to and remove) that mercury. That should take away some of the worry.

One of our favorite sources of wild-caught fish (and lots of other healthy cool foods) is Vital Choice in Alaska, a company deservedly famous for sustainability and quality. Both Dr. Sinatra and Dr. Jonny get our salmon from Vital Choice, which you can find online.

Free-Range Poultry: Another Great Source of Heart-Healthy Protein

A rich source of protein, healthy fats, and nutrients, chicken and turkey make excellent and versatile meats for salads, main dishes, and even preworkout snacks.

The nutrient profile of dark and light meat is slightly different, but it's all good, so eat whichever you prefer (or mix 'em up!). Poultry is rich in heart-healthy monounsaturated fat, the same fat that's found in olive oil and that's such a huge component of the much-touted Mediterranean diet.

As with all meats, quality matters. Go for free-range, organic poultry whenever possible and get to know your sources.

Eggs: Truly Nature's Most Perfect Food (Including the Yolks!)

Eggs are one of the best and least-expensive sources of high-quality protein you can possibly buy. In addition, they contain good fat and a host of nutrients such as *choline* for the brain, and *lutein* and *zeaxanthin* for the eyes. Eggs got a bad and undeserved reputation for raising cholesterol, but thankfully that myth has now been firmly debunked. Dietary cholesterol contributes little to blood levels of cholesterol, and even if it did, by now you know how little cholesterol contributes to heart disease.

Eggs are also anti-inflammatory. One study in *Nutrition and Metabolism* found that a low-carb diet that included eggs decreased inflammatory C-reactive protein (CRP), an important marker for overall cardiovascular health. Researchers also found that the cholesterol in eggs increases HDL (the so-called "good" cholesterol), whereas the antioxidant lutein modulates certain inflammatory responses.

To increase that anti-inflammatory benefit, look for omega-3-enriched, organic eggs. Better yet, hit up your farmers' market for eggs from barnyard-raised chickens, which tend to be higher in vitamin D and other nutrients.

Vegetables: The One Type of Food Everyone Agrees On!

Put nine health experts on stage and you're pretty much guaranteed to run into some major disagreements about the ideal diet. So when you find one area of nutrition just about every expert agrees on, it's time to pay attention. And the single principle that just about everyone agrees on is this: We should all be eating more vegetables.

Vegetables are loaded with heart-healthy antioxidants, anti-inflammatories, and other plant chemicals such as flavonoids, flavanols, catechins, polyphenols, and other botanical wonders. We don't know anyone alive who wouldn't benefit from eating more vegetables, and this includes our friends in the Paleo and low-carb communities.

Now, there are vegetable rock stars and there are ancillary players. The A-listers include green, leafy veggies (spinach, for instance, and Swiss chard) and cruciferous ones (broccoli, Brussels sprouts, kale, cabbage, and cauliflower). Broccoli, for example, is a flavonoid powerhouse that also packs an anti-inflammatory, antioxidant punch.

You could eat bushels of spinach and take in fewer calories than you'd get in half a slice of pizza, so consider green vegetables essentially as a "free food," even if you're trying to lose weight. We cook ours with olive oil, coconut oil, butter, or sometimes a combination of the three. These healthy fats provide flavor and also help you better absorb the fat-soluble nutrients in green vegetables. It's a win-win.

Fruit: A Heart-Healthy Staple

There's no such thing as a bad fruit: They all contain valuable nutrients. That said, the "free food" stipulation doesn't extend to fruits, especially higher-sugar fruits like bananas and grapes. Although most people can handle a certain amount of fructose, which is naturally found in fruit, too much can create inflammation, fatty liver, and the other problems fructose is associated with, so keep fruit to a couple of portions a day and give a little more weight to the "vegetables" member of the "fruits and vegetables" duo.

When it comes to fruits, you can't go wrong with berries. First, they're low glycemic, meaning they don't create a big blood sugar spike. Second, they're loaded with anti-inflammatory compounds like *anthocyanins*. Third of all, they have a great assortment of antioxidants. And fourth, they contain fiber.

Blueberries, for instance, contain a compound called *pterostilbene* that prevents arterial plaque deposit and oxidized cholesterol damage. Raspberries and strawberries have *ellagic acid*, which also offers protection against oxidized LDL. And, though not a berry, cherries are also a tremendous source of anthocyanins that perform like natural anti-inflammatory COX-2 inhibitors.

So eat as many kinds of berries (and cherries) as you can. One of our favorite desserts is frozen berries stirred into unsweetened Greek yogurt. (You don't see dairy on this list because we're not huge fans of cow's milk, but unflavored, unsweetened Greek yogurt with the live and active culture seal is one of several healthy exceptions.)

After berries, look for medium-glycemic fruits like apples, which contain a ton of phytochemicals like *quercetin* and *chlorogenic acid*, both of which provide serious antioxidant benefits against cardiovascular disease. Grapefruit is another terrific choice.

Nuts: Protein, Fat, and Minerals in a Heart-Protecting Snack

When we were growing up, the conventional wisdom was that nuts were fattening. Later, in the decades commencing around 1970, the critique of nuts became more specific—they're high in fat! Finally, as we rounded the 1990s, the powers that be grudgingly admitted that all fat was not bad and pronounced the fat in nuts "healthy." There's probably a lesson in all this, but other than "be careful of listening to conventional wisdom," we're not sure what it is.

What we do know is that nuts are one of the heart-healthiest foods on the planet. Most of the fat in almonds, macadamia nuts, and other types comes from monounsaturated fat, the same stuff in olive oil and avocado. Almonds, for instance, are about 70 percent monounsaturated fat. The fat in walnuts and pecans is also mostly monounsaturated fat, with walnuts having some omega-3s as well. As for the relatively small amount of saturated fat in nuts, well, we've already told you what we think about that—you have little to fear from saturated fat in whole food sources such as nuts.

Nuts are one of the heart-healthiest foods on the planet.

Five large studies, in fact, showed eating nuts several times a week was associated with a 30 to 50 percent lower risk of heart attack or heart disease.

One of the many reasons nuts are so good for your heart is that they are a rich source of an amino acid called *arginine*. Arginine protects the inner lining of your artery walls (the endothelium), making them less susceptible to atherogenesis. Arginine also helps make nitric oxide, an important molecule that is needed to relax blood vessels and increase blood flow. In addition, nuts provide a great source of numerous heart-healthy antioxidant phytonutrients to protect against coronary heart disease.

Let's face it, nuts pack some serious calories and are not an "unlimited" or free food. But in the long-running Nurses' Health Study II, women who reported eating nuts two or more times a week had slightly less weight gain over time than those who rarely ate nuts at all and had a slightly lower risk of obesity.

Beans: A Fiber Heavyweight for the Heart

"Studies have shown that foods that have a lot of fiber are clearly associated with lower risk of heart disease," says Alice H. Lichtenstein, D.Sc., American Heart Association spokeswoman and director of the cardiovascular nutrition research program at Tufts University's Jean Mayer USDA Human Nutrition Research Center on Aging. We agree. We think fiber is one of the most important things you can ingest.

And one of the best foods to get it from is beans.

Though we've been fed a crock of you-know-what about cereals and breads being "needed" for fiber, the truth is that most cereals (and breads) provide pathetic amounts; if you want to talk fiber heavyweights, it's all about the beans. Garbanzo beans (also known as chickpeas) pack almost 13 grams per cup. Black beans provide about 15 grams. But the winner might well be lentils, which have 16 grams of fiber along with 18

If you want to talk fiber heavyweights, it's all about the beans. The winner might well be lentils, which have 16 grams of fiber along with 18 grams of protein.

grams of protein. Nice. (For comparison, you're lucky to find a slice of bread or a cup of cereal with more than 2 to 3 grams at best.) Our Paleolithic ancestors ate between 50 and 100 grams a day of fiber. Most mainstream health organizations, which are not known to be wide-eyed radicals on the subject of nutritional requirements, recommend between 25 and 38 grams a day. The average American gets between 4 and 11 grams. Do the math. Legumes are an easy way to meet the quota.

Foods high in fiber provide good protection against cardiovascular disease, and, according to one study from the scientific journal *PLOS One*, the effect is particularly marked in women. "Women who ate a diet high in fiber had an almost 25 percent lower risk of suffering from cardiovascular disease compared with women who ate a low-fiber diet," lead researcher Peter Wallstrom of Lund University told *ScienceDaily*. "In men the effect was less pronounced. However, the results confirmed that a high-fiber diet does at least protect men from stroke."

Although the exact reason for the differences between the sexes is not known, it's been suggested that women consumed most of their fiber from fruits and vegetables while men consumed most of theirs from bread.

Besides being fiber heavyweights, legumes are also a rich source of antioxidants. At one time, the U.S. Department of Agriculture ranked foods by antioxidant capacity, using a measure known as the ORAC scale. Small red dried beans had the highest antioxidant capacity per serving size of any food tested, and several other beans topped the list. Most beans are also rich in folate (folic acid), a key player in reducing homocysteine, an important culprit in heart disease.

Dark Chocolate: A Health Food for the Ages

Dark chocolate for your heart? Yup. (We thought you'd like that one!) Dark chocolate is a rich source of flavonoids, the same antioxidant compounds you find in tea, strawberries, and red wine.

The particular flavonoids in cocoa are a subgroup called *cocoa flavanols*, which prevent fatlike substances from clogging your arteries, therefore reducing your risk for heart attack. Flavanols also stimulate the production of nitric acid for healthy blood flow and optimal cardiovascular health.

When we say chocolate, we're not talking about the stuff you get at the drugstore front counter or convenience store, which is often loaded with sugar (especially high-fructose corn syrup), bad fats, and artificial crap. Bypass that stuff for high-quality dark chocolate with at least 70 percent cacao and very little sugar.

Dark chocolate is far less "fattening" than you might think. The typical high-quality bar contains 210 calories, but a half—or even a quarter—of a bar is very satisfying. Because dark chocolate isn't cloyingly sweet, it's nonaddictive, and a small portion, even a couple of squares, goes a long way.

Worth knowing: A few years ago, the *British Medical Journal* published a piece on the perfect meal, one that—if eaten consistently—would be projected to lower the risk for heart disease and premature death by double digits. The seven foods this perfect meal contained were cold-water fish (salmon), vegetables, nuts, garlic, beans, red wine, and—wait for it—dark chocolate. Thought you'd want to know!

Turmeric: The Superstar of Spices

In Dr. Jonny's bestseller, *The 150 Healthiest Foods on Earth*, several foods, spices, and beverages received "stars" for being—even in a sea of outstanding performers—superstars. One of them was turmeric.

Turmeric is the spice that gives curries and Indian foods their orange-yellow color. And it deserves its reputation as a superfood. Among its many benefits, turmeric is a powerful anti-inflammatory, in addition to which it has anticancer activity. Its antioxidant benefits help quench the oxidized LDL that contributes to inflammation and heart disease.

The benefits of turmeric come mainly from a group of plant compounds called curcuminoids, the primary one being *curcumin*. We like curcumin so much we included it in our recommended supplements for heart health (see chapter 6 for more information). For now, let's just say this compound packs one heck of a serious anti-inflammatory punch.

Turmeric adds a nice kick to food, so sprinkle this spice everywhere you can. We love it on poached and scrambled eggs and sautéed spinach, and in, of course, curries and Middle Eastern dishes.

Green Tea: Health Insurance in a Teacup

Green tea is a beverage rock star, thanks mainly to an anticancer compound called *epigallocatechin gallate*. Sure, green tea lowers cholesterol, but more importantly it lowers *fibrinogen*, a substance in the body that can cause clots and strokes. (We discuss fibrinogen at greater length in *The Great Cholesterol Myth*.) Bottom line: One study concluded "the more green tea patients

> Green tea drinkers rarely get the jitters. Why? Because green tea contains an amino acid called *L-theanine*, which has a calming effect on your brain.

consume, the less likely they are to have coronary artery disease."

Consider this: Green tea drinkers rarely get the jitters. Why? Because green tea contains an amino acid called *L-theanine*, which has a calming effect on your brain. It helps your brain release the neurotransmitter GABA, which is very calming. (In Asia, L-theanine is frequently prescribed for anxiety and has been available as a supplement for decades.) Because stress, you'll remember, is a major contributor to heart disease, anything that can calm the brain is a good thing!

But it's not just green tea that's great for the cardiovascular system. Every type of tea is good: Oolong, black, and white teas all provide their own benefits. Black tea, for instance, lowers triglycerides and helps trigger the antioxidant *superoxide dismutase*. And a tea from a completely different plant—yerba maté—has been found to be extremely high in antioxidants. Drink them all, and often.

Olive Oil: The Not-So-Secret Ingredient in the Mediterranean Diet

The Mediterranean diet is practically synonymous with heart health, and one of the big stars of the Mediterranean diet, no matter which version of it you're talking about, is olive oil. The main fat in olive oil is a monounsaturated fatty acid called *oleic acid*. Among its many health benefits, olive oil contains polyphenols that are powerful antioxidants.

Always choose extra-virgin olive oil, which has the least amount of processing, is not processed at high temperatures, and is by far the healthiest kind of olive oil. Because light can damage olive oil's fragile amino acids, always buy extra-virgin olive oil in opaque glass containers. And for goodness' sake, don't heat extra-virgin olive oil to very high temperatures, as that defeats the purpose of using the more expensive extra-virgin variety! Instead, use it for sautéing and for drizzling.

Garlic: A Global Remedy for Heart Health

Garlic is the closest thing to a universal remedy. This much-studied bulb, a member of the lily family (which includes onions, shallots, and chives) carries quite a résumé. It's antithrombotic, anti-blood coagulation, antihypertensive, and antioxidant. In other words, garlic provides serious cardiovascular protection.

To get these numerous benefits, you need to freshly chop or crush the garlic. The compound most responsible for garlic's many benefits–*allicin*–is made when you crush the garlic and starts to degrade almost as soon as it's produced, so fresher garlic is better.

Garlic is easy to incorporate into foods. Meats become more flavorful, and we really love sautéing spinach (or other green veggies) in garlic and coconut oil. Just remember to chop it fresh, and avoid eating too much on first dates!

Pomegranate Juice: Oxidized Cholesterol's Worst Enemy

Pomegranate juice is one of the highly touted superantioxidant juices that has actually lived up to the hype. Israeli researchers found that pomegranate juice had the highest antioxidant capacity compared to other juices, red wine, and green tea. In one study, published in the *American Journal of the College of Cardiologists*, forty-five patients with ischemic heart disease drank either a daily dose of 8 ounces of pomegranate juice or a placebo. Those who drank the juice had significantly less oxygen deficiency to the heart during exercise, which suggests increased blood flow to the heart.

Equally terrific, pomegranate juice has also shown a greater ability to inhibit the oxidation of LDL cholesterol than other beverages. Remember, only *oxidized* cholesterol is a problem, so anything that helps prevent oxidation of cholesterol is a good thing. And if that weren't enough, at least five other studies have demonstrated a beneficial effect of pomegranate juice on cardiovascular health, including a study that showed a whopping 30 percent reduction in arterial plaque.

With pomegranate juice you want to get the pure stuff, not mixed with a bunch of other juices in a pomegranate "fruit drink" and sweetened to within an inch of its life. It'll be more expensive, but worth it.

Pulling It All Together

Incorporating heart-healthy foods becomes easy and delicious once you get a "big picture" idea of what a typical day's menu looks like. We've created a sample menu that, once you get the hang of it, becomes easy whether you're on the road, vacation, juggling a hectic workload, or just enjoying a relaxing weekend at home. Also, see chapter 7 for a month's worth of sample menus using the 100 heart-healthy recipes in this book.

Breakfast

Three-egg organic omelet with sautéed spinach, broccoli, feta cheese, and salsa

Green tea

Lunch

Spinach salad topped with garlic chicken, avocado, tomato, and extra-virgin olive oil and vinegar

Filtered water

Snack

1 ounce raw almonds or 2 tablespoons almond butter

Apple slices

Dinner

Wild-caught salmon

Asparagus sautéed in olive oil and garlic

Steamed cauliflower

Fresh organic blueberries for dessert

Glass of pinot noir (optional)

6 SUPPLEMENTS FOR A HEALTHY HEART

What you need to know about citrus bergamot, coenzyme Q_{10}, L-carnitine, magnesium, D-ribose, omega fatty acids, vitamins C and D, curcumin, and resveratrol

This is what we say when people ask us, "Do I need nutritional supplements?"

"No. Nor do you need indoor plumbing and electricity. But why in the world would you choose to live without them?"

Nutritional supplements are just a high-tech delivery system for nutrients that your body absolutely needs. The key word in the supplement controversy here is "need." For decades dietitians and medical doctors saw nutritional needs only as necessary to prevent deficiency diseases. Most of the recommendations we're saddled with today came from a culture that looked at vitamin C "needs" only in terms of what would prevent scurvy, vitamin D "needs" in terms of what would prevent rickets, etc.

Neither of us has ever seen a clinical case of scurvy. Nor rickets. Nor beriberi, for that matter. But we have seen hundreds, if not thousands, of cases where people were consuming considerably less than the optimal amount of certain nutrients. And we have been around long enough to know the difference between the amount of a nutrient necessary to prevent a vitamin deficiency disease and the amount of a nutrient needed for optimal health.

What's more, the heart is a special case. It consumes more than its share of coenzyme Q_{10} (CoQ_{10}), a nutrient that is essentially impossible to get in significant amounts from the diet unless you're a big fan of organ meats. Heart patients in recovery have been shown to benefit significantly from nutrients like D-ribose and L-carnitine, and we suspect that those same nutrients, which benefit an ailing heart, will also benefit a healthy one, hopefully upping the odds that said heart *remains* healthy!

So we're big believers in the benefits of supplements. If you can incrementally reduce your risk factor for heart disease and improve cardiovascular health with a few inexpensive, readily available nutrients in healthy doses, we don't see any drawbacks.

At the same time, you can't eat a crappy diet, live a sedentary existence, stress out on a daily basis, and then expect amazing results swallowing some supplements. These are *supplements*, and they're meant to complement, not replace, a healthy diet and lifestyle.

Simply put, these are the raw materials your heart requires to work, and, if the machinery has broken down, assist in repairing it. Although there's a potential danger in putting too much emphasis on supplementation, there's an equal if not bigger danger in completely ignoring it.

Here we chose the most effective supplements for cardiovascular health. These are the heart-healthy A-listers, and there's a significant amount of science to support their use.

But in this book, we didn't want to bog you down with studies. *The Great Cholesterol Myth* discusses the science behind these and other supplements, and even a cursory search of www.pubmed.com will yield enough research on each of these nutrients to keep even the most voracious data-lover occupied for weeks.

For the purpose of this book, we kept things simple and streamlined, with a compelling argument for why you should take these supplements followed by a simple way to use them in a heart-healthy protocol. (Those wanting research citations should start with the studies referenced in *The Great Cholesterol Myth*.)

Choosing supplements can be daunting. Though we've provided an essential cardioprotective nutrient plan, we encourage you to find an integrative physician or qualified nutritionist who can create a protocol for your specific needs.

CoQ_{10}: THE SPARK OF LIFE

CoQ_{10} is a vitally important nutrient that literally recharges the energy production furnaces in the cells (known as the *mitochondria*). It's one of the greatest nutrients for energy on the planet, and because the heart produces more energy than any other organ, CoQ_{10} and the heart are a natural fit. Indeed, CoQ_{10} has been approved as a drug for congestive heart failure in Japan since 1974—it's that effective at helping the heart produce energy.

Nearly every cell in your body makes CoQ_{10}, but as we age, we produce substantially less. And don't think you're going to make up the difference with food—as mentioned previously, CoQ_{10} is found mainly in organ meats (heart, liver, and kidney). Other foods that have it, such as sardines and beef, contain tiny amounts—you'd need a ton of these foods to get even 30 mg a day, the absolute minimum dose for healthy folks needing general protection.

CoQ_{10} is required for your body to manufacture a molecule with the unwieldy name of *adenosine triphosphate* (ATP). ATP, you may recall from high school science class, is the molecular "gasoline" that makes every cell run and every muscle move. Without ATP, you would have no energy. Without ATP, frankly, you wouldn't even be alive.

ATP becomes especially crucial for heart health because your heart is your most metabolically active tissue; it demands a constant supply of these energy molecules. That's where CoQ_{10} comes in. Simply put, without CoQ_{10}, there's no ATP. It's hardly surprising that the greatest concentration of CoQ_{10} in your body is found in the heart. No wonder. Your heart *loves* CoQ_{10}, as it guarantees a supply of ATP!

Now, here's a dirty little secret about statin drugs, one we spent a considerable amount of time on in *The Great Cholesterol Myth*: Statin drugs deplete CoQ_{10}. When you interfere with cholesterol production, you also interfere with CoQ_{10} production. When that happens, your heart suffers as well as the muscles that support your heart. (It's hardly a coincidence that muscle pain, fatigue, and energy crashes are some of the most common side effects of CoQ_{10}-depleting statin drugs.) How ironic it is that the same drugs that supposedly benefit heart health at the same time deplete one of the heart's most vital nutrients, one that is required for your heart to pump effectively!

So why doesn't every doctor who prescribes statin drugs also tell patients to stop by their vitamin store for CoQ_{10}?

Good question. Perhaps because most of them never took a nutrition course in medical school? Even today, when we have countless studies that confirm statins deplete CoQ_{10}, many doctors aren't recommending this crucial nutrient.

If you're on a statin drug, you must also be on CoQ_{10}. If your doctor says you don't need it, or doesn't know what CoQ_{10} is, find another doctor. Even if you're not on statin drugs, CoQ_{10} can still provide numerous benefits for heart health. We both take CoQ_{10} on a daily basis, as we do all of the supplements in this section. Because CoQ_{10} is a fat-soluble supplement, you need to take it with a meal containing fat.

L-CARNITINE: THE SHUTTLE BUS FOR FAT

L-carnitine is a molecule similar to an amino acid that loads up fatty acids and transports them into the cell mitochondria, where they can be burned for energy. Along with CoQ_{10}, L-carnitine helps "recycle" ATP rather than build it from scratch.

Your heart gets about 60 percent of its energy from fat, and L-carnitine plays a crucial role in getting those fatty acids into your heart's muscle cells. In addition to its fat-shuttling duties, this workhorse nutrient performs triple duty as a powerful cardioprotective antioxidant that also lowers triglycerides. (Triglycerides are the main form of fat found in the body and are always measured on a standard blood test.)

The strongest research evidence for the benefit of L-carnitine supplementation comes from studies of patients being treated for various forms of cardiovascular disease. People who take L-carnitine supplements soon after suffering a heart attack may be less likely to suffer a subsequent heart attack, die of heart disease, experience chest pain and abnormal heart rhythms, and develop congestive heart failure (a condition in which the heart loses its ability to pump blood effectively). A well-designed study of seventy heart-failure patients found that three-year survival was significantly higher in the group receiving 2 grams a day of L-carnitine compared to the group receiving a placebo.

L-carnitine also appears to improve exercise capacity in people with coronary artery disease. In one study, the walking capacity of patients with intermittent claudication—a painful cramping sensation in the muscles of the legs due to decreased oxygen supply—improved significantly when they were given oral L-carnitine. In another study, patients with peripheral arterial disease of the legs were able to increase their walking distance by 98 meters when supplemented with carnitine, almost twice what those given a placebo were able to do. Congestive heart failure patients have experienced an increase in exercise endurance on only 900 mg of carnitine per day. It also appears to help alleviate the symptoms of angina.

Nutritionists have long used the combination of L-carnitine and CoQ_{10} as an "energy" cocktail. Though it doesn't necessarily give you more get-up-and-go (although for many people it does just that!), it definitely helps give your heart the tools it needs to function optimally.

Look for the fumarate and tartrate forms of L-carnitine, which seems to be absorbed better than other formulas. Ideally you should take L-carnitine on an empty stomach before breakfast and lunch. We especially like it with a cup of organic coffee for a pre-workout boost.

D-RIBOSE: THE MISSING LINK

We've discussed sugar's evils and how you could live just fine without ever touching the stuff again. But in nutrition, as in life, exceptions exist for nearly every rule. D-ribose is an exception to the sugar-is-bad rule—it's one sugar that's not only healthy but absolutely *essential* for life.

D-ribose is a five-carbon sugar that provides the scaffolding for ATP. It's literally needed to manufacture ATP, much like steel beams are needed to make a building. Simply put: Without ribose, you don't make ATP. Without ATP, you have no energy.

Your cells make D-ribose, and your body uses it in numerous ways for optimal cellular function. Any time your muscles' energy reserves become depleted, whether via exercise or a heart condition, supplementing with D-ribose can restore them. We know many athletes, in fact, who supplement religiously with D-ribose. We do it ourselves.

D-ribose's benefits become apparent with heart health. Those benefits include helping to reverse heart failure, assisting in recovery from cardiac surgery, restoring energy to stressed skeletal muscles, and reducing free-radical formation in tissues deprived of oxygen.

Remember, your heart depends on ATP. When blood flow and oxygen are compromised, such as in ischemia (an insufficient supply of blood to the heart, usually as a result of blockage), your heart can lose a large amount of its ATP, and cells can't make enough D-ribose to replace the lost energy quickly.

Likewise, when oxygen or blood flow deficits become chronic, as they do in heart disease, tissues can never make enough D-ribose, and cellular energy levels are constantly depleted. Supplementation can restore those D-ribose levels.

Physiologist Heinz-Gerd Zimmer at the University of Munich first discovered the ribose-heart connection in 1973, when he found energy-starved hearts recovered much faster when D-ribose was replenished prior to or immediately following ischemia. In fact, D-ribose can help recovery and function return to normal in one to two days for ischemia patients.

Five years later, Zimmer demonstrated that the energy-draining effects of certain drugs used to make the heart beat could be significantly lessened when people take D-ribose along with the drugs. Zimmer discovered D-ribose contributes significantly to restore energy and normal diastolic cardiac function. (Diastolic dysfunction is basically a kind of heart failure.)

D-ribose can be of great benefit to people without heart disease, including athletes. Athletes place a lot of strain on their muscles' energy metabolism. And though it might take a lot for trained athletes to subject their muscles to this kind of stress and strain on energy reserves, a less-conditioned person might experience it while gardening or participating in weekend warrior activities.

Anytime the energy reserves of the muscle are depleted, whether it's done through exercise or because of a heart condition, ribose supplementation can help. An adequate dose of ribose—usually 5 grams—will usually result in symptom improvement very quickly.

D-ribose comes in capsules, though we recommend the powder, which is easier for taking therapeutic doses. D-ribose has a mildly sweet taste that mixes well in water and can easily be added to shakes as well.

MAGNESIUM: THE GREAT RELAXER

Magnesium, the fourth most abundant mineral in your body, aids in more than 300 enzymatic reactions, many of which affect your heart. Researchers estimate about 75 percent of us are deficient in magnesium. And a deficiency in this vital nutrient can adversely affect numerous heart conditions.

Among its benefits, magnesium helps you relax. Think about one of the most relaxing things you can do—soaking in an Epsom salt bath. When you soak in that bath you're delivering a large dose of magnesium to your body, absorbed right through your skin. And if you've ever gotten a vitamin drip from an integrative physician, you already know that there's nothing like magnesium for making you sleep like a baby.

Magnesium is a cofactor in manufacturing our old friend ATP, the cellular energy molecule. One study linked magnesium deficiencies with ischemic heart disease, and countless others connect low levels of magnesium with poor cardiovascular health. Simply put: Low magnesium levels in your cells trigger heart tissue destruction, which can lead to a heart attack.

Magnesium helps widen and relax blood vessels by affecting the muscle cells found in arterial walls. Relaxed arteries also mean your heart can more easily pump blood, thereby reducing blood pressure. Studies show an inverse relationship between magnesium intake and blood pressure; people who consumed *more* magnesium had *lower* blood pressure.

Magnesium also inhibits platelet aggregation—the tendency of red blood cells to clump together. (Platelet aggregation is a big factor in the development of clots.) On top of that, magnesium is a kind of natural calcium channel blocker. That's important because coronary artery calcification is a huge risk factor for heart disease. You want to keep calcium in your bones, not in your arteries.

Many people find taking magnesium before bed helps them sleep better and aids morning bowel movements. (Note: if you're constipated, we recommend magnesium oxide, as it has a "loosening" effect. If you don't want that effect, we suggest you stick with something like magnesium glycinate.)

OMEGA-3S FROM FISH OIL: THE ULTIMATE WELLNESS MOLECULES

Blood levels of omega-3 fatty acids are one of the best predictors of sudden heart attacks, and people with the lowest levels are at highest risk for heart attacks. Among their numerous benefits, these essential fatty acids help reduce inflammation, blood pressure, and triglyceride levels.

Fish oil supplements reduce triglyceride levels by up to 40 percent in some research, an astonishingly high amount. The Agency for Healthcare Research and Quality analyzed 123 studies on omega-3 fatty acids and concluded that "omega-3 fatty acids demonstrated a consistently large, significant effect on triglycerides—a net decrease of 10 to 33 percent." The effect is most pronounced in those with high triglycerides to begin with. Even the extremely conservative American Heart Association recommends 2 to 4 grams of the two omega-3 fats found in fish oil (EPA and DHA) for patients who need to lower triglycerides.

Another major risk factor for heart disease is hypertension, or high blood pressure. Fish oil lowers blood pressure, albeit modestly. But its effect on cardiovascular disease overall is anything but modest. Study after study has shown that consuming the omega-3 fatty acids found in fish reduces the risk of death, heart attack, stroke, and abnormal heart rhythms (arrhythmias). It's been estimated that proper omega-3 fatty acid intake could reduce the rate of fatal arrhythmias by 30 percent and save more than 70,000 lives every year.

The other benefit of omega-3s is that they lower inflammation. If you read *The Great Cholesterol Myth*, you already know that we consider inflammation to be one of the four major promoters of heart disease. Omega-3s are among the most anti-inflammatory molecule on the planet; our bodies make our own anti-inflammatory compounds (called *eicosanoids*) out of omega-3s, so it's vitally important to get enough of them.

Omega-3s are beginning to be recognized as critical for heart health even by the conservative medical establishment. In Britain, heart attack survivors are now prescribed fish oil supplements for life in keeping with the guidelines of the British National Institute for Health and Clinical Excellence. Many physicians also consider supplementation with omega-3 fatty acids an important part of nutritional treatment for diabetes and metabolic syndrome, both of which significantly increase the risk for heart disease.

To get optimal amounts of these essential fatty acids, eat plenty of wild-caught fish, preferably three or four times a week. As we mentioned in the previous chapter, sourcing makes all the difference: Wild-caught fish provide a more impressive omega-3 profile than farm-raised fish, which suffer all the problems of feed-lot cattle.

Even if you eat fish, we believe, you should also supplement with omega-3s for optimal cardioprotective benefits. But remember, you're dosing on the amount of EPA and DHA contained within the fish oil, not the total amount of fish oil per se. EPA and DHA are the "gold nuggets" in the prospector's tin. Many cheaper supplement brands boast that they contain 1,000 mg of omega-3s per serving, but that number is useless: All that matters is the amount of EPA and DHA found within each capsule or spoonful. Read the label—it will tell you exactly how much EPA and DHA are found in each dose.

In addition to EPA and DHA, there is a third type of omega-3 fatty acid called *alpha-linolenic acid*, or ALA, but it is found primarily in plant foods (flaxseeds, hempseeds, and chia seeds and their oils). ALA is a precursor to both EPA and DHA, and a powerful anti-inflammatory essential fatty acid in its own right. (But never cook with flaxseed oil and keep it refrigerated because it can go rancid within a few months.)

Ideally, you'll combine wild-caught fish with ALA-rich foods such as flax and chia seeds and a high-quality EPA and DHA supplement. (If you rely solely on plant foods such as flaxseed oil for your omega-3s, take *at least* 1 tablespoon per 100 pounds of body weight to get an appropriate amount.) And quality matters: Fish oil goes rancid just like fish does, so look for a professional brand that contains antioxidants such as tocopherols (vitamin E) to reduce oxidation, and check its manufacturing date.

We hear people complain about fish burp, which usually signifies fish oil gone bad. Every so often, bite into one of your capsules to test for rancidity. Trust us, oxidized fish oil does more harm than good, so skip those bargain-basement and warehouse-store softgels.

Whether you opt for liquid or softgel form, always take fish oil with a meal containing fat for optimal absorbency.

VITAMIN C: THE ULTIMATE ANTIOXIDANT

With regard to heart disease, the simplest argument for vitamin C supplementation goes like this:

Oxidative damage is one of the four major promoters of heart disease.

Vitamin C is one of the most powerful antioxidants in the world.

Therefore, vitamin C should help prevent—or at least slow down—one of the strongest promoters of heart disease, oxidative damage.

The fact that vitamin C fights free-radical damage (i.e., oxidation) is reason enough to supplement with it. Remember, cholesterol is never a problem until it's oxidized—oxidized (damaged) LDL cholesterol particles (along with other metabolic debris) may get trapped in pockets underneath the lining of the artery, leading to inflammation, more oxidation, and ultimately plaque.

But there's another reason to take vitamin C.

See, one of the main determinants of plaque rupture is the balance between the synthesis and degradation of something called *collagen*. (Collagen is a protein used to connect and support other body tissues, giving them firmness and strength. You've probably heard of collagen in connection with skin care.) And collagen requires—you guessed it—vitamin C. Now stay with us for a minute, because this gets a bit complicated.

The most abundant amino acids in collagen are proline and lysine, and when collagen is damaged, these two amino acids become exposed. Then a highly atherogenic particle of oxidized cholesterol called *lipoprotein*(a), also known as Lp(a), will attach itself to these damaged strands of collagen.

The attachment of Lp(a) to these damaged strands of collagen is "an attempt by the body to repair damage to the collagen of the artery walls in the absence of adequate levels of vitamin C," writes Andrew W. Saul, M.S., Ph.D. "When vitamin C levels are low, the body manufactures more cholesterol, especially Lp(a). Conversely, when vitamin C levels are high, the body makes less cholesterol."

Saul adds: "If high blood cholesterol were the primary cause of heart disease, all bears and other hibernating animals would have become extinct long ago. One reason bears are still with us is simple: They produce large amounts of vitamin C in their bodies, which stabilizes the artery walls, and there is therefore no tendency to develop cholesterol deposits or plaque."

Though this may seem theoretical, we have hard data to show an association between low vitamin C levels and heart disease. A 2011 study in the *American Heart Journal* found that blood levels of vitamin C did indeed predict incident heart failure in both men and women. In other words, the lower the level of vitamin C in the blood, the higher the risk for heart failure.

A few things to remember about vitamin C. High doses are incredibly safe, but start low and gradually work up to 1,000 mg daily. Too much at once may upset your stomach. (It's harmless, but annoying, and may result in mild diarrhea.)

Vitamin C also increases the iron you absorb from food. This is usually not a problem in premenopausal women, but men and postmenopausal women need to watch that their iron stores don't go too high. We do not recommend taking more than 100 mg of vitamin C daily for anyone with the gene for hemochromatosis (iron storage disease). For those who can tolerate higher dosing, we recommend a vitamin C powder combined with magnesium, potassium, and other nutrients in the morning and after dinner.

VITAMIN D: THE SUPERSTAR NUTRIENT THAT DOES JUST ABOUT EVERYTHING

One of the many things cholesterol does in the body (in addition to being the parent molecule for sex hormones) is serve as the precursor for vitamin D.

And studies show that a low level of vitamin D is a risk factor for cardiovascular disease. In fact, low concentrations of 25-hydroxyvitamin D [25 (OH) D] are an independent risk factor for cardiovascular events, in particular strokes and sudden cardiac deaths.

What's more, few of us get enough of this spectacularly important vitamin. A number of studies in the last decade have suggested that vitamin D deficiency is widespread. Because vitamin D has been found to help with everything from heart health to osteoporosis to depression to physical performance to weight loss, low levels of vitamin D are a serious problem indeed.

Very few foods contain good amounts of vitamin D. We know, we know—they fortify milk with the stuff, but for many reasons we're not huge fans of pasteurized, homogenized milk. For example, cow's milk is fortified with the synthetic (and inferior) form of vitamin D, *ergocalciferol*. So to get optimal amounts of this terrific nutrient—and to reap the many health benefits of it—we need to spend more time in the sun, supplement, or, ideally, do both. (For what it's worth, Dr. Jonny lives in Southern California and plays tennis outdoors 2 hours a day—and he still supplements with 5,000 IUs of vitamin D_3.)

Many of us have become sun-phobic, slathering sunscreen for even a short jaunt to the store with our dog. Dark-skinned individuals, those who live in dark climates, or those who just don't spend enough time outdoors just aren't making adequate vitamin D.

An easy way to identify and correct deficiencies is a 25-hydroxy vitamin D test, which is becoming standard practice at most doctors' offices. Most knowledgeable integrative practitioners like to see levels between 50 ng/ml and 80 ng/ml. If yours aren't up to par, work with a practitioner to get your levels up. Once you hit your mark, supplement with 2,000 IUs as a maintenance dose, though many people, us included, use considerably more. (No toxicity has been found in humans at levels up to 10,000 IUs daily, and it's probably safe at higher levels as well; we just don't have research studies on it.) Spending 10 to 15 minutes a day a few times a week in the sun without sunscreen is another way to help your body make vitamin D.

CITRUS BERGAMOT EXTRACT: A NEW SUPERSTAR ON THE HORIZON

Citrus bergamot is a fruit that's endemic to the Calabrian region in Southern Italy, and if it lives up to its promise, which it seems to be doing, it may turn out to be one of the most important supplements for the prevention of metabolic syndrome (also known as pre-diabetes). Metabolic syndrome is a collection of symptoms (high blood sugar, high triglycerides, high blood pressure, abdominal fat, etc.) that greatly increases the risk for heart disease.

Here's what citrus bergamot does: It lowers blood sugar. It lowers triglycerides. It also appears to *raise* HDL cholestero. As Dr. Sinatra says, "this is a trifecta of cardiovascular health."

As with all of the other supplements, but especially resveratrol, curcumin, and fish oil, you need to pay attention to the label and ingredients. To get the effects seen in the research, the bergamot extract must contain 38 percent polyphenols; several companies produce a less potent product, but that's not the one that has the demonstrated benefits. Citrus bergamot extract of 38 percent polyphenols has been demonstrated to suppress inflammation, inhibit plaque formation, and improve arterial responsiveness, thus contributing mightily to cardiovascular health.

GARLIC: THE GLOBAL REMEDY

Garlic is one of the oldest medicinal foods on the planet. It's lipid-lowering, antithrombotic, anti–blood coagulation, antihypertensive, antioxidant, antimicrobial, antiviral, and antiparasitic. And all of those incredible benefits have been well documented in more than 1,200 pharmacological studies.

The irony of it is that garlic seems to be accepted even by conventional doctors as an agent for lowering cholesterol, which it actually does (and it does it without lowering HDL). It has also lowered triglyceride levels by up to 17 percent!

But even more impressive, to us, is the fact that garlic can reduce plaque. In one study, those receiving 900 mg of garlic powder for four years in a randomized, double-blinded, placebo-controlled study had a regression in their plaque volume of 2.6 percent; a matched group of subjects given a placebo saw their plaque increase over the same time period (by 15.6 percent, no less!).

One of the active ingredients made when you crush garlic is something called *allicin*, which has significant antiplatelet activity. Platelets in the blood can tend to stick together more than they should, ultimately forming clots (not good). To understand how important garlic's antiplatelet activity is, consider that many heart attacks and strokes are believed to be caused by spontaneous clots in the blood vessels. The anticoagulant effect of garlic is a very important health benefit.

If all that weren't enough, consider this: Garlic can lower blood pressure, something that's been demonstrated in quite a number of studies. In addition, it appears to have other wide-ranging benefits that extend beyond cardiovascular health. We consider garlic one of our favorite heart-healthy supplements.

CURCUMIN: POWERFUL NATURAL MEDICINE FROM A SUPERSTAR SPICE

Curcumin is the name given to a collection of compounds called *curcuminoids*, which are the active anti-inflammatory compound found in the superspice turmeric. (Turmeric is the spice that gives Indian foods and curries their yellow color.) In fact, curcuminoids are the primary reason turmeric is a superspice.

Curcumin is not only a powerful anti-inflammatory, it also provides antioxidant, antithrombotic, and cardiovascular protective benefits. Among its heart duties, curcumin reduces oxidized LDL cholesterol. In animal studies, curcumin protects arterial wall linings from the damage caused by homocysteine (an inflammatory amino acid found in the blood). High homocysteine is a risk factor for heart disease.

One study found that curcumin could preserve cardiac function after ischemia and reperfusion (the restoration of blood flow to the heart after a heart attack). "Curcumin has potential as a treatment for patients who have had a heart attack," researchers concluded. We think it's got a lot more than just "potential," and consider it an important supplement for heart health.

You get some curcumin from turmeric but not very much. To get therapeutic anti-inflammatory benefits you'll need to supplement. Which presents another problem, as curcumin is difficult to absorb. When you buy curcumin supplements, make sure they use BCM-95 curcumin. Meriva or Turmeracin are good options as well. They all have good absorption.

RESVERATROL: RED WINE'S GIFT TO HEART HEALTH

Resveratrol, an anti-aging nutrient found primarily in red wine and the skins of dark grapes, protects your arteries against blood clots, improves elasticity, and reduces blood pressure as well as oxidized LDL. A powerful antioxidant, resveratrol inhibits several inflammatory enzymes that can trigger heart disease. It also stops certain molecules from sticking to artery walls, where they hang out and create inflammation.

Recently, the findings of the 2010 Resveratrol Conference in Denmark were made public. Almost 3,700 published studies were analyzed, and the findings were profound. Experts identified twelve mechanisms of action by which resveratrol may act to combat the diseases of aging and protect the body against the five leading causes of death among Americans (number one, of course, being heart disease).

Among the mechanisms cited, resveratrol

- lowers inflammation
- is a powerful antioxidant
- can prevent damage to DNA
- can stimulate bone formation
- can lower the incidence of hypertension
- is neuroprotective

When you're purchasing a resveratrol supplement, understand that they aren't all created equal. The total amount of resveratrol in a capsule isn't as important as the amount of *trans-resveratrol*, the particularly potent and bioactive form that has all the benefit. Trans-resveratrol content is what you need to pay attention to. Some high-end manufacturers will actually tell you

Supplement Prescription Pad for Heart Health

We like to think about nutrients the way people think about great sports teams, or great bands, such as The Rolling Stones or The Beatles. Great bands are almost always greater than the sum of their parts, always greatest when they perform together. (How many solo Keith Richards albums can you name?) And it's the same with nutrients. Though there are undoubtedly superstars in the nutrient galaxy, their benefits can often be dwarfed by what happens when they work together synergistically. Simply put, the right nutrients in efficacious doses, working together (and as a supplement to a healthy eating and living plan) contribute mightily to a cardiovascular-protection protocol that strengthens and protects your heart.

Let's be clear: We don't think supplements can take the place of medicine. We do, however, think that medicines should be used judiciously, and only when lifestyle changes, diet modification, and supplementation are not enough. Our view is that the more you can stay out of the medical "system," the better for *you*. The less medicine you can get away with (and still be healthy), the better off you are. So while the following prescription isn't meant to substitute for any prescription drugs your doctor feels you need, it is an excellent way to support a healthy heart.

Our fondest hope is that following the program outlined in this book will diminish the need for powerful pharmaceuticals in the first place.

Daily Supplement Prescription for Heart Health

Coenzyme Q_{10}: 100 to 300 mg

L-carnitine: 1,500 to 2,500 mg

Magnesium: 400 mg

D-ribose: 5 grams

Curcumin: 500 to 1,000 mg

Vitamin D: 2,000 to 3,000 IUs as a maintenance dose once your 25-hydroxy levels reach 50 to 60 ng/ml

Trans-resveratrol: 25 to 200 mg (look for the *trans* variety, which is the active component of resveratrol)

Vitamin C: 1,000 to 2,000 mg

Fish oil: 1 to 2 grams combined EPA and DHA

Garlic: 600 to 1,200 mg

Citrus bergamot (38 percent polyphenols): 1,300 mg (650 mg 2 times a day)

how much trans-resveratrol is in every capsule (you'll want to take at least 25 mg and up to a maximum of 200 mg daily). Others will say "standardized to 20 percent trans," which means that only 20 percent of the total amount in the capsule is the important trans-resveratrol form. (A 500-mg capsule of resveratrol standardized to 20 percent trans would deliver 100 mg of trans-resveratrol per capsule.)

In addition to the all-stars listed previously, three other supplements are worth considering if you don't mind a couple of extra pills.

Cocoa flavanols. The active ingredient in dark cocoa—cocoa flavanols—has been found to have wide-ranging cardiovascular benefits, most notably the ability to lower blood pressure. Studies on the Kona people of Panama, where cocoa is a staple drink, have consistently found that they have remarkably low blood pressure. Though correlation isn't cause, much other research has reported on the ability of cocoa flavanols to lower blood pressure and stimulate *nitric oxide*, an important molecule that helps keep your arteries open, healthy, and relaxed. In studies, flavanol-rich cocoa and chocolate increased plasma antioxidant capacity and reduced scores on something called the *platelet reactivity test*, a good predictor of heart issues. About 450 mg a day of cocoa flavanols is an excellent dose.

Olive leaf complex. We've long been a fan of olive leaf complex for its antimicrobial effects and its ability to support the immune system, but recently a new benefit was added to its résumé: Olive leaf complex lowers blood pressure. Researchers divided twenty pairs of identical twins with borderline hypertension into two groups, the first of which took 1,000 mg of olive leaf extract while the second group took 500 mg. At the end of eight weeks, those taking the higher dose had the greatest benefit, significantly lowering systolic blood pressure by an average of 11 points, from 137 mmHg to 126 mmHg. Those taking the smaller dose also saw a drop, but by an average of 5 points.

Vitamin K. This vitamin that's only recently begun to get the attention it deserves. Its role in bone health is well established, but we are just beginning to understand that it has a significant effect on cardiovascular health as well.

Here's why. Vitamin K is necessary for the actions of a group of proteins that inhibit calcium buildup in the blood vessels. Calcium buildup in the blood vessels translates into arterial calcification—that is, calcium-hardened plaques, which is associated with increased cardiovascular and morbidity. Vitamin K helps prevent that calcification, which makes it an important nutrient to include in a comprehensive heart-protection program.

Its two main forms are vitamin K_1, found in green leafy vegetables, and vitamin K_2, which is widely believed to be the more potent and cardio-protective form, found in foods such as natto, and several types of cheese. Vitamin K_2 itself has several forms, the most famous of which are MK-4 and MK-7.

Though vitamin K deficiency is rare, most of the vitamin K in the Western diet is vitamin K_1, but the heart-protective actions of this vitamin clearly come from vitamin K_2. At least one major study has found that a high intake of vitamin K_2 could protect against coronary heart disease.

• SECTION 2 •

How to Eat Well for a Long and Healthy Life

7

100 DELICIOUS AND NUTRITIOUS RECIPES YOUR HEART WILL LOVE

A collection of nutritionally balanced dishes rich in heart-healthy essential nutrients, low in sugar, and bursting with flavors to suit any tastes and desires

GOOD START BREAKFASTS

Quick Weekday Breakfasts

Get-Up-And-Go Banana Berry Quinoa Porridge

Melt-in-Your-Mouth Baked Granola

Protein-Powered Muesli with Coconut and Raisins

Regenerating Herb Scrambled Eggs

Fortifying Flourless Chicken Flapjacks

Leisurely Weekend Breakfasts

Brain-Boosting Salmon Eggs Benedict

Strengthening Sun-Dried Tomato and Feta-Chive Omelet

Hearty Mediterranean Frittata

Super-Energizing Baked Beans

Zesty Digestive Herb and Cheddar Breakfast Muffins

MIDDAY MEALS AND ANYTIME SNACKS

Salads for all Seasons

Almighty Avocado and Black Bean Salad

Mood-Boosting Chicken and Pineapple Coleslaw with Coconut-Lime Dressing

Vitalizing Broccoli and Cauliflower Salad

Cardioprotective Salmon Caesar Salad

Energizing Thai Spice Chicken Salad

Pumping Jumping Bean Salad

Delicious Dressings

Simply Nourishing Salad Dressing

Cardioprotective Caesar Salad Dressing

Energizing Thai Spice Salad Dressing

Holy-Moly Guacamole Dressing

Lunch Box-worthy Meals

Stress-Less Turkey, Avocado, and Veggie Nori Wrap

Gluten-Free Mediterranean Veggie Pizza

Vibrant Avocado and Veggie Salsa Collard Wraps

Feel-Good Turkey or Salmon Tomato Panini

Heartwarming Soups & Broths

Nutritive Chicken Stock

Digestive Vegetable Stock

Heart-Protective Carrot Ginger Soup with Chives

Love-Your-Heart Red Lentil Soup

Immune-Boosting Basque Bean and Cabbage Soup

Build-Me-Up Butternut and Macadamia Nut Bisque

Satisfying Snacks

Low-Carb Herbed Cheddar Crackers

Blood-Sugar Balancing Butternut & Leek Pies

High-Energy Chicken & Cauliflower Croquettes

Turkey, Lamb, or Beef Koftas with a Heart-Healthy Kick

Spiced Honey-Glazed Nuts

Calming Coconut-Date Balls

Detoxifying Lima Bean Blinis with Artichoke Herbed Dip

ON THE DINNER MENU

Meatless Main Dishes

Spicy Moroccan Tempeh with Lentils

Hi-Fibe Red Bean Burgers

Protein-Packed Vegetarian Shepherd's Pie

Nutrient-Rich Roasted Quinoa with Mushrooms, Cumin, and Coriander

High-Fiber Butternut Gnocchi with Herbed Cream Sauce

Revitalizing Vegetable Biryani

Comforting Cheddar and Broccoli Quiche with Quinoa Crust

Strengthening Spinach, Feta, and Rice Casserole

Immune-Boosting Thai Tempeh Cakes with Sweet Spicy Dipping Sauce

Stress-Less Shiitake and Asparagus Risotto

BEEF, SEAFOOD, AND POULTRY MAINS

Beef

Easy Beef Sauté with Fresh Herbs

Favorite Sweet, Spicy, and Crunchy Meatloaf

Nice and Spiced Beef or Chicken Stir-Fry

Seafood

Fisherman's Omega-3 Fish Fingers

Mega-Omega Spice-Crusted Salmon

Tantalizing Thai Fish Cakes

Soul-Warming Tuna Lasagna

Healing Baked Halibut or Salmon and Shiitake

Spicy Shrimp and Tomato Kebabs with Herbed Lima Beans

Poultry

Mighty Moroccan Chicken Tagine

Metabolism-Boosting Chicken Curry Feast

Tantalizing Chicken Satay with Powerful Peanut Coconut Sauce

Supercharged Chicken or Turkey Meatloaf

Anti-Inflammatory Turmeric Turkey Burgers

Vegetables, Grains, and Beans on the Side

Get-Up-and-Go Indian Chickpea Delight

Fragrant Cauliflower-Quinoa Risotto

Luscious Lima Bean Mash

Anti-Ox Pumpkin and Cauliflower Mash

Sautéed Shiitake Mushrooms with a Kale Kick

Zesty Broccoli with Garlic and Ginger

Balancing Basmati Almond Rice

Sumptuous Spinach and Swiss Chard with Pine Nuts

Cardioprotective Green Beans

Sustaining Ginger-Sesame Carrots

NOURISHING ACCOMPANIMENTS AND MENU ENHANCEMENTS

Choice Condiments

Mediterranean Black Olive Tapenade

Super-Healthful Hummus

Bone-Strengthening Lemon Tahini

Heart-Healthy Almond Mayonnaise

Succulent Sauces

Punchy Peanut-Coconut Sauce

Spice-it-Up Sweet Chili Sauce

Health-Giving Hollandaise Sauce

Antioxidant BBQ Sauce

Powerful Preserves & Fabulous Ferments

Antioxidant Ginger, Date, and Orange Chutney

Berry-Buzz Jelly

Immune-Building Lemon Ginger Butter

Bone-Building French Cream

Restorative Cucumber-Yogurt Raita

Immune-Boosting Yogurt

Probiotic Fruit Chutney

SWEET ENDINGS: DESSERTS AND OTHER DELIGHTS

Cookies, Cakes, & Breads

Hearty Hazelnut Rounds

Luscious Lemon-Pineapple Yogurt Cake

Health-Gratifying Grapefruit and Orange Cake

Almighty Almond and Walnut Pumpernickel Bread

Powerhouse Pumpkin, Spice, and Almond Bread

Nourishing Crusty Onion and Parmesan Rolls

Puddings & Pies

Fortifying Fig and Minty Blueberry Brûlée

Energy-Giving Coconut, Almond, and Raisin Custard

Blueberry and Apple Crumble Gone Nuts

Berry-Beneficial Blueberry and Pecan Pie

Anti-Ox Orange Mousse

Soothing Pear, Date, and Almond Pudding with Grapefruit Cream Sauce

Sweet Brown Rice Pudding with an Antioxidant Twist

No-Bake Superfood Fudge Brownies

· GOOD START · BREAKFASTS

- **QUICK WEEKDAY BREAKFASTS** 81
- **LEISURELY WEEKEND BREAKFASTS** 85

Breakfast is the most important meal of the day because it sets the pace for your metabolism, making it more or less efficient. Eating breakfast allows you to restock the energy stores that have been depleted overnight and begin the day with a tank full of the right fuel. All of the recipes in this chapter include a variety of healthy proteins and fats, and low-on-the-glycemic-index carbohydrates to ensure a steady supply of fuel. These recipes provide you with the nutrition necessary for energy production and keep you nourished and satisfied. You may even lose a few inches around your waist, too!

You'll find a ready selection of quick weekday breakfasts that take little time to prepare when you're adhering to a busy schedule. Weekends often afford us some extra time to spend in the kitchen, and you'll find recipes that take a little longer to make but offer a combination of choices and flavors to suit any taste sensations and desires. Variety is the spice of life, and you will thrive when you start your day out with a heart- and brain-healthy breakfast.

GET-UP-AND-GO BANANA BERRY QUINOA PORRIDGE

If you've never tried quinoa for breakfast, you're in for a treat. Quinoa is great combined with the sweet taste of fruit and spices or served with more savory items such as vegetables and herbs. It is a dieter's dream because it is satisfying, filling, rich in fiber, and full of all nine essential amino acids that make it a complete protein. Quinoa is digested slowly and has a low glycemic index, helping keep your blood sugar levels stable for hours. Quinoa dates back several thousand years, when the Incas discovered and prized it because they believed it increased the stamina of their warriors.

4 cups (680 g) quinoa

1 cup (160 g) dates

1 banana

1 cup (145 g) berries, fresh or frozen

1 teaspoon ground nutmeg

1 teaspoon ground cinnamon

1 cup (120 g) chopped walnuts

Soak the quinoa overnight in filtered water and drain the next morning. Soak the dates overnight in 1½ cups (355 ml) filtered water. The next morning, drain the dates but reserve the soak water. Blend the quinoa, dates, soak water, banana, berries, nutmeg, and cinnamon in a blender until smooth. Sprinkle with walnuts and serve cold or at room temperature.

Yield: 12 servings

Note: Quinoa is a flavorful source of plant-derived calcium, so it helps regulate contraction of the heart and facilitates nerve and muscle function. It also contains impressive amounts of potassium, magnesium, and zinc.

Reasons to Crave Quinoa

If you're looking for a high-protein substitute for cereal, look no further. Although quinoa is technically a seed, it cooks up like a grain and is a terrific substitute for wheat. The protein quality and quantity in quinoa is often superior to that of the more common cereal grains—certainly superior to wheat—and, according to the Food and Agricultural Organization of the United Nations, the nutritional quality of quinoa is comparable to dried whole milk. It's also high in iron (about 8 mg per ½ cup) and has a hefty 5 grams of fiber to boot!

[NUTRITIONAL ANALYSIS]

Per serving: 336.5 calories; 10.2 g fat; 10.1 g protein; 55.1 g carbs; 6.5 g fiber; 15.3 mg sodium.

MELT-IN-YOUR MOUTH BAKED GRANOLA

If you love the crunch, texture, and flavor of granola, look no further than this delicious treat. This granola is high in heart-healthy fiber and flavors, sprinkled with a wide range of nutrients that are fun to eat.

6 cups (480 g) rolled oats

3 cups (360 g) rye flakes

2 cups (160 g) shredded coconut

1 cup (145 g) sunflower seeds

1 cup (144 g) sesame seeds

1 cup each almonds (145 g), pecans (110 g), and walnuts (120 g), chopped

¾ cup (90 g) barley malt powder

⅔ cup (160 ml) coconut oil

1 cup (235 ml) pure maple syrup

1 teaspoon vanilla extract

1 tablespoon (15 ml) pure almond extract

¼ teaspoon pure maple extract

1 cup (145 g) raisins

Preheat the oven to 375°F (190°C, gas mark 5). In a large bowl, combine the oats through the walnuts. Set aside.

In a separate bowl, stir together the barley malt powder, oil, maple syrup, and vanilla, almond, and maple extracts. Add the wet mixture to the dry mixture and mix well. (For granola that sticks together more, use a food processor to combine the wet and dry mixtures.) Spread the combined mixture onto a large baking sheet and bake for 50 minutes, or until the mixture is lightly browned. Let cool for 30 minutes.

Mix in the raisins and serve immediately or store in an airtight, sealable container for future breakfasts. It will keep for 10 days or slightly longer if refrigerated.

Yield: 24 servings

Note: Oats are naturally high in iron, an essential mineral for healthy red blood cells to reduce your risk of iron-deficiency anemia.

[NUTRITIONAL ANALYSIS]
Per serving: 387.3 calories; 23.7 g fat; 7.8 g protein; 39 g carbs; 7.4 g fiber; 5.8 mg sodium.

PROTEIN-POWERED MUESLI WITH COCONUT AND RAISINS

Loaded with fiber and rich in antioxidants, this sublimely tasty muesli is nutrient rich, crunchy, and flavorful. It will satisfy your appetite and keep your system working like a well-oiled machine for hours. Enjoy this dish as part of a nourishing breakfast or filling snack.

- **2 cups (160 g) rolled oats**
- **1 cup (120 g) rye flakes**
- **1 cup (160 g) dried dates, chopped**
- **1 cup (145 g) raisins**
- **1 cup (145 g) almonds, chopped roughly**
- **½ cup (60 g) walnuts, chopped roughly**
- **½ cup (55 g) pecans, chopped roughly**
- **½ cup (72 g) sunflower seeds**
- **⅓ cup (27 g) shredded coconut**
- **1 teaspoon pure vanilla extract**
- **¼ teaspoon ground nutmeg**
- **½ teaspoon ground cinnamon**
- **4 cups (946 ml) apple cider**
- **1 banana**
- **1½ cups (220 g) blueberries**

In a large bowl, combine the oats through the cinnamon. Mix well. Place the mixture in an airtight, sealable container and stir in the apple cider. Cover, refrigerate overnight, and serve in the morning with chopped banana and blueberries.

Yield: 8 to 10 servings

Note: Nuts and seeds provide protein, essential fatty acids, and several antioxidant vitamins and minerals.

———————**[NUTRITIONAL ANALYSIS]**———————
Per serving: 455.5 calories; 20.9 g fat; 9.4 g protein; 63.2 g carbs; 9.7 g fiber; 16.1 mg sodium.

REGENERATING HERB SCRAMBLED EGGS

In addition to containing all nine essential amino acids that make up protein, eggs contain choline, a nutrient important for neurotransmitter function, the nervous system, and the cardiovascular system. This delicious and nutritious combination of garlic and fresh herbs, coupled with the additional nutrients in the greens they are served over, provides fiber and potent antioxidant activity that strengthen your entire system.

- **4 eggs**
- **1 clove garlic, minced**
- **1 tablespoon (4 g) chopped fresh parsley**
- **½ teaspoon chopped fresh basil**
- **Pinch of salt, Celtic or sea**
- **Pinch of cayenne pepper (optional)**
- **2 tablespoons (28 ml) Bone-Building French Cream (page 157)**
- **2 to 3 finely chopped scallions**
- **1 tablespoon (15 ml) extra-virgin olive or coconut oil**
- **2 cups mixed lettuce greens (110 g), romaine lettuce (110 g), or spinach (60 g)**

Whisk the eggs in a medium bowl with the garlic, parsley, basil, salt, cayenne, and cream. Stir in the scallions. Heat the oil in a medium skillet over medium heat. Pour in the egg mixture and scramble with a spatula, slowly turning and breaking up the egg mixture until it reaches desired doneness. Turn the off heat before most of the moisture has evaporated. Serve over mixed lettuce greens, romaine lettuce, or spinach.

Yield: 2 servings

———————**[NUTRITIONAL ANALYSIS]**———————
Per serving: 258 calories; 19.7 g fat; 13.7 g protein; 3.5 g carbs; 1.5 g fiber; 221 mg sodium.

FORTIFYING FLOURLESS CHICKEN FLAPJACKS

Good-choice breakfasts contain a full profile of essential amino acids that turn on brain neurotransmitters and provide energy to help carry you over the morning hungries. These delicious chicken pancakes are no exception! They will keep your weight in check and your heart healthy thanks to vitamins B_6 and B_3, both of which are known for their energy-giving benefits. Vitamin B_6 in particular assists the heart by keeping homocysteine levels low, thereby reducing damage to the walls of the blood vessels. Apart from the delicious taste sensation, the addition of turmeric, avocado, and spinach in this dish will ensure the healthy functioning of your digestive and immune systems.

> **1 cooked chicken breast, chopped**
>
> **3 eggs**
>
> **½ teaspoon ground turmeric**
>
> **1 tablespoon (15 ml) coconut or grapeseed oil**
>
> **2 cups (110 g) salad greens or raw or lightly steamed spinach**
>
> **½ avocado, pitted, peeled, and sliced**
>
> **3 to 4 tablespoons Simply Nourishing Salad Dressing (page 97)**

Blend the chicken, eggs, and turmeric in a food processor until completely smooth. (The mixture will look just like thick pancake batter.)

In a medium skillet, melt the oil over medium-high heat. Pour ¼ cup of the chicken mixture into the skillet. You may need to spread the batter a bit so that it is not too thick. Cook for 1 to 2 minutes on each side (these pancakes cook much faster than regular flour pancakes, so watch them closely).

Serve over a bed of fresh salad greens or spinach and top with avocado slices. Drizzle with the dressing.

Yield: 4 to 5 pancakes

Note: Organic, free-range, hormone- and antibiotic-free chicken does not contain chemicals that may, over time, cause harm.

--------[NUTRITIONAL ANALYSIS]--------

Per serving: 217.1 calories; 14.6 g fat; 14.6 g protein; 4.5 g carbs; 1.2 g fiber; 94 mg sodium.

BRAIN-BOOSTING SALMON EGGS BENEDICT

You have nothing to fear and much to gain when it comes to eating eggs. They are a good source of high-quality protein and vitamins D, B_2, B_5, and B_{12}, as well as iodine, selenium, and tryptophan, all of which help improve overall health. In this dish, the addition of omega-3 fatty acids in the salmon and abundance of vitamin K in the spinach greatly contribute to a healthy metabolism, nervous system, and brain function. Flavorful and delicious in every way.

1 tablespoon (15 ml) extra-virgin olive or coconut oil

1 salmon fillet (4 ounces [115 g])

5 cups (150 g) spinach

1 tablespoon (15 ml) vinegar (e.g., apple cider or white)

4 eggs

Health-Giving Hollandaise Sauce (page 153)

Dash of black pepper

Preheat the oven to warm. In a medium-size pan, melt the oil over medium heat and sauté the salmon for about 4 minutes on each side until just cooked through. Keep it warm in the oven.

While the salmon is cooking, place a steamer basket in a small saucepan, add the spinach, and steam lightly for about 3 minutes, or until wilted. Place the spinach in the oven with the salmon to keep it warm.

Fill a medium-size skillet halfway with water and add the vinegar. Heat the water until simmering and then crack the eggs into the pan, one at a time, being careful not to break the yolks. The eggs will be done when the whites have become solid, about 4 to 5 minutes.

Remove the spinach and salmon from the oven and divide among 4 plates, placing the spinach on first, topped with the salmon, and then a poached egg. Serve with hollandaise sauce and sprinkle with freshly ground black pepper.

Yield: 4 servings

Note: Choose organically farmed, free-range eggs because they provide a higher quality nutrient content and lack the harmful growth hormones that can compromise your health.

———————[NUTRITIONAL ANALYSIS]———————

Per serving: 161.2 calories; 8.4 g fat; 13.4 g protein; 2 g carbs; 0.8 g fiber; 100.7 mg sodium.

STRENGTHENING SUN-DRIED TOMATO AND FETA-CHIVE OMELET

This easy and delicious omelet is packed with heart-healthy goodness. Tomatoes are loaded with lycopene, a natural pigment produced by plants and a potent antioxidant that offers cardiovascular benefits. The inclusion of feta cheese adds a bold and tangy flavor and supplies key vitamins D and B_{12} plus calcium and iron, all of which support overall metabolism.

4 eggs, separated

1 tablespoon (15 ml) Bone-Building French Cream (page 157)

1 clove garlic, minced

1 tablespoon (3 g) chopped fresh chives

¼ teaspoon salt, Celtic or sea

Dash of black pepper

1 teaspoon coconut oil or extra-virgin olive oil

¼ cup (28 g) oil-packed and drained sun-dried tomatoes, sliced, divided

¼ cup (37 g) sheep or goat feta cheese, sliced, divided

In a medium bowl, whisk the egg yolks, cream, garlic, chives, salt, and pepper until light and fluffy. In a separate bowl, whisk the egg whites until stiff, about 3 to 5 minutes, and then fold them into the other whisked ingredients.

Heat a nonstick saucepan over medium heat with the oil. Pour in half the egg mixture, swishing it around to leave a thin layer of egg on the sides of the pan. Cook for a few minutes and then add half the sun-dried tomatoes and half the feta on top of one side of the omelet. Using a spatula, flip the other side of the omelet on top of the filling. Cook for a few more minutes. Place the omelet aside and keep warm. Repeat the process for the other omelet.

Serve immediately. These omelets can be served with any other fillings desired and go well with Spice-It-Up Sweet Chili Sauce (page 152).

Yield: 2 omelets

Note: No other system in the body has greater need for antioxidant protection than the cardiovascular system. And when it comes to heart health, tomatoes are loaded with three important cardioprotective antioxidants: vitamins C, E, and lycopene, a powerful carotenoid.

[NUTRITIONAL ANALYSIS]

Per serving: 278.3 calories; 18 g fat; 18 g protein; 9.7 g carbs; 2.1 g fiber; 494.1 mg sodium.

HEARTY MEDITERRANEAN FRITTATA

Load up on fresh vegetables that pack a wallop of vitamins, minerals, antioxidant nutrients, and fiber that explode with flavor and a cheesy texture with each bite. This is a delicious breakfast or any-time dish combining elements of the heart-healthy Mediterranean diet.

1 tablespoon (15 ml), plus 1 teaspoon extra-virgin olive oil, butter, or ghee

1 cup each chopped broccoli florets (71 g) and bell pepper (150 g)

2 cups (60 g) chopped spinach

½ cup (50 g) pitted and halved black olives

⅔ cup (110 g) chopped onion

1 clove garlic, minced

2 tablespoons (5 g) chopped fresh or 1 teaspoon dried basil

8 eggs, lightly beaten

¼ cup (60 ml) Bone-Building French Cream (page 157)

¼ teaspoon salt, Celtic or sea

Dash of black pepper

1 teaspoon dried oregano

½ cup (50 g) grated Parmesan cheese

½ cup (55 g) oil-packed and drained sun-dried tomatoes, sliced

Preheat the oven to 350°F (180°C, gas mark 4). Grease a 9-inch (23-cm) baking dish with the teaspoon of oil. Evenly arrange the broccoli, bell pepper, spinach, and olives in the dish.

In a medium saucepan, add the remaining tablespoon of oil or ghee and sauté the onion and garlic until tender, about 3 minutes, over medium to high heat. Add the basil and sauté until wilted, about 30 seconds. Remove from the heat and let cool. Whisk the eggs with the cream, salt, and pepper until creamy. Add the oregano, Parmesan, and sun-dried tomatoes, blend together, and then pour over the vegetables. Bake for 30 minutes, or until the frittata is firm to the touch. Let cool for 10 minutes before serving, or serve cold.

Yield: 4 to 6 servings

Note: A five-year Spanish study conducted on 7,500 people and published in April 2013 in the New England Journal of Medicine *concluded that people who ate a Mediterranean diet (which focuses on olive oil, nuts, produce, and seafood) had a 30 percent reduction in stroke and other cardiovascular diseases compared to control subjects, who were low-fat dieters.*

———————[NUTRITIONAL ANALYSIS]———————
Per serving: 252 calories; 15.5 g fat; 13.7 g protein; 11.3 g carbs; 2.3 g fiber; 302.1 mg sodium.

SUPER-ENERGIZING BAKED BEANS

The humble baked bean is the perfect breakfast food. Navy beans, used in this recipe, are a nutritional powerhouse of plant protein, fiber, iron, magnesium, copper, and calcium that supports cellular energy and an overall healthy metabolism. The pureed tomatoes are tasty and also a good source of the antioxidant lycopene. You'll love the savory and flavorful addition of the herbs and spices that enhance the cardioprotective benefits of this dish.

2 cups (416 g) dried navy beans

2 tablespoons (28 ml) extra-virgin olive oil or ghee

2 cups (320 g) chopped onions

1 clove garlic, minced

2 cups (248 g) tomato puree

½ cup (170 g) organic honey

2 tablespoons (28 ml) apple cider vinegar

¼ teaspoon ground nutmeg

½ teaspoon ground cinnamon

3 bay leaves

½ teaspoon each ground turmeric and cumin

¼ teaspoon each salt, Celtic or sea, and black pepper

Soak the beans overnight. Drain and rinse under cold water. Add the beans to a large pot, cover with water, and bring to a boil. Reduce the heat to a simmer and cook for up to 2 hours.

Preheat the oven to 300°F (150°C, gas mark 2).

Drain the beans and place them in a large casserole dish. In a small skillet, heat the oil or ghee and sauté the onions and garlic until browned, about 3 or 4 minutes. Add the onions and garlic to the beans and mix together. Add all the other ingredients and stir to combine. With the lid on, bake the beans for 3 hours, stirring frequently. Check the moisture level and add water if needed. After 3½ hours, remove the cover and bake for another 30 minutes.

Serve with Zesty Digestive Herb and Cheddar Breakfast Muffins (page 89). Refrigerate the beans in an airtight jar, where they will keep for up to 1 week.

Yield: 1 quart or 8 servings

Note: The insoluble fiber in baked beans is not fully digested but moves into the large intestine or colon, where friendly bacteria thrive on it to produce beneficial B-complex vitamins, enzymes, and short-term fatty acids.

———— **[NUTRITIONAL ANALYSIS]** ————

Per serving: 314.8 calories; 4.2 g fat; 12.4 g protein; 56.1 g carbs; 14.1 g fiber; 16.6 mg sodium.

ZESTY DIGESTIVE HERB AND CHEDDAR BREAKFAST MUFFINS

These wholesome almond flour muffins are high in plant protein and fiber as well as calcium and heart-protective vitamin E. Almond flour imparts a satisfying taste to baked goods and is more filling than grain-based flours, so you will probably eat less. The fresh ginger and orange zest will help give your digestive system a boost and keep your metabolism running smoothly.

1 teaspoon butter or extra-virgin olive oil

1 whole egg

2 eggs, yolks and whites separated

¼ cup (56 g) butter, softened

¼ cup (60 g) Immune-Boosting Yogurt (page 158)

1 teaspoon organic honey

1 tablespoon (6 g) minced fresh ginger, peeled

1 teaspoon grated orange peel

¼ teaspoon salt, Celtic or sea

½ cup (60 g) grated Cheddar cheese

2 cups (230 g) almond flour

1 teaspoon baking soda

2 hard-boiled eggs, peeled

Preheat the oven to 325ºF (170ºC, gas mark 3). Lightly oil a large, 6-hole muffin tin using 1 teaspoon butter or oil.

In a large bowl, combine the whole egg with the two egg yolks, butter, yogurt, honey, ginger, orange peel, and salt and whisk until light and fluffy, about 3 minutes. Add the Cheddar and combine well. In a separate bowl, mix the almond flour with the baking soda and add to the egg mixture. Beat the 2 egg whites until stiff, about 3 or 4 minutes, and gently fold into the dough. Chop the hard-boiled eggs into large chunks and fold into the mixture. Evenly distribute the dough among the muffin tin holes and bake for 30 minutes, or until the muffins feel spongy. Let cool for 10 minutes before serving warm with butter or alongside your favorite breakfast dishes.

Yield: 6 servings

Note: Almond flour is heavier and coarser than wheat flours, causing baked goods not to rise as much. They usually rise in the oven and then sink when cooled.

[NUTRITIONAL ANALYSIS]

Per serving: 420.8 calories; 33.5 g fat; 14 g protein; 10.7 g carbs; 4.1 g fiber; 368.5 mg sodium.

· MIDDAY MEALS ·
AND ANYTIME SNACKS

- **SALADS FOR ALL SEASONS** 91
- **DELICIOUS DRESSINGS** 97
- **LUNCH-BOX-WORTHY SANDWICHES** 99
- **HEARTWARMING SOUPS & BROTHS** 103

Including plenty of antioxidant vitamin- and mineral-laden foods, the raw, lively salads and energy-sustaining soups and sandwiches in this section are vital to your heart- and brain-healthy diet. These recipes contain foods to balance your metabolism, boost your immune system, and fight stress, thereby warding off the tendency to reach for high-glycemic carbohydrate foods. Many of the recipes contain heart-strengthening minerals such as potassium and magnesium, plus ample amounts of vitamins A, C, and E. In addition, you'll find vitamin B–complex-rich foods to strengthen your blood vessels, arteries, and heart, plus lots of fiber to keep your metabolism efficient. I recommend eating at least one raw salad every day—notice what happens to your health when you do. You'll be pleasantly delighted, I am certain.

Experiment until you find the right balance of foods that makes you feel best, as no two people are identical. Gradually you will learn how to eat to protect your heart and improve your entire health. Your taste buds will enjoy the journey, also.

ALMIGHTY AVOCADO AND BLACK BEAN SALAD

Apart from their smooth nutty flavor, avocados are rich in monounsaturated fat, which is easily burned for energy. They are an excellent source of fiber, folate, vitamins E, C, B_6, and B_5, and potassium, all of which have cardioprotective benefits. Black beans are high in plant protein and fiber plus an impressive array of essential antioxidant vitamins and minerals that reduce inflammation and benefit the whole body. This combination together with the herbs and spices in this salad is a dieter's dream dish.

2 cups (388 g) dried black beans

1½ tablespoons (1.5 g) chopped fresh cilantro

1½ tablespoons (6 g) chopped fresh parsley

1 tablespoon (15 ml) fresh lime juice

¼ teaspoon salt, Celtic or sea

¼ teaspoon black pepper

½ cup (90 g) chopped tomatoes

½ cup (73 g) diced avocado

2 tablespoons (12 g) chopped scallions

1 teaspoon chopped green chile pepper, seeded

4 cups (220 g) salad greens

Soak the beans overnight. Drain, rinse, and place into a medium-size pot. Cover with water, bring to a boil, and reduce to a simmer. Cook for up to 2 hours, until the beans have softened. Drain.

Whisk together the cilantro, parsley, lime juice, salt, and pepper in a large bowl. Add the beans, tomatoes, avocado, scallions, and pepper, and toss well. Cover and chill for 2 hours. Combine with the salad greens shortly before serving.

Yield: 4 servings

Note: One cup of avocado has 23 percent of the recommended daily value of folate. Studies have shown that folate improves heart health and is protective against strokes.

[NUTRITIONAL ANALYSIS]

Per serving: 183.9 calories; 2.8 g fat; 19.3 g protein; 50 g carbs; 34.7 g fiber; 176.1 mg sodium.

MOOD-BOOSTING CHICKEN AND PINEAPPLE COLESLAW WITH COCONUT-LIME DRESSING

Delight your taste buds as you improve your health with the delicious combination of spices and nutrients in this dish. Coleslaw is made from one of the most powerful health-promoting vegetables in the food kingdom–cabbage. Cabbage is rich in fiber and vitamins A, C, and K, all of which are natural antioxidants that help prevent heart disease. The addition of chicken to this dish adds complete protein along with vitamins B_6 and B_3, which support energy metabolism throughout the body.

FOR THE COLESLAW:

1 pound (455 g) chicken breast

1 cup (235 ml) filtered water

1 cup (110 g) carrots, peeled and grated

3½ cups (315 g) savoy cabbage, thinly sliced

1 cup (155 g) diced fresh pineapple

2 scallions, chopped

¼ cup each chopped fresh cilantro (4 g) and mint (24 g)

FOR THE DRESSING:

1 cup (235 ml) coconut milk

¼ cup (60 ml) fresh lime juice

2 tablespoons (28 ml) fish sauce

1 tablespoon (20 g) organic honey

To make the coleslaw: Place the chicken and 1 cup (235 ml) filtered water in a saucepan over medium heat and steam until cooked through, about 15 to 20 minutes. Let it cool, then shred. Place the chicken in a large bowl and combine with the remaining coleslaw ingredients.

To make the dressing: In a separate bowl, whisk together all the dressing ingredients and pour over the top of the chicken.

Yield: 4 servings

Note: Apart from its high content of vitamin C, fiber, potassium, and other nutrients, cabbage has the fewest calories and least fat of any vegetable. Store cabbage whole in the refrigerator, which will help to retain its vitamin C content.

[NUTRITIONAL ANALYSIS]

Per serving: 314 calories; 14.9 g fat; 28.3 g protein; 18.6 g carbs; 3.9 g fiber; 799.2 mg sodium.

VITALIZING BROCCOLI AND CAULIFLOWER SALAD

Together, these two superfoods, broccoli and cauliflower, will provide your body with its daily dose of fiber, antioxidants, and essential vitamins and minerals. Botanically, they are part of the cruciferous family of vegetables, which are loaded with B-complex vitamins like niacin, riboflavin, pantothenic acid, thiamine, and folate, as well as vitamin K, potassium, calcium, magnesium, and iron. The nutrients are made even more bioavailable by steaming them first, which we've done here. The antioxidants in the spices combine to make this salad a winner when it comes to providing sustained energy, and the natural flavor companions in this stunning dish are simply delicious.

1½ cups each cauliflower (150 g) and broccoli florets (107 g), chopped into bite-size pieces

1 cup (130 g) chopped carrots

3 tablespoons (45 ml) Bone-Building French Cream (page 157)

2 tablespoons (28 ml) apple cider vinegar

1 teaspoon organic honey

¼ teaspoon salt, Celtic or sea

⅛ teaspoon ground fresh ginger, peeled

½ teaspoon ground cumin

¼ teaspoon each ground coriander and nutmeg

Dash of cayenne pepper

2 tablespoons (12 g) chopped scallions

Place the cauliflower, broccoli, and carrots in a vegetable steamer and steam for about 3 minutes. Rinse under cold water, drain well, and place in a large bowl.

In a separate bowl, combine the cream, vinegar, and honey and mix well. In a third bowl, combine the salt, ginger, cumin, coriander, nutmeg, and cayenne and add to the cream mixture. Pour this over the cooled vegetables and garnish with the scallions. Serve.

Yield: 4 servings

Note: To ensure freshness and higher nutrient content, purchase whole rather than precut broccoli and cauliflower and store it in the refrigerator. Once cooked, you should consume it within a couple days to avoid spoilage.

[NUTRITIONAL ANALYSIS]

Per serving: 69.1 calories; 3.8 g fat; 2.4 g protein; 8.1 g carbs; 2.9 g fiber; 157.3 mg sodium.

CARDIOPROTECTIVE SALMON CAESAR SALAD

Adding salmon to a traditional Caesar salad increases the flavor and omega-3 fatty acid content by a mile. The protein in salmon is easy to digest and absorb, which speeds up your metabolism and keeps blood sugar levels in check. The eggs, romaine lettuce, and dressing meld nicely in this dish to satisfy your palate, all the while contributing to a healthy lifestyle.

FOR THE SALAD:

2 salmon fillets (4 ounces [115 g] each)

½ teaspoon salt, Celtic or sea

¼ teaspoon black pepper

4 cups (220 g) romaine lettuce, washed, roughly shredded

4 hard-boiled eggs, shelled and cut into quarters

Cardioprotective Caesar Salad Dressing (page 97)

Rub the salmon with the salt and pepper and steam it, covered, in a small skillet over medium heat, with a little water (about ½ cup [120 ml]) for about 10 minutes, until just cooked through. Set aside and let cool. Cut into slices. Place the romaine lettuce into a large bowl and add the salmon and quartered eggs. Toss with the dressing and serve immediately.

Yield: 4 servings

Note: Omega-3 essential fatty acids not only strengthen your heart muscle but help your brain work better and improve memory.

Salmon: High Quality Protein and Nutrition

Salmon is a superb source of omega-3 fatty acids, which strengthen your heart muscle and help your brain and memory function better. It's also a great source of high-quality protein. One 3-ounce serving of wild salmon gives you more than 18 g of protein, plus 360 mg of potassium and almost half the Daily Value (DV) of the important cancer-fighting mineral, selenium. It also contains more than half the DV for vitamin B_{12} and 30 percent of the DV for niacin.

Although we'll eat farm-raised salmon in a pinch, our first choice—by far—is wild Alaskan salmon. Here's why. Farm-raised salmon are raised on grain—hardly their natural diet—and have higher amounts of inflammatory omega-6 fatty acids. Like factory-farmed cattle, they're also frequently given antibiotics. And farm-raised salmon are a significant source of PCBs. Whenever possible, opt for wild Alaskan salmon.

---[NUTRITIONAL ANALYSIS]---

Per serving: 177.5 calories; 5.3 g fat; 18.3 g protein; 2.1 g carbs; 1 g fiber; 272 mg sodium.

ENERGIZING THAI SPICE CHICKEN SALAD

There's something balanced about Thai food because of the sweet, salty, and sour combination of flavors in the dishes. It's also one of the healthiest cuisines because of the wide use of fresh medicinal herbs. This recipe is no exception.

FOR THE MARINADE:

1 teaspoon salt, Celtic or sea

6 cloves garlic

2 tablespoons (28 ml) fresh lemon or lime juice

1 cup (16 g) chopped fresh cilantro

1 teaspoon black pepper

FOR THE SALAD:

2 cups (140 g) finely shredded cabbage

1½ cups (83 g) mixed lettuce greens

1 cup (40 g) shredded fresh basil

1 fresh red chile pepper, minced

2 chicken breasts (4 ounces [115 g] each)

FOR THE DRESSING:

See Energizing Thai Spice Salad Dressing (page 97)

To make the marinade: Place all the marinade ingredients into a food processor and blend until minced.

To make the salad: Combine the cabbage, mixed lettuce greens, basil, and pepper in a large bowl. Set aside.

Place the chicken and marinade in a saucepan with ½ cup (120 ml) filtered water and simmer, covered, for about 20 minutes, or until the chicken is cooked through. Let cool. Shred the cooled chicken by hand. Toss with the dressing and serve immediately over the mixed greens.

Yield: 4 servings

Note: Cilantro is one of the richest herbal sources for vitamin K and a good source of potassium, calcium, iron, and magnesium, all of which support healthy metabolism and cellular energy.

───[NUTRITIONAL ANALYSIS]───
Per serving: 99.8 calories; 2.2 g fat; 15.8 g protein; 4.2 g carbs; 1.8 g fiber; 371.5 mg sodium.

PUMPING JUMPING BEAN SALAD

Keep your blood sugar balanced while you enjoy the delicious nutty flavors of this legume-filled salad, which is high in plant protein and fiber and loaded with health-supportive nutrients to give you energy. The pine nuts are high in vitamins E and K, copper, magnesium, and iron, all of which are heart healthy.

FOR THE SALAD:

1 can (13¾ ounces [390 g]) garbanzo beans, drained and rinsed

½ cup (80 g) chopped red onion

1 cup (120 g) diced celery stalks

1 cup (130 g) diced carrots

½ cup (30 g) chopped fresh parsley

1 cup (135 g) seeded and diced cucumber

1 cup (150 g) diced red bell pepper

½ cup (70 g) pine nuts

For the dressing:

Simply Nourishing Salad Dressing (page 97)

Combine all the salad ingredients in a large bowl and toss with Simply Nourishing Salad Dressing. Cover and chill for 1 hour before serving.

Yield: 4 servings

Note: If using dry beans, soaking them for several hours before cooking or consuming them helps to break down the antinutrients and hard-to-digest components of the legume and at the same time, release the beneficial nutrients. This recipe, which calls for canned beans, was adapted from one that came from my book Foods That Fight Fibromyalgia.

Recipe Variations

Bean recipes are very tolerant to substitutions but color, texture, and flavor are also criteria to consider. For the Pumping Jumping Bean Salad, you might switch out the garbanzo beans for black beans if you prefer a meatier texture and a flavor that has been compared to mushrooms. To turn up the heat on a summer's day, you may like to add some fresh mango, lime juice, fresh cilantro, and a jalapeño.

―――――[NUTRITIONAL ANALYSIS]―――――

Per serving: 235 calories; 13.4 g fat; 8.2 g protein; 26.5 g carbs; 7.3 g fiber; 411.9 mg sodium.

SIMPLY NOURISHING SALAD DRESSING

This dressing provides a good balance of essential fatty acids and tastes delicious. Make it in bulk and keep a fresh supply on hand to add to raw salads or drizzle it over your favorite steamed veggies.

1 clove garlic, minced

4 tablespoons (60 ml) extra-virgin olive oil

2 to 4 tablespoons (28 to 60 ml) flaxseed oil

2 tablespoons (28 ml) fresh lemon or lime juice

2 tablespoons (28 ml) apple cider vinegar

1 teaspoon dry mustard powder

¼ teaspoon salt, Celtic or sea

Dash of black pepper

Dash of cayenne pepper (optional)

Place all the ingredients into a food processor and blend until smooth, or place all the ingredients in a jar with a tight-fitting lid and shake vigorously until well blended. Taste, and adjust seasonings as desired. Serve over mixed lettuce leaves or other favorite salad ingredients.

Yield: 1 cup

Note: Flaxseed oil is easily oxidized and therefore should never be heated, always refrigerated, and purchased in opaque bottles that have been refrigerated.

CARDIOPROTECTIVE CAESAR SALAD DRESSING

The anchovies in this tasty dressing deliver health benefits in the form of essential fatty acids, protein, calcium, and magnesium, all of which combine to keep your heart in good shape. The other ingredients simply add to the nutritional profile and pack a flavorful punch.

5 anchovies

1 egg

¼ teaspoon dry mustard powder

1 tablespoon (15 g) Dijon mustard

1 clove garlic

¾ cup (175 ml) extra-virgin olive oil

2 tablespoons (28 ml) fresh lemon or lime juice

Place the anchovies, egg, mustard powder, Dijon mustard, and garlic into a food processor and blend until smooth. Add a little of the oil, about 2 tablespoons (28 ml), and blend again. Keep adding the oil slowly while still blending. Then add the lemon or lime juice and keep blending until the dressing starts to thicken. Refrigerate in an airtight container. Serve over top of the Cardioprotective Caesar Salad (page 94).

Yield: 1 cup

Note: Anchovies packed in cans or jars are frequently high in sodium. The best way to eliminate some of the excess salt is to rinse or soak them first in cold water.

———————— [NUTRITIONAL ANALYSIS]————————

Per tablespoon: 60.7 calories; 6.9 g fat; 0 g protein; .2 g carbs; 0 g fiber; 35.4 mg sodium.

———————— [NUTRITIONAL ANALYSIS]————————

Per tablespoon: 98.2 calories; 10.9 g fat; 0.7 g protein; 0.1 g carbs; 0 g fiber; 72.4 mg sodium.

ENERGIZING THAI SPICE SALAD DRESSING

Fragrant and full of flavor—these are some of the words used to describe this delectable dressing. The kaffir lime leaf adds an unmistakable, refreshing taste that is used in many Thai dishes and provides an array of digestive nutrients. The spices in this dish will dress up any raw salad greens with delightful flavors.

1 tablespoon (15 ml) fish sauce

1 tablespoon (4 g) lemongrass

1 kaffir lime leaf

1 clove garlic

1 tablespoon (20 g) organic honey

1 teaspoon grated fresh ginger, peeled

2 tablespoons (28 ml) fresh lime juice

½ cup (8 g) chopped fresh cilantro

1 teaspoon Spice-It-Up Sweet Chili Sauce (page 152)

5 tablespoons (75 ml) filtered water

Place all the ingredients into a food processor and process until finely minced. Serve over Energizing Thai Spice Chicken Salad (page 95). Refrigerate in an airtight container.

Yield: ⅓ cup

Note: Kaffir lime leaves are used in many Thai dishes, where they not only add aromatic fragrance but are believed to brighten a person's mental outlook as well.

───────[NUTRITIONAL ANALYSIS]───────

Per tablespoon: 5.8 calories; 0 g fat; 0.1 g protein; 1.5 g carbs; 0 g fiber; 88 mg sodium.

HOLY-MOLY GUACAMOLE DRESSING

A member of the fruit family, avocados are considered one of the healthiest foods on the planet. They contain more than twenty-five nutrients, including essential fatty acids, vitamins C, E, K, and the heart-healthy minerals magnesium, selenium, and zinc. This delicious guacamole has zingy flavors to match the nutrient density and antioxidants in it.

1 avocado, pitted and peeled

1 small tomato, diced

¼ cup (60 ml) lemon or lime juice

1 tablespoon (1 g) chopped fresh cilantro

1 spring onion, chopped

1 clove garlic, chopped

¼ teaspoon cayenne pepper

Place all the ingredients in a blender or food processor and blend until coarse in texture. Spread the dressing over toast or crackers, or serve on top of mixed salad greens.

Yield: 1 cup

Note: A firm, green avocado can be ripened more quickly by placing it in a paper bag or fruit basket at room temperature. The used ripe portion should be stored in the refrigerator, where it will maintain freshness for several days. Sprinkle with lemon juice to avoid brown spots.

───────[NUTRITIONAL ANALYSIS]───────

Per tablespoon: 21.3 calories; 1.7 g fat; 0.3 g protein; 1.8 g carbs; 0.9 g fiber; 1.8 mg sodium.

STRESS-LESS TURKEY, AVOCADO, AND VEGGIE NORI WRAP

Turkey is high in protein and the amino acid trypto-phan, which produces the feel-good neurochemical serotonin. In addition to being deliciously tasty, nori seaweed is a great way to obtain natural iodine, a trace mineral that stimulates the thyroid to produce hormones required for healthy metabolism. Adding avocado is simply icing on the nutrient-rich cake, or wrap, as the case may be.

- **4 raw nori sheets**
- **4 romaine lettuce leaves**
- **4 tablespoons (60 g) Bone-Strengthening Lemon Tahini (page 151), divided**
- **4 slices turkey (1 ounce [28 g] each)**
- **1 cup (50 g) alfalfa sprouts**
- **1 carrot, peeled and julienned**
- **½ cup (75 g) cherry tomatoes, halved**
- **1 avocado, peeled, pitted, and sliced into quarters**
- **¼ cup (60 ml) filtered water**

Lay out 1 nori sheet and place 1 lettuce leaf across the end. Spread 1 tablespoon (15 g) of the tahini on top of the lettuce leaf. Layer the lettuce leaf with 1/4 of the sprouts, carrot, tomatoes, and avocado on top (ensure vegetables are distributed evenly). Dip your fingers in the water to dampen them and begin rolling the nori sheet into a wrap. The water will make it easy to stick together. Repeat the process with the other 3 sheets.

Yield: 4 wraps

───── **[NUTRITIONAL ANALYSIS]** ─────

Per serving: 139.8 calories; 8.5 g fat; 7.6 g protein; 8.7 g carbs; 3.7 g fiber; 278.1 mg sodium.

GLUTEN-FREE MEDITERRANEAN VEGGIE PIZZA

Rich in flavor and Mediterranean goodness, this pizza is made with heart-healthy olive oil, protein-rich nuts, and colorful, fiber-rich vegetables that will sustain you for hours. Feel free to add chicken or shrimp on top if you want extra protein.

FOR THE CRUST:

- **½ cup (80 g) brown rice flour, plus a little extra for dusting**
- **½ cup (68 g) whole grain sorghum flour**
- **½ cup (58 g) almond meal**
- **¼ cup (26 g) ground flaxseed**
- **½ teaspoon salt, Celtic or sea**
- **¼ teaspoon garlic powder**
- **2 tablespoons (30 g) Bone-Strengthening Lemon Tahini (page 151; optional)**
- **2 tablespoons (28 ml) filtered water**
- **2 tablespoons (28 ml) extra-virgin olive oil**

FOR THE TOPPING:

- **1 to 2 tablespoons (15 to 28 ml) extra-virgin olive oil**
- **½ red onion, thinly sliced**
- **1 cup (150 g) chopped red bell pepper**
- **1 tablespoon (4 g) oregano, fresh or dried, chopped finely**
- **1 small zucchini, sliced into thin strips**
- **2 cloves garlic, chopped finely**
- **1 cup (70 g) portobello mushrooms, chopped into ¼-inch (6-mm) cubes**

───── **[NUTRITIONAL ANALYSIS]** ─────

Per slice: 139.4 calories; 7.4 g fat; 3.7 g protein; 16 g carbs; 2.2 g fiber; 122.4 mg sodium.

Dash each of cayenne and black pepper

3 tablespoons (45 g) Mediterranean Black Olive Tapenade (page 150)

1 cup (115 g) shredded mozzarella

4 ripe tomatoes, thinly sliced (or use sun-dried tomatoes if preferred)

1 cup (100 g) grated Parmesan cheese

Preheat the oven to 400°F (200°C, gas mark 6).

To make the crust: Combine all the crust ingredients in a bowl and mix thoroughly. Cover the dough and refrigerate overnight, or about 8 to 12 hours. The next day, remove the dough from the refrigerator and let it sit at room temperature for 1 hour before using. Prepare the surface of a baking sheet with a light rub of coconut or olive oil. Lay a few overlapping pieces of waxed paper on a countertop to cover a large rolling area and lightly dust the surface with brown rice flour. Place the dough on top. Dust a rolling pin with more flour and roll the dough into a 1/8-inch (3-mm) layer to fit the size of your baking sheet. Reshape and patch rolled areas as needed.

To transfer the dough to the baking sheet, lay the sheet face down on top of the dough. Slide one hand underneath the waxed paper and place the other hand on top of the baking sheet. Quickly flip the two over and peel away the waxed paper. Bake for 20 minutes.

To make the toppng: In a large saucepan, heat the oil over medium heat. Add the onion, pepper, and oregano and sauté for 5 minutes. Stir in the zucchini, garlic, and mushrooms and sauté for 5 more minutes. Remove from the heat and add the cayenne and black peppers.

When the crust is ready, remove from the oven and evenly spread black olive tapenade over it. Sprinkle mozzarella over the crust. Top with the tomatoes. Layer the cooked vegetables on top and sprinkle with Parmesan and mozzarella cheeses. Bake for 10 minutes, or until the cheeses melt and brown slightly. Cut into slices with a pizza roller and serve hot with a tossed green salad or refrigerate and serve cold.

Yield: 1 pizza (8 slices)

Recipe Variation

The crust for this pizza is more of a crackerlike flat bread, so be sure to roll it thinly enough so that it bakes nice and crispy. If you want a more puffy, doughy texture, add 1 teaspoon of xanthan gum, and, after the refrigeration stage, add 1/4 teaspoon of instant yeast dissolved in 1 tablespoon (15 ml) water to the dough.

VIBRANT AVOCADO AND VEGGIE SALSA COLLARD WRAPS

Why use bread when you can use the tasty collard green to wrap your veggies? High in heart-healthy vitamin C and soluble fibers, collard greens are renowned for their ability to strengthen immunity.

FOR THE SALSA:

1 cup (180 g) diced tomatoes

1 clove garlic, minced

½ medium shallot, minced

½ jalapeño pepper, deseeded and minced

1 tablespoon (15 ml) fresh lime juice

FOR THE WRAPS:

4 large collard greens, without rips or holes

2 avocados, peeled and pitted

¼ teaspoon salt, Celtic or sea

4 raw nori sheets, cut in half

2 cups (110 g) mixed baby greens

2 cups (100 g) sprouts (mung bean, sunflower, or your favorite)

2 cups (220 g) shredded carrots

To make the salsa: Combine all the salsa ingredients together in a medium bowl. Refrigerate for a minimum of 30 minutes before serving to allow the flavors to meld.

To make the wraps: Blanch the collard greens by dipping each leaf in boiling water for 10 seconds, then immediately submerging in a bath of ice water. Dry them thoroughly before using. Lay 1 leaf at a time flat on a cutting board and cut off the end stem so that it's flush with the leaf edge. Repeat with the remaining leaves and set aside.

In a medium bowl, mash the avocados with a fork. Add the salsa and salt and mix together. To assemble the wraps, take a leaf and lay it on a flat surface with the lighter side facing up and the spine vertical to you. Lay a nori strip horizontally across each leaf, about 2 inches (5 cm) up from the bottom end. Spread the avocado salsa along the nori, leaving about an inch (2.5 cm) from each horizontal side. Layer with baby greens, sprouts, and carrots. Using your fingers, pack the ingredients together and roll the collard green tightly over the filling. Cut the wrap on a diagonal in half to serve. Repeat the process for the remaining wraps.

Yield: 4 wraps

Note: Wash collard greens thoroughly before cooking or eating them, as they tend to collect dirt and soil.

[NUTRITIONAL ANALYSIS]

Per serving: 205.9 calories; 11.4 g fat; 7.3 g protein; 22.6 g carbs; 8.1 g fiber; 298.9 mg sodium.

FEEL-GOOD TURKEY OR SALMON TOMATO PANINI

Turkey or salmon with summer-ripe tomato slices in-between a creamy spread full of Parmesan and fresh basil combine to make this savory hot sandwich your favorite go-to snack or mealtime solution. The fresh tomatoes, basil, and avocados are a treasure of anti-oxidants such as vitamin A and C that provide support at the cellular level, which is increased further with the addition of lime juice. The wholesome goodness is further enhanced by protein with the addition of turkey or salmon. Make double the amount and save one for later.

3 tablespoons (42 g) Heart-Healthy Almond Mayonnaise (page 151)

2 tablespoons (30 g) Immune-Boosting Yogurt (page 158)

2 tablespoons (10 g) shredded Parmesan cheese

2 tablespoons (5 g) chopped fresh basil

1 teaspoon lemon or lime juice

Dash of freshly ground black pepper

4 slices gluten-free bread or Nourishing Crusty Onion and Parmesan Rolls (page 166)

4 slices deli turkey or ½ cup (112 g) canned red salmon

4 tomato slices

½ avocado, pitted, peeled, and mashed

1 teaspoon extra-virgin olive oil

In a small bowl, combine the mayonnaise, yogurt, Parmesan, basil, lemon or lime juice, and black pepper. Spread about 2 teaspoons of the mixture on each slice of bread. Divide the turkey or salmon and tomato, place on top of the bread, and cover with sliced avocado. Place the remaining bread on top.

In a medium skillet, heat the olive oil over medium heat. Place the 2 panini in the pan and cook until golden brown on one side, about 2 minutes. Reduce the heat to low and flip the panini. Cook until the second side is golden, about 1 to 3 minutes. Alternatively, place the sandwiches under the grill for 5 minutes. Cut in half diagonally and serve immediately.

Yield: 2 sandwiches

Note: Grass-fed, organically raised turkey, as opposed to factory farmed, offers substantially higher nutritional content and conveys the most health benefits.

[NUTRITIONAL ANALYSIS]

Per serving (with salmon): 565.9 calories; 36.7 g fat; 20.4 g protein; 42.4 g carbs; 2.5 g fiber; 653.4 mg sodium.

NUTRITIVE CHICKEN STOCK

In addition to being simple, easy, and cost effective, preparing your own chicken stock provides your body with many essential minerals and vitamins to rejuvenate your entire system. Enjoy this tasty, nourishing stock on its own as a broth or use it as a base when cooking grains, legumes, or any other recipe that calls for stock or water.

- 4 quarts (3.8 L) filtered water
- 1 chicken carcass
- 1 pound (455 g) chicken thighs, with bones
- 1 cup (160 g) onions, peeled and chopped into chunks
- 1 cup (120 g) diced celery
- 1 cup (130 g) diced carrots
- 4 cloves garlic, chopped
- 2 bay leaves
- 2 sprigs fresh thyme, chopped, or 1 teaspoon dried thyme
- 1 bunch parsley stems, chopped
- 2 tablespoons (28 ml) apple cider vinegar

Place the water, chicken carcass, and thighs in a large stockpot and bring to a boil over high heat. Reduce the heat to low and skim off the foam that rises during the first 10 to 15 minutes of simmering. Add the remaining ingredients. Simmer for 2½ to 3 hours. Turn the heat off and let stand, cooling, for 1 to 2 hours. Pour through a strainer, pushing with the back of a spoon to extract as much liquid as possible. Discard the vegetables and meat and other solids or fat from the surface of the stock, then transfer the stock to a variety of container sizes, including ice-cube trays. The stock can be refrigerated and used within 3 days, or it can be frozen for up to 3 months.

Yield: 3 quarts (2.8 L)

Recipe Variation

Change the chicken to beef if you want to include more red meat in your diet or if the dish you are preparing calls for beef stock.

[NUTRITIONAL ANALYSIS]

Per cup: 83 calories; 2.7 g fat; 11 g protein; 3.4 g carbs; 1.3 g fiber; 60.8 mg sodium.

DIGESTIVE VEGETABLE STOCK

Vegetable stock is loaded with healing nutrients that will alkalize your system, making it easier to cleanse and detoxify and boost your metabolism. Enjoy this tasty, nourishing stock on its own as a broth or use it as a base when cooking grains, legumes, or any other recipe that calls for stock or water.

2 quarts (1.9 L) filtered water

2 cups (260 g) chopped carrots

4 cups (480 g) diced celery

1 parsnip, chopped

1 cup (160 g) chopped onion

2 leeks, white and light green parts only, trimmed, rinsed, and thinly sliced

1 bunch parsley stems, chopped

3 cloves garlic, chopped

1 tablespoon (5 g) whole black peppercorns

2 sprigs fresh thyme, chopped, or 1 teaspoon dried thyme

2 bay leaves

Pour the water into a stockpot and add the remaining ingredients. Bring to a boil over high heat, then reduce the heat to low and simmer the stock, uncovered, for 1 hour. Turn the heat off and let cool for 1 to 2 hours.

Pour through a strainer, discarding the vegetables and solids. Allow the stock to cool at room temperature. Spoon into smaller containers, including ice-cube trays. Refrigerate a portion for upcoming use and store the rest in the freezer, where it will keep for up to 3 months.

Yield: 2 quarts (1.9 L)

Recipe Variation

The recipe can be varied according to taste. For example, you can add more root vegetables in the winter such as potatoes and turnips, or add more herbs.

The Culinary Advantages of Using Stock

You may think it's not necessary to use vegetable stock if you're making a vegetarian or vegan dish that includes the same vegetables, but that's not the case. Using stock creates a much more richly flavored dish that can't be replicated by increasing the quantity of vegetables cooked in it.

—— [NUTRITIONAL ANALYSIS] ——

Per cup: 63.9 calories; 0.4 g fat; 1.9 g protein; 14.7 g carbs; 4.2 g fiber; 85.7 mg sodium.

HEART-PROTECTIVE CARROT-GINGER SOUP WITH CHIVES

Tangy, tasty, and warming from the inside out, the combination of carrots with ginger will delight not only your taste buds but your entire digestive system. This soup is packed with the antioxidants vitamin A and beta-carotene, together with tons of fiber and B-complex vitamins. It doesn't get better than this for high-energy, nutrient-dense soups.

2 tablespoons (28 ml) extra-virgin olive oil or coconut oil

1 large onion, chopped

6 large carrots, chopped

2 cups (280 g) chopped butternut squash, skin on

5 cups (1.2 L) Digestive Vegetable Stock (page 104)

½ teaspoon salt, Celtic or sea

1 teaspoon chopped fresh ginger, peeled

¼ teaspoon each ground cumin, coriander powder, and garlic powder

1 cup (60 g) chopped fresh parsley

6 tablespoons (90 g) Immune-Boosting Yogurt (page 158)

2 tablespoons (6 g) chopped fresh chives

Melt the oil in a large pot. Add the onions and cook for several minutes over medium heat until they begin to sweat. Add the carrots and butternut squash and cook for about 3 minutes. Add the vegetable stock, salt, ginger, cumin, and coriander and garlic powders. Bring to a boil, reduce the heat, and simmer, about 15 to 20 minutes, or until you can pierce the pieces easily with a fork.

Purée the soup in a blender or food processor with the parsley. Serve with 1 tablespoon of yogurt in each bowl and top with fresh chives.

Yield: 6 servings

Note: Ginger is a stimulating herb that gets the blood flowing and the circulation going. Because of this, it can make you feel warm when nothing else seems to do the trick.

───[NUTRITIONAL ANALYSIS]───
Per serving: 183.3 calories; 6.3 g fat; 4.5 g protein; 30.6 g carbs; 8.3 g fiber; 256.1 mg sodium.

LOVE-YOUR-HEART RED LENTIL SOUP

Enjoy a warm bowl of this tasty lentil soup with its classic herbs and vegetables reminiscent of Northern Italy. Lentils are one of the healthiest sources of plant-based protein around in addition to their numerous other nutritional benefits. They are packed with heart-healthy soluble fiber, which helps moderate blood sugar levels and promote digestive health.

2 cups (384 g) dried red lentils

2 bay leaves

6 cups (1.4 L) Digestive Vegetable Stock (page 104) or filtered water

3 tablespoons (45 ml) extra-virgin olive oil

2 cups (320 g) diced onions

3 cloves garlic, diced

2 cups (360 g) chopped fresh tomatoes

2 cups (240 g) sliced zucchini

1½ tablespoons (4.5 g) dried oregano

2 tablespoons (5 g) chopped fresh basil

2½ tablespoons (35 ml) apple cider vinegar

2½ teaspoons onion powder

1 tablespoon salt, Celtic or sea

⅓ cup (90 g) canned tomato paste

1 tablespoon (15 ml) balsamic vinegar

½ teaspoon black pepper

Wash and drain the lentils. Place in a large pot with the bay leaves and stock and bring to a boil. Reduce the heat to medium and cook, stirring occasionally, for 30 minutes, or until the lentils are soft.

In a large skillet, heat the oil over medium heat and sauté the onions and garlic for about 10 minutes, or until the onions are golden brown. Stir in the tomatoes, zucchini, oregano, basil, apple cider vinegar, and onion powder and sauté for about 5 minutes. Set aside.

When the lentils are nearly soft, add the salt and reserved tomato, zucchini, and herb mixture. Stir in the tomato paste, balsamic vinegar, and pepper and simmer for 10 minutes. Remove the bay leaves and serve immediately.

Yield: 6 servings

Recipe Variation

To increase the complete protein content, add ¼ or ½ cup (47 to 95 g) of brown rice and decrease the lentils by the same amount.

[NUTRITIONAL ANALYSIS]

Per serving: 413.5 calories; 9.4 g fat; 20.6 g protein; 61.8 g carbs; 15.3 g fiber; 919.8 mg sodium.

IMMUNE-BOOSTING BASQUE BEAN AND CABBAGE SOUP

This delicious, simple soup is a hearty staple of the Basques, an ethnic group of people from France and Spain that primarily inhabits an area traditionally known as the Basque Country. The white beans give it body in the form of fiber and protein, while the cabbage provides tons of vitamin C and other heart-healthy nutrients. Like any thick soup or stew, it tastes even better the day after it is made, so make this one a day ahead of consuming it.

1½ cups (312 g) dried white navy beans

2 tablespoons (28 ml) olive oil

1 medium onion, chopped

3 cloves garlic, minced

1 medium carrot, chopped

½ cup (50 g) chopped celery

8 cups (1.9 L) Digestive Vegetable Stock (page 104)

1 tablespoon (7 g) ground paprika

2 tablespoons (13 g) ground flaxseed

¼ cup (15 g) chopped fresh parsley

1 teaspoon dried thyme

1 bay leaf

¾ pound (340 g) redskin potatoes, scrubbed and cut into ¾-inch (2-cm) cubes

6 cups (420 g) firmly packed shredded green cabbage

1 teaspoon salt, Celtic or sea

½ teaspoon black pepper

Soak the beans overnight. Next morning, rinse the beans under cold water and drain. In a large pot, heat the oil over medium-high heat. Add the onion, garlic, carrot, and celery. Cook for about 5 minutes, or until the onions are translucent, stirring frequently. Add the beans, stock, paprika, flaxseed, parsley, thyme, and bay leaf. Bring to a boil over high heat, then reduce the heat to low and simmer the soup, partially covered, for about 45 minutes, or until the beans are almost tender.

Add the potatoes and cabbage and cook for an additional 20 to 25 minutes, or until the vegetables are very tender. Remove and discard the bay leaf, season with salt and pepper, and serve immediately.

Yield: 8 servings as an appetizer or 6 as an entrée

Note: The soup can be prepared up to 2 days in advance and refrigerated, tightly covered. Reheat over low heat, covered, until hot, stirring occasionally.

[NUTRITIONAL ANALYSIS]

Per serving: 306.9 calories; 5.3 g fat; 14.4 g protein; 54.3 g carbs; 18.5 g fiber; 182.7 mg sodium.

BUILD-ME-UP BUTTERNUT AND MACADAMIA NUT BISQUE

This creamy, delicious dish is rich in antioxidants, fiber, and anti-inflammatory omega-3s that are particularly important for inclusion in your heart-healthy diet. Butternut squash is warming and good for stabilizing blood sugar levels to keep your system balanced for hours. Macadamia nuts contain essential vitamins and minerals including potassium, manganese, thiamine, and fiber, all of which help your body defend against disease and increase overall energy.

2 tablespoons (28 ml) extra-virgin olive oil

1 cup (160 g) chopped onions

¾ cup (101 g) macadamia nuts, roughly chopped

2 teaspoons grated fresh ginger, peeled

1 clove minced garlic

1 teaspoon ground turmeric

1 cup (150 g) green apples, peeled, cored, and diced

1 medium to large butternut squash, peeled, seeded, and diced

1 cup (235 ml) Nutritive Chicken (page 103) or Digestive Vegetable Stock (page 104)

4 tablespoons (60 g) Immune-Boosting Yogurt (page 158)

4 teaspoons (68 g) macadamia nuts, roughly chopped

Heat the oil in a large pot. Add the onions, macadamia nuts, ginger, and garlic and sauté until lightly browned, about 3 to 5 minutes. Stir in the turmeric. Add the apple and squash. Stir for about 3 minutes, coating them with the other ingredients, and then add the stock. Cover and cook for about 20 minutes, until the squash is quite soft. Pour all the ingredients into a food processor and blend until smooth and creamy. Add a little hot water if the soup is too thick or for a thinner consistency. Serve with a large dollop of yogurt and a teaspoon of macadamia nuts.

Yield: 4 servings

Note: Macadamia nuts are a good source of protein and vitamin E, a powerful antioxidant that not only protects your cells from free-radical damage but reduces your risk of gastrointestinal cancer.

[NUTRITIONAL ANALYSIS]

Per serving: 476 calories; 40.2 g fat; 6.3 g protein; 30.8 g carbs; 7.8 g fiber; 44.2 mg sodium.

LOW-CARB HERBED CHEDDAR CRACKERS

These are moist and delicious, so I like to make a large batch to keep on hand for all occasions. Believe it or not, topping these savory, delectable crackers with sweet spreads is simply scrumptious.

- **2 teaspoons butter**
- **2 cups (230 g) almond flour**
- **2 cups (240 g) grated sharp Cheddar cheese**
- **1 teaspoon fresh thyme, or ½ teaspoon dried**
- **1 teaspoon fresh sage, or ½ teaspoon dried**
- **¼ teaspoon cayenne pepper**
- **1 teaspoon baking soda**
- **6 tablespoons (90 ml) cold filtered water**

Preheat the oven to 300°F (150°C, gas mark 2). Grease 2 baking sheets with butter. In a large bowl, combine the almond flour, Cheddar, thyme, sage, cayenne, and baking soda. Add the cold water, mix, and form into a flat dough. Cover and refrigerate for about 30 minutes.

Remove the dough from the refrigerator. Take 1 teaspoon dough, roll it into a ball, and squeeze down with your fingers onto the prepared baking sheet. Continue this process until all of the dough has been used. Each cracker should be about ⅛-inch (3 mm) thick and at least ¾-inch (2 cm) away from the next cracker. Bake in the oven for 30 minutes, or until the edges start to brown. The crackers should look pale in the center. Turn the oven down to 200F (95°C).

Remove the sheets from the oven and let cool for 5 minutes. Turn each cracker over and return the trays to the oven. Bake for 20 minutes, turn the oven off, and let the crackers sit in the oven until the oven has cooled somewhat, about 10 minutes. Remove the sheets from the oven and cool completely. The crackers should be slightly browned, but still pale. Serve these topped with your favorite condiments. Store the crackers between waxed paper in an airtight container.

Yield: About 50 crackers

Note: Almond flour is not only gluten free, but also low in carbohydrates and sugars and high in protein.

[NUTRITIONAL ANALYSIS]

Per serving: 38.7 calories; 3.1 g fat; 2 g protein; 0.9 g carbs; 0.4 g fiber; 64 mg sodium.

BLOOD SUGAR–BALANCING BUTTERNUT & LEEK PIES

You'll love the sweet, subtle flavors and smooth texture of these satisfying and delectable pies. The high-fiber and antioxidant-laden butternut squash marries nicely with the sweet, delicate flavor of leeks, all the while adding impressive amounts of the B vitamin folate. Folate supports the cardiovascular system by keeping homocysteine in proper balance. Warning: You may need to eat more than just one.

1 cup (140 g) butternut squash, peeled, seeded, and diced

1½ tablespoons (21 g) butter

¾ cup (78 g) chopped leeks

1 tablespoon (20 g) organic honey

1 clove garlic, minced

10 eggs

⅓ cup (33 g) grated Parmesan cheese

⅓ cup (80 ml) Bone-Building French Cream (page 157)

Dash of cayenne pepper

½ teaspoon salt, Celtic or sea

½ teaspoon black pepper

Preheat the oven to 350°F (180°C). Lightly oil a large, 6-hole muffin tin.

In a medium-size pot, steam the squash in a small amount of water for about 10 minutes, or until it starts to soften. Drain and set aside. Heat the butter in a small skillet and add the leeks. Stir and sauté for about 3 minutes, or until the leeks start to wilt. Add the honey and garlic and cook, stirring, for 3 to 4 minutes. Remove from the heat and set aside.

In a large bowl, combine the eggs, Parmesan, and cream and mix well. Add the squash, leeks, cayenne pepper, salt, and black pepper. Divide the mixture evenly among the muffin tin holes and bake for 30 to 40 minutes, until the tops of the pies feel firm. Remove from the oven and let cool for a few minutes before removing from the molds. Serve at room temperature or cold. Refrigerate in an airtight container, where they will keep for up to 5 days.

Yield: 6 servings

Note: Leeks, like onions and garlic, are part of the sulfur-containing Alliaceae family, which are high in antioxidant flavonoids well known for their anti-inflammatory properties.

[NUTRITIONAL ANALYSIS]

Per serving: 243.1 calories; 16.8 g fat; 13.7 g protein; 9.6 g carbs; 1.2 g fiber; 361.6 mg sodium.

HIGH-ENERGY CHICKEN & CAULIFLOWER CROQUETTES

Gain more energy when you nosh on these high-protein and fiber-filled goodies. The chicken and cauliflower pair nicely with the fresh herbs and Parmesan cheese to create a creamy and crunchy texture that will explode with flavor in your mouth.

- ½ cup (80 g) chopped onions
- 1 tablespoon (15 ml) extra-virgin olive oil
- 1 pound (455 g) chicken, minced
- 1 cup (100 g) chopped cauliflower
- 1 teaspoon fresh thyme
- 1 tablespoon (4 g) chopped fresh parsley
- ½ teaspoon salt, Celtic or sea
- ½ teaspoon pepper
- 2 eggs, divided
- ½ cup (50 g) grated Parmesan cheese
- 1 cup (115 g) almond flour
- ⅓ cup (80 ml) coconut oil

In a medium to large skillet over medium heat, sauté the onions in olive oil until tender, about 5 minutes. Add the chicken and cook for about 20 minutes on low until all the moisture has evaporated. In a separate pot, steam the cauliflower until just soft, about 8 minutes. Drain and place into a food processor with the chicken and onions and add the thyme, parsley, salt, pepper, and 1 egg and blend until smooth. Refrigerate the mixture for 30 minutes.

Mix the Parmesan cheese with the almond flour and spread onto a large, flat plate. Whip the remaining egg in a bowl until light and fluffy. Remove the chicken mixture from the refrigerator and form into small croquettes, about 1 by 2 inches (2.5 by 5 cm). Dip them into the beaten egg and roll in the almond and cheese flour until well covered. Heat the coconut oil in a nonstick pan and fry the croquettes, turning them frequently, until golden brown. When cooked, place the croquettes onto a double layer of kitchen paper towels to remove excess oil. Serve warm with Antioxidant BBQ Sauce (page 154) or Spice-It-Up Sweet Chili Sauce (page 152).

Yield: About 16 croquettes

Recipe Variation

Change the protein content by swapping the chicken with salmon, shrimp, or any white-meat fish you prefer.

[NUTRITIONAL ANALYSIS]

Per serving: 151.4 calories; 12.1 g fat; 9.5 g protein; 2.6 g carbs; 1 g fiber; 132.8 mg sodium.

TURKEY, LAMB, OR BEEF KOFTAS WITH A HEART-HEALTHY KICK

Spiced with tasty herbs and spices, these delicious treats will satisfy your palate and keep you well nourished at the same time. Kofta is a type of spicy meatball or kebab made popular in the Middle East, South Asia, and the Balkans. The ground meat in this dish provides texture and all nine essential amino acids. The spices add extra flavor along with exemplary heart-healthy benefits.

1 pound (455 g) turkey, lamb, or beef, minced

½ cup (80 g) finely chopped onion

1 clove garlic, minced

1 teaspoon each dried coriander, cumin, and turmeric

½ teaspoon ground cinnamon

½ teaspoon finely chopped dried chile pepper

1 teaspoon tomato paste

1 tablespoon (6 g) chopped fresh mint

1 tablespoon (1 g) chopped fresh cilantro

3 tablespoons (45 ml) coconut oil

In a large bowl, combine the turkey, lamb, or beef with all the other ingredients except the coconut oil and mix well, using your hands. Form into 12 to 15 small balls, using about a heaped teaspoon per ball. Heat the coconut oil in a large, nonstick frying pan over medium to high heat and cook the koftas until browned all over, about 3 minutes. Layer a bowl with crumpled-up paper towels and place the koftas into the bowl to remove any excess oil. Serve hot or cold with Antioxidant BBQ Sauce (page 154), Spice-It-Up Sweet Chili Sauce (page 152), or another sauce of your choosing.

Yield: 12 to 15 koftas

Recipe Variation

Turn these koftas into a vegetarian dish by removing the meat and using brown rice, bulgur, or beans instead.

[NUTRITIONAL ANALYSIS]

Per serving: 109.5 calories; 9.2 g fat; 5.5 g protein; 0.8 g carbs; .2 g fiber; 29.8 mg sodium.

SPICED HONEY-GLAZED NUTS

Enjoy a handful or two of these sweet, delicious, and flavorful nuts packed with notable health-benefiting nutrients. Heart-friendly fiber, essential fatty acids, protein, and antioxidant vitamins and minerals are loaded in every bite from the nuts, which are made even better by the addition of honey and herbs to spice things up.

- **1 cup each raw almonds (145 g), walnuts (120 g), pecans (100 g), and cashews (145 g) or macadamia nuts (135 g)**
- **¼ cup (85 g) organic honey**
- **1 teaspoon ground cinnamon**
- **1 pinch ground cloves**
- **¼ teaspoon each ground turmeric, coriander, and cumin**
- **1 teaspoon coconut oil**

Preheat the oven to 350°F (180°C, gas mark 4). Spread the nuts onto a large baking sheet and bake for 5 to 10 minutes, or until they are crisp and lightly browned, ensuring they do not get overbrowned. Remove from the oven and allow to cool.

Combine the honey and all the spices in a bowl and mix well. Heat a large, nonstick frying pan over medium heat and add the nuts. Sprinkle the spice and honey mixture over the nuts and stir for about 5 minutes, or until the nuts start to turn golden. The honey will heat and become thinner and coat the nuts. Using a wooden spoon, gently separate the nuts if they start to stick together. When the nuts are cooked, remove them from the heat, spread them onto the baking sheet coated with coconut oil, and allow them to cool. Store the nuts in an airtight container.

Yield: 16 servings

Note: Raw honey contains a full spectrum of essential vitamins and minerals and is an excellent source of antioxidants. Whenever possible, purchase locally grown, organic raw honey, as it will be of higher nutrient content. Pasteurizing honey through heating removes some of its best qualities. In recipes that require heating the honey, don't use raw honey but go for plain honey and choose organic whenever you can.

[NUTRITIONAL ANALYSIS]

Per serving: 414 calories; 37.6 g fat; 9.6 g protein; 16.6 g carbs; 5.1 g fiber; 1.8 mg sodium.

CALMING COCONUT-DATE BALLS

These sweet, delicious treats are rich in heart-healthy nutrients such as fiber, potassium, and magnesium, along with numerous antioxidants. The coconut adds a nice, chewy texture plus provides essential fatty acids. A couple of these are enough to satisfy any sweet tooth and keep your appetite satiated for hours.

- **1 cup (160 g) pitted, halved dates**
- **1 cup (130 g) dried apricots**
- **1 cup (145 g) raisins**
- **1 cup walnuts (120 g)**
- **1 tablespoon (15 ml) maple syrup**
- **3 tablespoons (45 ml) fresh orange juice**
- **¼ teaspoon salt, Celtic or sea**
- **1 cup (80 g) shredded coconut, unsweetened, divided**

Place the dates, apricots, raisins, walnuts, maple syrup, orange juice, and salt in a food processor and grind to a paste. Add half the coconut and process again until smooth. Check the consistency: Pinch the dough and make sure that it sticks together. If the dough is too dry, add a teaspoon or two of water until it sticks.

Place some cold water in a bowl and dip your fingers in the bowl. With moist hands, form small balls out of the date paste and roll in the remaining coconut. Refrigerate in an airtight container.

Yield: 30 to 35 balls

Note: Soaking your dates and dried fruits helps release essential vitamins and minerals and makes them easier to digest. The soak water is fortifying for the heart.

———————[NUTRITIONAL ANALYSIS]———————

Per serving: 76.9 calories; 3.9 g fat; 1.1 g protein; 11 g carbs; 1.4 g fiber; 11.3 mg sodium.

DETOXIFYING LIMA BEAN BLINIS WITH ARTICHOKE HERBED DIP

Well known for their meaty texture and mild buttery flavor, lima beans are a good source of protein, providing all nine essential amino acids. These deliciously buttery beans are also an excellent source of both soluble and insoluble dietary fiber that are well known for their digestive benefits. The combination of antioxidant-laden artichokes and herbs adds greatly to the many medicinal benefits of this delicious and satisfying dish.

FOR THE BLINIS:

- **1 cup (156 g) dried lima beans**
- **6 eggs**
- **1 tablespoon (15 ml) Bone-Building French Cream (page 157)**
- **2 cloves garlic, minced**
- **1 tablespoon (1.7 g) chopped fresh rosemary**
- **1 teaspoon salt, Celtic or sea**
- **½ teaspoon black pepper**
- **Dash of cayenne pepper**

FOR THE DIP:

- **1 can (13¾ [390 g] ounces) artichoke hearts in water, drained, rinsed, and coarsely chopped**
- **8 ounces (225 g) cream cheese, diced into small cubes**
- **⅓ cup (75 g) Heart-Healthy Almond Mayonnaise (page 151)**
- **½ cup (50 g) grated fresh Parmesan cheese**
- **¼ cup (15 g) chopped fresh parsley**
- **2 tablespoons (5 g) chopped fresh basil**
- **1 teaspoon grated lemon zest**
- **½ teaspoon black pepper**
- **Dash of cayenne pepper**

———————[NUTRITIONAL ANALYSIS]———————

Per serving: 53.8 calories; 2.9 g fat; 3.1 g protein; 4.5 g carbs; 1.2 g fiber; 109.2 mg sodium.

To make the blinis: Soak the beans overnight. The next day, drain and rinse them under cold water. Place the beans in a medium-size pan, add water to cover the beans, cover the pot, bring to a boil, and reduce to a simmer for 1 hour, until the beans are quite soft. Drain the beans and set aside.

Preheat the oven to 350°F (180°C, gas mark 4).

In another bowl combine the eggs and cream and whip until fluffy. Pour into a food processor along with the beans, garlic, rosemary, salt, pepper, and cayenne. Blend until smooth.

Lightly grease a 12-hole muffin tin with coconut or olive oil. Pour about 1 inch (2.5 cm) of the mixture into each muffin hole and bake for about 10 minutes. The blinis only need to set firmly; they do not need to brown. Repeat this process until all of the blinis are made. Let cool and then refrigerate in an airtight container. These will keep for a few days and are great with any other toppings.

Yield: 30 blinis

To make the dip: Preheat the oven to 425°F (220°C, gas mark 7).

In a medium bowl, mix all the dip ingredients together. Transfer to a lightly oiled ovenproof casserole dish or 9-inch (23-cm) pie pan and bake for about 20 minutes, until hot and bubbly. Serve on top of the blinis and with cut-up raw vegetables such as celery and carrots.

Yield: Approximately 3 cups

Note: Thanks to their high antioxidant content, artichokes have been ranked number seven in a study conducted by the U.S. Department of Agriculture that examined antioxidant levels of one thousand different foods. Among their many powerful antioxidants, artichokes also contain two important components, luteolin and cynarin, which are believed to provide heart-healthy benefits.

· ON THE · DINNER MENU

- **MEATLESS MAIN DISHES**.. 117

- **BEEF, SEAFOOD, & POULTRY MAINS** 127

- **VEGETABLES, GRAINS, & BEANS ON THE SIDE** 141

More than a family ritual, your last meal of the day is just as important as your first, because it provides an opportunity to consume nutrients that may have been lacking during the day. A balanced, nutrient-packed dinner also provides your body with essential vitamins and minerals to help it repair, rebuild, and regenerate your cells, organs, and tissues during sleep.

In this section you'll find tantalizing, balanced options that pack in the antioxidants and vitamins while providing a diversity of both nutrition and flavor. From meatless main dishes to poultry, seafood, and beef, all are stocked with nature's most powerful ingredients. There's also a hearty selection of irresistible vegetables, grains, and beans, which by no means should only be reserved for the side of the plate. Experiment a little and have fun with your meals. Perhaps rather than making meat the mainstay of your meal, try filling half your plate with vegetables or building your dishes around the ingredients that offer the greatest nutritional benefits and bang for the bite.

SPICY MOROCCAN TEMPEH WITH LENTILS

Tempeh is more than just a delicious meat substitute for vegetarians. It is made from fermented soybeans, which are a rich source of probiotics, friendly micro-organisms that help maintain a healthy digestive system and boost immunity. Tempeh has the added advantage of soaking up the flavors of whatever other items it is cooked with and has a rich, chewy texture that many meat eaters often can't tell apart from meat. Together, the tempeh and lentils in this recipe provide plenty of healthy, plant-based protein, fiber, and an array of heart-healthy vitamins and minerals.

1 package (8 ounces [225 g]) tempeh, cut into 1-inch (2.5-cm) cubes

1 tablespoon (15 ml) each wheat-free tamari and brown rice vinegar

2 tablespoons (28 ml) coconut oil, divided

1 small onion, diced

2 cloves garlic, minced

2 medium celery stalks, diced

2 small carrots, diced

2 tablespoons (32 g) tomato paste

¼ cup (60 ml) red or white wine

1 teaspoon each ground cumin and turmeric

1 cup (192 g) brown lentils

5½ cups (1.3 L) Digestive Vegetable Stock (page 104)

1 teaspoon salt, Celtic or sea

1 teaspoon capers

1 tablespoon (15 ml) extra-virgin olive oil

Preheat the oven to 375°F (190°C, gas mark 5). Toss the tempeh with the tamari and vinegar and let sit for at least 20 minutes. Toss with 1 tablespoon (15 ml) of coconut oil and transfer to a baking sheet. Bake for 15 minutes and set aside.

Heat the remaining tablespoon of coconut oil in a large pan over medium heat. Add the onion, garlic, celery, and carrots and sauté until they are tender and start to brown, about 8 to 10 minutes. Add the tomato paste and sauté a few more minutes, until it starts to brown. Add the wine and stir to release any browned bits from the bottom of the pan. Add the cumin, turmeric, lentils, and stock. Cover and simmer gently until the lentils are soft, about 40 minutes. Add the salt and capers and simmer for 5 to 10 more minutes. Toss in the baked tempeh and cook until warmed. Serve hot, drizzled with the olive oil.

Yield: 4 servings

Note: The fermentation process that soy undergoes to become tempeh makes it more easily digestible and metabolized by the body than traditional soy products, and it is much healthier. One 4-ounce (115-g) serving of tempeh provides more than a third of the average daily protein requirement.

───────[**NUTRITIONAL ANALYSIS**]───────

Per serving: 394.8 calories; 15.3 g fat; 19.7 g protein; 45.4 g carbs; 17.3 g fiber; 836 mg sodium.

HI-FIBE RED BEAN BURGERS

Chock-full of tasty herbs and spices and loaded with heart-healthy nutrients, these delicious meatless burgers can hold their own against any frozen burger you'd buy in a supermarket. They are so easy to make and you'll be pleased to have created such a vegetarian delight.

1 cup (250 g) dried red kidney beans

2½ cups (570 ml) Digestive Vegetable Stock (page 104) or filtered water

½ cup (70 g) sunflower seeds and ½ cup (70 g) pumpkin seeds

½ cup (55 g) peeled, grated carrots

½ cup (80 g) finely chopped onion

½ cup (75 g) finely chopped green bell pepper

1 teaspoon ground cumin

1 tablespoon (4 g) finely chopped fresh parsley

1 tablespoon (1 g) finely chopped cilantro

1 teaspoon salt, Celtic or sea

½ teaspoon black pepper

4 eggs

1 tablespoon (15 ml) fresh lemon or lime juice

2 tablespoons (28 ml) coconut oil

Soak the beans overnight. Drain and wash under cold water until the water runs clear. Place the beans into a pot and cover with stock or water, bring to a boil, reduce the heat to a simmer, and cook for up to 2 hours, or until soft but not mushy. They should still have a slight firmness to them. Grind the sunflower and pumpkin seeds in a food processor or use a coffee grinder until the consistency resembles a cereal meal, about a minute or less.

Place the kidney beans into a food processor and process until coarsely chopped. Combine with the sunflower and pumpkin seed meal, carrots, onion, bell pepper, cumin, parsley, cilantro, salt, pepper, eggs, and lemon or lime juice and knead with your hands until mixed through. Divide into 4 pieces and form into patties.

Add the coconut oil to a large, nonstick skillet over medium heat. Cook each patty for approximately 10 minutes on each side, or until they are slightly browned on the outside. Serve hot or cold with Antioxidant BBQ Sauce (page 154), Spice-It-Up Sweet Chili Sauce (page 152), or another sauce of your choosing.

Yield: 4 burgers

Note: Put a little olive oil on your hands when shaping the patties to prevent sticking.

[NUTRITIONAL ANALYSIS]

Per serving: 555.4 calories; 29.8 g fat; 26 g protein; 51.1 g carbs; 17.3 g fiber; 479.9 mg sodium.

PROTEIN-PACKED VEGETARIAN SHEPHERD'S PIE

Shepherd's pie is pure comfort food, and this vegetarian version will satisfy the taste buds of meat eaters and vegetarians alike. The goat cheese adds a slightly sweet and sometimes salty undertone, plus it's loaded with calcium, vitamin D, protein, and the amino acid tryptophan, which is a feel-good chemical that relaxes you. Numerous other heart-healthy nutrients, such as potassium, B_2, and fiber, are loaded into the mix to help give you energy and contribute to good health.

1 cup (208 g) each dried black and navy beans

½ cup each (96 g) green split peas and green lentils

4 cups (946 ml) Digestive Vegetable Stock (page 104), divided

2 ½ cups (250 g) roughly chopped cauliflower

½ teaspoon each salt, Celtic or sea, and black pepper

¼ teaspoon ground nutmeg

⅓ cup (43 g) peeled, chopped carrots

⅓ cup (33 g) chopped celery

1 cup (160 g) chopped onion

1 cup (150 g) chopped green bell pepper

¼ cup (56 g) butter or ghee

¾ cup (135 g) peeled, sliced tomatoes

¼ teaspoon cayenne pepper

¼ teaspoon freshly cracked black pepper

½ cup (75 g) goat cheese

½ cup (50 g) grated Parmesan cheese

Soak the black and navy beans overnight. Drain and rinse under cold water. Place the black beans into a large pot with the split peas and lentils and add 2½ cups (570 ml) vegetable stock and a little salt. Cover and simmer gently for up to 2 hours, or until the pulses have absorbed the stock and are soft. Remove them from the heat and mash just a little with a fork. At the same time, place the navy beans into another pot and cover with the remaining stock, cover, and cook for up to 2 hours. Remove and drain.

Preheat the oven to 375°F (190°C, gas mark 5). Steam the cauliflower until soft, about 5 minutes. Toss the cauliflower and navy beans into a food processor and blend until smooth, adding the salt, black pepper, and nutmeg. Set aside. Next, take the carrots, celery, onion, and bell pepper and process in the food processor until finely chopped.

Melt the butter or ghee in a large skillet over medium heat and add the vegetables. Cook for about 10 to 15 minutes, or until they are soft and tender. Set aside. Add the cooked vegetables to the pulse mixture and combine well. Pour the mixture into a 10-inch (25-cm) square baking dish and arrange the tomatoes in overlapping slices on the top.

Combine the mashed cauliflower and navy bean mixture with the goat cheese and season with cayenne pepper, and freshly cracked pepper. Spread the mixture over the tomatoes in the baking dish. Top with grated Parmesan cheese and bake on the top shelf in the oven for about 30 minutes, or until the top is lightly browned. Remove from the oven and let sit for 10 minutes. Serve. Store covered in the refrigerator.

Yield: 4 servings

———————[**NUTRITIONAL ANALYSIS**]———————
Per serving: 668.9 calories; 21.3 g fat; 40.7 g protein; 97 g carbs; 37.3 g fiber; 619.7 mg sodium.

NUTRIENT-RICH ROASTED QUINOA WITH MUSHROOMS, CUMIN, AND CORIANDER

Light, fluffy, and easy to prepare, quinoa is chock-full of nutrients such as protein and fiber and an array of essential vitamins and minerals. It's great for ensuring a healthy digestive system because the complex carbohydrates digest slowly to keep you feeling full longer. The spices add extra goodness and flavor.

1 cup (170 g) quinoa, rinsed and drained

1 cup (70 g) diced porcini mushrooms

1½ cups (355 ml) Digestive Vegetable Stock (page 104)

½ teaspoon salt, Celtic or sea

1 tablespoon (7 g) ground cumin

1 tablespoon (6 g) ground coriander

Dash of cayenne pepper

½ cup (8 g) chopped fresh cilantro

1 tablespoon (15 ml) fresh lemon or lime juice

Preheat the oven to 350°F (180°C, gas mark 4). Place the quinoa on a baking sheet and bake for about 10 minutes, or until you get a crispy texture. Transfer to a medium-size pot and add the mushrooms, stock, and salt. Set aside.

Place the cumin and coriander in a dry skillet over medium heat. Toast them, stirring often, about 1 to 2 minutes. Add them to the quinoa mixture. Bring to a boil, reduce the heat, cover with a lid, and simmer for about 10 minutes to allow flavors to meld together. Transfer into a serving dish, fluff with a fork, and stir in the fresh cilantro and lemon or lime juice.

Yield: 2 servings

Recipe Variation

To add more plant protein to dishes that call for rice, use quinoa instead. It cooks quickly and is generally done when the water has been absorbed and the germ has separated from the seed.

[NUTRITIONAL ANALYSIS]

Per serving: 378 calories; 5.4 g fat; 14.3 g protein; 70.8 g carbs; 9.7 g fiber; 416.3 mg sodium.

HIGH-FIBER BUTTERNUT GNOCCHI WITH HERBED CREAM SAUCE

Sublimely delicious and with all-around goodness, this flavorsome dish transforms butternut squash into something special. With its tangerine hue indicating an abundance of the antioxidants known as carotenoids, butternut squash also delivers an ample dose of dietary fiber, making it an exceptionally heart-friendly choice. The delicious mix of herbs in the cream sauce provides a ton of antioxidants to boost your health and increase the flavor.

FOR THE GNOCCHI:

2 pounds (910 g) fresh butternut squash, unpeeled, seeded, and cut into large chunks

3 eggs

½ teaspoon salt, Celtic or sea

¼ teaspoon ground nutmeg

½ cup (50 g) grated Parmesan cheese

1 cup (115 g) almond flour

FOR THE SAUCE:

⅓ cup (75 g) butter

1 clove garlic, minced

1 tablespoon each fresh basil (2.5 g), parsley (4 g), and tarragon (4 g), all finely chopped

4 sage leaves, finely chopped

1 cup (235 ml) Bone-Building French Cream (page xx)

⅓ cup (33 g) grated Parmesan cheese, divided

½ teaspoon salt, Celtic or sea

¼ teaspoon black pepper

Preheat the oven to 320°F (160°C).

To make the gnocchi: Place the butternut squash in an ovenproof dish and bake for 30 to 40 minutes, or until soft.

Start making the cream sauce while the squash is baking (see directions that follow). When the squash is cooked, remove it from the oven and let it cool a little. Place it into a food processor and process until smooth. Add the eggs, salt, nutmeg, cheese, and almond flour and process to combine. Pour the mixture into a 9- by 13-inch (23- by 33-cm) baking dish lined with parchment paper and bake for 1 hour, or until the gnocchi feels firm. Remove from the oven and let sit for 5 minutes. Cut the gnocchi into squares or triangle shapes and serve hot with the Herbed Cream Sauce.

Yield: Approximately 4 servings (1 cup each)

To make the sauce: Melt the butter in a small skillet on medium heat. Add the garlic, basil, parsley, tarragon, and sage and stir for approximately 1 minute. Add the cream and half the Parmesan. Stir and cook until the Parmesan has melted. Add the salt and pepper. Do not boil the mixture, just sauté on low heat until all ingredients have combined to a creamy consistency, about 2 to 3 minutes. Serve hot over top of the sliced gnocchi and garnish with the remaining Parmesan.

Yield: Approximately 4 servings

[NUTRITIONAL ANALYSIS]

Per serving: 337.8 calories; 20.1 g fat; 17.1 g protein; 29.5 g carbs; 9.3 g fiber; 399.7 mg sodium.

REVITALIZING VEGETABLE BIRYANI

Warming spices combined with basmati rice lend a distinctive Indian aroma and flavor to this high-fiber, heart-healthy dish. The colorful addition of saffron provides a richness of flavor as well as many vital antioxidants and vitamins, including folic acid, niacin, riboflavin, and vitamins A and C. Basmati rice is a good source of soluble fiber as well as the heart-healthy and fat-soluble vitamin E, which is an antioxidant known for preventing blood platelets from clumping and reducing the risk of heart disease. The cashews add healthy fats and give the dish a nice, crunchy texture.

1½ cups (270 g) white basmati rice

2½ cups (570 ml) Digestive Vegetable Stock (page 104) or filtered water

1 teaspoon salt, Celtic or sea

Pinch of saffron threads

2 tablespoons (28 g) ghee or coconut oil

½ cup (80 g) diced onion

1 tablespoon (6 g) minced fresh ginger, peeled

1 teaspoon ground turmeric

1 to 2 cloves garlic, minced

1 small carrot, diced

¾ cup (98 g) frozen peas

½ cup (75 g) raisins

½ cup (72 g) whole raw cashews

1 tablespoon (1 g) chopped fresh cilantro

Rinse and drain the rice. Combine the rice, stock or water, salt, and saffron in a large pot with a fitted lid and bring to a boil over medium-high heat. Reduce the heat to low, cover, and cook until the rice is tender, about 12 to 15 minutes. Turn off the heat and let stand, covered for a few minutes, before fluffing with a fork.

Heat the ghee or oil in a pan over medium-high heat. Add the onion, ginger, turmeric, garlic, and carrot and sauté until softened, about 5 to 8 minutes. Remove from the heat, add the peas and raisins, and set aside.

Uncover the rice and gently fluff with a fork. Add the carrot mixture and cashews and gently combine. Garnish with fresh cilantro and serve hot.

Yield: 4 servings

Note: Basmati rice comes in brown and white colors, and it is generally best to soak it for up to 2 hours prior to cooking with it. Soaking it first separates the grains and allows for a more fluffy, less sticky rice.

[NUTRITIONAL ANALYSIS]

Per serving: 357 calories; 13 g fat; 7.7 g protein; 54 g carbs; 6.4 g fiber; 556 mg sodium.

COMFORTING CHEDDAR AND BROCCOLI QUICHE WITH QUINOA CRUST

You can take comfort in knowing that this dish is superhigh in overall nutrient richness to promote optimum health. Quinoa is especially high in plant protein, folate, magnesium, and tryptophan. Sweet-tasting Swiss chard contains more than 800 percent of your daily intake of vitamin K, which is needed throughout the body for myriad functions from bone health to regulating normal blood clotting. Broccoli contains high amounts of vitamins A, C, folic acid, fiber, and calcium, all of which ensure an efficiently running metabolism. The cheeses add a creamy finish to this tasty dish that will leave you feeling good all over.

- **1 cup (170 g) quinoa**
- **2 tablespoons (28 ml) extra-virgin olive or coconut oil**
- **1 medium red onion, diced**
- **1 tablespoon (10 g) chopped garlic**
- **2 cups (110 g) Swiss chard, roughly chopped**
- **4 cups (284 g) medium-size broccoli florets**
- **1 cup (120 g) grated Cheddar cheese**
- **12 eggs**
- **2 cups (475 ml) whole milk**
- **2 tablespoons (5 g) fresh thyme leaves**
- **½ teaspoon salt, Celtic or sea**
- **Dash of black pepper**
- **¼ cup (25 g) grated Parmesan cheese**

Preheat the oven to 350°F (180°C, gas mark 4). Rinse the quinoa well and set aside to drain. Heat the oil in a pan over medium heat. Add the onion and garlic and sauté until the onion begins to brown, about 8 minutes. Add the Swiss chard and broccoli and sauté for 1 minute, then turn off the heat. Cool slightly. Transfer the mixture to a lightly greased 9- by 13-inch (23- by 33-cm) casserole dish and spread evenly. Sprinkle the Cheddar cheese evenly over the top of the vegetable mixture. Set aside.

In a large bowl, combine the eggs, milk, thyme, salt, pepper, and rinsed quinoa and whisk until thoroughly combined. Pour immediately over the cheese-topped vegetable mixture. Bake the casserole in the oven until cooked through and the top is just starting to brown, about 40 minutes. Remove the casserole from the oven and sprinkle the Parmesan over the top. Return to the oven and bake until the Parmesan is melted and just starting to brown, about 5 more minutes. Let the casserole sit for at least 10 minutes before serving. Serve with a mixed lettuce or spinach salad.

Yield: 6 to 8 servings

Recipe Variation

You can use kale instead of Swiss chard if you wish. Swiss chard eaten raw makes a nice base for smoothies, too, as it tends to be sweeter than kale.

[NUTRITIONAL ANALYSIS]

Per serving: 360 calories; 19.6 g fat; 20.8 g protein; 22.5 g carbs; 3.9 g fiber; 480.3 mg sodium.

STRENGTHENING SPINACH, FETA, AND RICE CASSEROLE

The feta and rice in this dish provide ample protein and a delicious, creamy texture that explodes with flavor in every mouthful. Spinach is a nutrition superstar that's loaded with fiber, vitamins, and minerals, some of which are hard to find in other foods. You can be certain of getting all your important and heart-healthy nutrients and then some in this dish.

1 cup (180 g) white basmati rice

¾ cup (175 ml) Digestive Vegetable Stock (page 104)

½ cup (75 g) raisins

2 tablespoons (28 g) ghee or coconut oil

1 small red onion, peeled and medium diced

1 tablespoon (10 g) minced garlic

1 teaspoon chopped fresh dill

½ teaspoon salt, Celtic or sea

¼ teaspoon black pepper

1 tablespoon (15 ml) white wine

1 teaspoon fresh lemon or lime juice

4 chops (120 g) chopped spinach

1½ cups (225 g) crumbled feta cheese

2 medium tomatoes, sliced

Preheat the oven to 350°F (180°C, gas mark 4). Lightly grease a 9- by 13-inch (23- by 33-cm) casserole dish and set aside. Rinse and drain the rice. Place the rice in a large pot with a fitted lid, add the stock, and bring to a boil. Reduce the heat to low, cover, and cook until the rice is tender, about 15 minutes. Fluff with a fork and gently mix in the raisins. Cover and set aside.

Heat the ghee or oil in a pan over medium heat. Add the onion and garlic and sauté until the onion is tender, about 5 minutes. Add the dill, salt, pepper, and wine and sauté a few more minutes. Add the lemon or lime juice and spinach and stir until well combined. Remove from the heat and allow to cool. Toss in the feta cheese.

Cover the bottom of the greased casserole dish with the rice mixture. Layer the spinach mixture over the rice. Cover with the tomato slices. Cover with foil and bake until heated through, about 30 to 40 minutes. Serve hot, garnished with extra feta cheese and a drizzle of extra-virgin olive oil, if desired.

Yield: 6 to 8 servings

Note: Spinach contains oxalic acid, which can block the absorption of calcium and iron. Lightly steaming spinach first reduces oxalic acid and makes the minerals more bioavailable to your body.

[NUTRITIONAL ANALYSIS]

Per serving: 234.2 calories; 8.5 g fat; 7.5 g protein; 33 g carbs; 3.5 g fiber; 451.3 mg sodium.

IMMUNE-BOOSTING THAI TEMPEH CAKES WITH SWEET SPICY DIPPING SAUCE

These delicious tempeh cakes are one of my favorite go-to dishes for taste, flavor, and nourishment. They taste just like the ones you would get in a Thai restaurant, only they are healthier. I also like to serve these delicious treats as an appetizer or snack.

1 tablespoon (4 g) lemongrass, fresh or dried

2 cloves garlic, chopped

⅓ cup (50 g) raisins, chopped

4 spring onions, chopped, divided in half

3 chiles, seeded, finely chopped, divided

1 teaspoon finely chopped fresh ginger, peeled

1 tablespoon (6 g) ground coriander

6 tablespoons (6 g) chopped fresh cilantro, divided

2¼ cups (374 g) tempeh, cut into strips

1 tablespoon (15 ml) fresh lime juice

3 tablespoons (21 g) almond flour

1 large egg, lightly beaten

½ teaspoon salt, Celtic or sea

Freshly ground black pepper, to taste

3 tablespoons (45 ml) each coconut oil, mirin, and white wine vinegar

To make the cakes: Place the lemongrass, garlic, raisins, 2 spring onions, 2 chiles, ginger, coriander, and 2 tablespoons (2 g) cilantro into a food processor. Blend into a coarse paste. Add the tempeh and lime juice and blend until combined. Add the almond flour, egg, salt, and pepper and blend again until the mixture forms a coarse, sticky paste.

Divide the mixture into 8 equal parts. Lightly cover your hands in flour to avoid sticking and form the paste into balls. Press the balls to form small cakes. Heat the coconut oil in a large frying pan over medium heat and cook the tempeh cakes for 5 to 6 minutes, turning once, until golden in color. Drain the cakes on paper towels and serve warm with dipping sauce, garnished with chopped cilantro.

To make the sauce: In a small bowl, mix together the mirin, white wine vinegar, and the remaining spring onions, chile, and the cilantro.

Yield: 8 cakes

Recipe Variation

Mirin is a sweet cooking wine made from rice. It is generally available at most supermarkets. You can use sake or sweet sherry instead of the mirin if you like. This recipe was adapted from one of my other books, Foods That Fight Fibromyalgia.

[NUTRITIONAL ANALYSIS]

Per serving: 201.5 calories; 12.2 g fat; 10.3 g protein; 13 g carbs; 1.3 g fiber; 177.7 mg sodium.

STRESS-LESS SHIITAKE AND ASPARAGUS RISOTTO

Your immune system will get a big boost from this nourishing, succulent, and tender dish, and so will your heart. Apart from their smoky flavor, shiitake mushrooms are known for their ability to lower blood pressure levels as well as their high levels of selenium, vitamin C, protein, and fiber. The addition of asparagus, a known anti-inflammatory vegetable, makes it a powerful duo.

1 teaspoon saffron threads

4 cups (946 ml) Digestive Vegetable Stock (page 104)

1 tablespoon (15 ml) extra-virgin olive oil or coconut oil

1 small onion, chopped

2 cloves garlic, chopped

1 teaspoon dried basil

1 teaspoon chopped fresh basil

2 sprigs fresh thyme

1 teaspoon salt, Celtic or sea

1½ cups (285 g) brown rice

½ cup (120 ml) dry white or red wine

6 asparagus spears, cut into 1-inch (2.5-cm) lengths

1 cup (70 g) sliced shiitake mushrooms

¼ cup (35 g) fresh or frozen peas

1 teaspoon grated lemon zest

1 tablespoon (2.5 g) chopped fresh basil

½ cup (30 g) chopped fresh parsley

Dash of black pepper

Place the saffron and stock in a medium pot and warm over low heat.

In a large pan, heat the oil over medium to high heat and add the onion and garlic until transparent, about 3 to 4 minutes. Add the dry and fresh basil, thyme sprigs, and salt and sauté for about 1 minute. Add the rice and stir and cook for several minutes. Add the wine and stir for 2 minutes. Add the asparagus, mushrooms, and peas and stir them into mixture. Add the saffron and vegetable stock, 1 cup (235 ml) at a time, and stir continuously. Remove the thyme sprigs and cook uncovered, stirring often, until most of the water is absorbed and the rice is thickened and slightly creamy, about 2 to 3 minutes. Add more stock if the rice is dry and needs it. Stir in the lemon zest, fresh basil, parsley, and black pepper. Serve immediately.

Yield: 4 servings

Note: When shopping for mushrooms, look for ones that are firm, ripe, plump, and clean. Avoid ones with wet, slimy spots. Prior to cooking, cleanse them in water and pat them dry with a paper towel so they do not become soggy. Always store fresh mushrooms in the refrigerator to ensure freshness and use them within a couple days of purchase.

[NUTRITIONAL ANALYSIS]

Per serving: 278.1 calories; 4.9 g fat; 7.1 g protein; 50.6 g carbs; 8.2 g fiber; 434.1 mg sodium.

EASY BEEF SAUTÉ WITH FRESH HERBS

Eating beef occasionally, especially when it's grass fed, gives you from two to six times more omega-3s than factory-farmed beef and is only surpassed by the vegetables you add to the dish. This one has got your heart health covered. Enjoy!

- 2 tablespoons (28 ml) extra-virgin olive oil
- 2 cloves garlic, minced
- 1 medium onion, minced
- 1 small chile pepper, minced
- 4 to 6 ounces (115 to 170 g) lean grass-fed beef, chopped into 1- to 2-inch (2.5- to 5-cm) cubes
- 1 cup (120 g) sliced zucchini
- 3 large carrots, sliced
- 8 cremini or shiitake mushrooms, sliced
- 1 large green bell pepper, chopped
- 2 tablespoons (28 ml) tamari
- ½ teaspoon each salt, Celtic or sea, and black pepper
- 2 tablespoons (8 g) chopped fresh parsley

In a skillet over medium-high heat, add the oil and sauté the garlic, onion, and chile pepper until softened, about 5 minutes. Add the beef and cook until tender, about 3 to 5 minutes. Add the remaining ingredients except the parsley. Cook, stirring often, until the vegetables are crisp and tender, about 2 to 3 minutes. Add the fresh parsley at the end. Serve immediately.

Yield: 2 servings

Note: Grass-fed beef contains conjugated linoleic acid (CLA) and the antioxidant vitamin E, both of which support a healthy cardiovascular system. Factory-farmed beef contains significantly lower amounts of these nutrients.

[NUTRITIONAL ANALYSIS]

Per serving: 374.8 calories; 60.4 g fat; 25.5 g protein; 29.5 g carbs; 6.8 g fiber; 1098.2 mg sodium.

FAVORITE SWEET, SPICY, AND CRUNCHY MEATLOAF

This dish is one of my favorite heartwarming meals. The vegetables ensure you are getting plenty of essential vitamins and minerals, the raisins add a particularly sweet flavor, and the nuts give this meal a crunchy texture.

2 tablespoons (28 g) butter or ghee

1 medium onion, chopped

3 cloves garlic, chopped

1 small zucchini, chopped

1 medium carrot, chopped finely

2 stalks celery, chopped finely

¼ cup (18 g) chopped shiitake mushrooms

1 small chile pepper, chopped finely (optional)

1 teaspoon ground turmeric

1 teaspoon ground cumin

1 teaspoon salt, Celtic or sea, divided

½ teaspoon black pepper, divided

1 pound (455 g) lean ground beef, grass fed and organically raised

1 to 2 eggs, beaten

1 tablespoon (15 ml) tamari

½ cup (60 g) roughly chopped walnuts

½ cup (75 g) raisins

4 tablespoons (64 g) unsweetened tomato paste

Preheat the oven to 350°F (180°C, gas mark 4). Melt the butter or ghee in a large frying pan, add the onion and garlic, and sauté on medium-high heat until the onion softens, about 4 minutes. Add the zucchini, carrot, celery, mushrooms, and chile and cook until they soften and brown, about 5 minutes. Add the turmeric, cumin, half the salt, and half the pepper, then turn the heat off and allow it to cool down to around room temperature (refrigerate to speed up the process if necessary).

In a large bowl, add the beef, eggs, tamari, walnuts, raisins, tomato paste, and remaining salt and pepper and mix together. Then add the cooked vegetables and herbs and blend together well. Transfer the mixture to a greased loaf pan or casserole dish and bake for 30 minutes. Serve hot or cold topped with Spice-It-Up Sweet Chili Sauce (page 152) or tomato sauce.

Yield: 4 servings

Recipe Variation

To increase the fiber in your meat loaf, add ½ cup (85 g) cooked brown rice, lentils, or quinoa. You may need to add an extra egg when you do this so it's moist enough.

[NUTRITIONAL ANALYSIS]

Per serving: 506.4 calories; 32.9 g fat; 27.5 g protein; 27.4 g carbs; 4.5 g fiber; 907.9 mg sodium.

NICE AND SPICED BEEF OR CHICKEN STIR-FRY

Enjoy the tender and tangy elements of the meat, ginger, and pineapple that cozy up to the hearty, sweet flavor of snow peas in this dish. This meal is nutritious and surprisingly simple, quick, and easy to prepare.

- **1 tablespoon (15 ml) extra-virgin olive or coconut oil**
- **1 pound (455 g) sirloin or tenderloin, cut into thin 2-inch (5-cm) strips, or 2 chicken breasts, thinly sliced**
- **½ red bell pepper, thinly sliced**
- **1 teaspoon chopped fresh ginger, peeled**
- **¼ teaspoon cayenne pepper**
- **1 cup (155 g) finely chopped pineapple**
- **½ teaspoon hot chile flakes**
- **3 tablespoons (45 ml) fresh lemon juice**
- **2 tablespoons (28 ml) tamari**
- **1 cup (75 g) snow peas, washed and halved**
- **1 green onion, thinly sliced**

In a large, nonstick frying pan, heat the oil over medium-high heat. Add the beef or chicken and cook for 3 to 4 minutes, until lightly cooked through. Add the bell pepper, ginger, cayenne, pineapple, chile flakes, lemon juice, tamari, and snow peas. Cook until tender-crisp, about 2 to 3 more minutes. Sprinkle with green onion and serve over rice or with vegetables.

Yield: 4 servings

Note: Snow peas provide us with good amounts of vitamins C and B complex, particularly the critical cardioprotective B vitamin, choline.

Which Foods to Brown?

For meat such as beef, browning is the initial step to a delicious dish; it's an optional step for poultry and pork, and totally unnecessary for fish and seafood. What browning accomplishes is actually enhancing the foods for better flavor.

[NUTRITIONAL ANALYSIS]

Per serving: 306.1 calories; 12.9 g fat; 36.5 g protein; 10.1 g carbs; 1.8 g fiber; 507.4 mg sodium.

FISHERMAN'S OMEGA-3 FISH FINGERS

High in omega-3 essential fatty acids, this dish has unexpected ginger and turmeric, making it distinctively healthy and delicious. Any kind of greens, particularly sautéed kale or spinach, or a spinach salad with red onions and vinaigrette, makes a great side.

1 pound (455 g) firm, white, deboned fish (mackerel, halibut, or trout)

1 egg

1 teaspoon minced fresh ginger, peeled

¼ teaspoon ground turmeric

½ teaspoon salt, Celtic or sea

½ teaspoon black pepper

1 cup (115 g) almond flour

2 to 3 tablespoons (28 to 45 ml) coconut oil

1 lemon, cut into wedges

Cut the fish into finger lengths. In a small bowl, combine the egg, ginger, turmeric, salt, and pepper. Place the almond flour onto a flat surface. Dip the fish into the egg mixture and then into the almond flour, turning it to cover on all sides.

Heat the oil in a nonstick frying pan over medium to high heat. Place the floured fish fingers into the frying pan and brown lightly until cooked through, about 3 to 4 minutes per side. Serve with a wedge of lemon.

Yield: 4 servings

Note: Apart from their high content of omega-3 essential fatty acids, cold-water varieties of fish, such as mackerel, tuna, salmon, halibut, sardines, and herring, provide other essential nutrients such as coenzyme Q_{10}, selenium, tryptophan, B vitamins, and potassium. All of these nutrients help to support a healthy heart.

Omega-3s Help More Than the Heart

Omega-3 fats lower both blood pressure and triglycerides. They protect the brain and the heart, support circulation, and boost mood. They've been studied for their effects on depression, cardiovascular health, skin, joints, and diabetes. Many studies of behavioral and mood problems have shown a correlation between these issues and low levels of omega-3s. Omega-3s are being studied at Harvard University for their role in combating depression. And a great deal of research has shown that omega-3s are great for the heart.

—————— **[NUTRITIONAL ANALYSIS]** ——————
Per serving: 431.5 calories; 29 g fat; 37.9 g protein; 7.4 g carbs; 3 g fiber; 326.2 mg sodium.

MEGA-OMEGA SPICE-CRUSTED SALMON

This meal is crunchy on the outside, melt-in-your-mouth delicious on the inside, and ready in just 10 minutes. Pair this dish with our Anti-Ox Pumpkin and Cauliflower Mash (page 144) and Sumptuous Spinach and Swiss Chard with Pine Nuts (page 147) and you'll create a restaurant-style meal that's heart-friendly, too!

- 1 tablespoon each coriander seeds (6 g), cumin seeds (6 g), and sesame seeds (8 g)
- ¼ teaspoon dried thyme
- 1 teaspoon salt, Celtic or sea
- ½ teaspoon black pepper
- 4 salmon fillets with skin on one side (about 3 to 4 ounces [85 to 115 g] each)
- 1 egg white, whisked
- 1 to 2 tablespoons (15 to 30 ml) coconut oil

Place a dry skillet over medium heat and toast the coriander seeds and cumin seeds, stirring constantly until they become fragrant, about 1 minute. Remove and place in a bowl. Repeat the process with the sesame seeds, remove from the heat, add to the coriander and cumin seeds, and crush with a pestle and mortar. Add the thyme, salt, and pepper and combine.

Dip the skin side of the salmon fillets into the egg white. Press into the spice mixture. Heat the coconut oil in the skillet over high heat and place the fillets into the pan with the seeded side on the oil. Fry for 2 minutes and then turn the heat to low. Flip the fillets and cook on low for up to 8 minutes, depending on how well done you would like them. Serve immediately.

Yield: 4 servings

Note: Farm-raised salmon is inferior in omega-3 essential fatty acid content when compared with wild-caught salmon. We prefer the Vital Choice brand of salmon because it is very high in omega-3s, and we discovered it to be free of harmful mercury and other toxins via independent lab testing. It truly is the best salmon in the world—wild, from Alaska. You can purchase it directly from their website at www.vitalchoice.com.

[NUTRITIONAL ANALYSIS]

Per serving: 197.2 calories; 10.7 g fat; 25 g protein; 2 g carbs; 1 g fiber; 482.1 mg sodium.

TANTALIZING THAI FISH CAKES

You'll love this delicious variation from regular grill-ing or baking, high in protein, rich in omega-3s, and bursting with the flavor of mixed Thai spices. The chiles add plenty of heat, so consider adding more or less depending on your palate. I like to pair this dish with Zesty Broccoli with Garlic and Ginger (page 145) or a mixed green salad with Simply Nourishing Salad Dressing (page 97).

¾ pound (340 g) firm, white, deboned fish (mackerel, halibut, or trout)

1 teaspoon chopped red chile peppers

1 tablespoon (20 g) organic honey

1 tablespoon (15 ml) fish sauce

1 tablespoon (1 g) chopped fresh cilantro

1 tablespoon chopped lemongrass

½ cup (50 g) green beans, finely sliced

½ cup (75 g) finely chopped red bell peppers

1 tablespoon (15 ml) coconut oil

Place the fish, chiles, honey, fish sauce, cilantro, and lemongrass in a food processor and process until smooth. Transfer the mixture to a bowl and add the beans and red bell pepper and mix thoroughly. Divide the mixture into 8 balls and shape into flat patties.

Heat the oil in a large frying pan over medium to high heat and add the patties. Fry evenly on each side for about 4 minutes, until golden and cooked through. Serve with Spice-It-Up Sweet Chili Sauce (page 152).

Yield: 8 cakes

Note: The American Heart Association recommends eating fatty fish, such as salmon, herring, sardines, albacore tuna, mackerel, and trout, at least 2 times per week to prevent heart disease, and 3 times per week if you are already at risk for or have heart disease.

How to Make Stock

Save the bones and head of the fish to make a healthy fish stock. It is quick and easy to make and a great standby to have in the freezer as to use as a base for soups and sauces. Wash any fish heads and bones well to remove any trace of blood, place them into a large saucepan, cover with water, add onion, peppercorns, lemon, and a few bay leaves, and simmer for twenty minutes. Remove from heat, strain out the solids, cool, and freeze until needed.

[NUTRITIONAL ANALYSIS]

Per serving: 89.3 calories; 3 g fat; 11.7 g protein; 3.6 g carbs; 0.4 g fiber; 163.4 mg sodium.

SOUL-WARMING TUNA LASAGNA

This tuna lasagna has become a family favorite ever since I started using tuna instead of beef in my lasagna dishes. You can make this dish several days before consuming it, which makes the flavors meld together for a richer flavor. It's a great dish for a dinner party, and there will be plenty left over for seconds, too! Serve it with a mixed green salad with our Simply Nourishing Salad Dressing (page 97).

1 tablespoon (15 ml) extra-virgin olive oil

1 cup (160 g) chopped onion

3 minced cloves garlic

½ cup (50 g) chopped celery

1 cup (130 g) chopped carrots

1 teaspoon fresh or ½ teaspoon dried thyme

1 tablespoon (2.5 g) chopped fresh basil

½ teaspoon salt, Celtic or sea

1 cup (248 g) tomato purée

1 cup (235 ml) Digestive Vegetable Stock (page 104)

1½ cups (270 g) chopped fresh tomatoes

2 cans tuna (7 ounces [195 g] each), in spring water

2 cups (240 g) chopped zucchini, sliced lengthwise

1 teaspoon ground nutmeg

1½ cups (150 g) grated Parmesan cheese, divided in half

Preheat the oven to 350°F (180°C, gas mark 4). Heat the olive oil in a large saucepan over medium to high heat. Add the onion and garlic and cook until tender, about 5 minutes. Add the celery, carrot, thyme, basil, and salt. In a small bowl, combine the tomato puree with the stock and gently add it to the pot, stirring constantly until evenly distributed. Add the tomatoes and tuna and mix in thoroughly.

Slice the zucchini lengthwise into thin slices. Pour a small amount of the sauce to cover the bottom of a 9- by 13-inch (23- by 33-cm) baking dish. Add a layer of zucchini slices, pour half of the sauce onto the zucchini layer, and top with half of the Parmesan. Add another layer of zucchini and top with sauce and the remaining cheese. Bake in the oven for about 40 minutes. Remove when cooked and serve immediately. This dish can be frozen and reheated in the oven at a later date.

Yield: 4 to 6 servings

Note: Because tuna fish is high on the food chain, it can contain higher mercury levels than smaller fish. That's why we prefer the canned albacore tuna that Vital Choice sells on its website, which uses only the younger, smaller albacore tuna (14 pounds [6.4 kg] or less) and contains optimal purity, flavor, and omega-3 levels.

[NUTRITIONAL ANALYSIS]

Per serving: 250.3 calories; 10.8 g fat; 23.6 g protein; 14.8 g carbs; 3.6 g fiber; 811.4 mg sodium.

HEALING BAKED HALIBUT OR SALMON AND SHIITAKE

This dish is simple and easy to prepare and loaded with immune-boosting, heart-healthy nutrients. In addition to adding a pungent, woodsy flavor and meaty texture, shiitake mushrooms provide an impressive array of vitamins and minerals that includes fiber, potassium, magnesium, selenium, zinc, and B complex. You'll love the textures and flavors in this satisfying dish.

1 tablespoon (14 g) butter

1 cup (70 g) chopped shiitake mushrooms

4 fillets salmon or halibut (4 ounces [115 g] each)

2 tablespoons (28 ml) fresh lemon or lime juice

1 tablespoon (14 g) butter, melted

1 tablespoon (7 g) almond flour

1 teaspoon ground paprika

1 teaspoon salt, Celtic or sea

½ teaspoon black pepper

1 tablespoon (4 g) chopped fresh parsley

Preheat the oven to 350°F (180°C, gas mark 4). In a small to medium pan, melt 1 tablespoon (14 g) butter over medium heat and toss in the shiitake mushrooms. Cook until just softened, about 2 to 3 minutes.

Place the fish fillets in a buttered baking dish. Pour the lemon or lime juice over them and brush with the melted butter. Pour the shiitake mushrooms over the top, sprinkle on the almond flour, and coat evenly. Sprinkle on the paprika, salt, and pepper and bake for 15 to 20 minutes, or until the fish is almost cooked.

Turn the heat to broil. Place under the broiler for about 1 minute until the flour browns. Sprinkle with fresh parsley and serve immediately.

Yield: 4 servings

Note: Dry-heat methods such as baking, broiling, and grilling work well for fattier fish such as halibut and salmon.

[NUTRITIONAL ANALYSIS]

Per serving: 291.2 calories; 18.6 g fat; 24 g protein; 5.5 g carbs; 1.1 g fiber; 402.2 mg sodium.

SPICY SHRIMP AND TOMATO KEBABS WITH HERBED LIMA BEANS

These shrimp kebabs are easy to make and bursting with flavor and goodness. Shrimp is an excellent source of protein and contains a variety of heart-healthy nutrients that include omega-3s, magnesium, selenium, tryptophan, choline, zinc, and B-complex vitamins. The herbed lima beans complement the flavorful kebabs nicely with added fiber and minerals.

1½ pounds (670 g) large, raw, uncooked shrimp, peeled, deveined, and cut in half

2 cups (300 g) cherry tomatoes

8 small cloves garlic, unpeeled

1 lemon, cut into 8 pieces

4 tablespoons (50 ml) extra-virgin olive oil, divided

1 teaspoon salt, Celtic or sea, divided

½ teaspoon black pepper, divided

1 can (15 ounces [425 g]) lima beans, rinsed

1 teaspoon chopped fresh sage

1 teaspoon chopped fresh basil

1 tablespoon (4 g) chopped fresh parsley

Soak 8 wooden skewers in water for about 15 minutes. In a medium bowl, combine the shrimp, tomatoes, garlic, lemon, 2 tablespoons (28 ml) of the oil, ¾ teaspoon of the salt, and ¼ teaspoon of the pepper.

Turn the broiler on. Thread the shrimp, tomatoes, garlic, and lemon pieces on the skewers and broil, turning occasionally, until the shrimp is cooked through and the lemon wedges are lightly charred, about 5 to 7 minutes.

Meanwhile, heat the remaining 2 tablespoons (28 ml) oil in a small saucepan over medium heat. Add the lima beans, sage, basil, and parsley, and the remaining salt and pepper. Cook, tossing occasionally, until the beans are warm and covered with the herbs, about 2 to 3 minutes. Serve with the kebabs.

Yield: 4 servings

Note: These kebabs can be assembled ahead of time and stored for up to 12 hours in the refrigerator. Simply reheat them in the oven for about 15 to 20 minutes at 275°F (140°C, gas mark 1) before serving.

[NUTRITIONAL ANALYSIS]

Per serving: 462.5 calories; 17.7 g fat; 43.6 g protein; 33.4 g carbs; 9.7 g fiber; 718.7 mg sodium.

MIGHTY MOROCCAN CHICKEN TAGINE

This healthy and traditional North African favorite requires minimal work and features braised chicken seasoned with fragrant spices and dried fruits. Its flavorsome, sweet sauce combines nicely and tenderizes the chicken, which just melts in your mouth. Feel free to add other vegetables such as cauliflower, carrots, tomatoes, or broccoli to increase its goodness.

1 tablespoon (15 ml) coconut oil

1 clove garlic, minced

1½ cups (240 g) diced onion

1 cup (150 g) chopped red bell pepper

1 teaspoon minced fresh ginger, peeled

2 pounds (910 g) chicken pieces, skin and bones removed

1 teaspoon each ground turmeric, coriander, cumin, and black pepper

2 cups (475 ml) Nutritive Chicken Stock (page 103)

⅔ cup (87 g) chopped dried apricots

½ cup (75 g) raisins

⅔ cup (117 g) prunes, pits removed

1 tablespoon (7 g) ground cinnamon

1½ tablespoons (10 g) almond flour

½ cup (55 g) slivered almonds

Melt the oil in a large pot over high heat and sauté the garlic and onion until soft, about 4 minutes. Add the bell pepper and ginger and sauté for about 2 more minutes, until soft. Add the chicken, turmeric, coriander, cumin, and black pepper and pour in the chicken stock. Half cover with a lid, turn the heat down, and cook for about 30 minutes. Add the apricots, raisins, prunes, cinnamon, and almond flour and cook for a further 15 minutes. In a small, dry pan, toast the slivered almonds. Serve decorated with the toasted almonds. This dish is delicious served with Luscious Lima Bean Mash or Anti-Ox Pumpkin and Cauliflower Mash.

Yield: 4 servings

Note: Tagine, which is often served with couscous, is traditionally cooked in an earthenware pot, also called a tagine, but you can use a heavy lidded pan or slow cooker if you don't have a tagine.

———————[NUTRITIONAL ANALYSIS]———————
Per serving: 655.2 calories; 16.9 g fat; 66.4 g protein; 61 g carbs; 8.9 g fiber; 890.5 mg sodium.

METABOLISM-BOOSTING CHICKEN CURRY FEAST

Because of its combination of spices, this traditional Indian dish has numerous health benefits, including the ability to stimulate your metabolism to feel full quicker, so you eat less and lose weight. Turmeric is one of the main spices used in curry, which also gives it the yellow pigment that brightens up most curry dishes. Coriander, small red or green chiles, cumin, ginger, and onion are also common ingredients in curry and burst with vital nutrients to keep your metabolism running efficiently.

- **3 tablespoons (45 ml) coconut oil or ghee**
- **2 cups (320 g) finely chopped onion**
- **4 cloves garlic, minced**
- **2 teaspoons minced fresh ginger, peeled**
- **1 teaspoon ground turmeric**
- **1 small red or green chile pepper, minced**
- **1 tablespoon (6 g) ground coriander**
- **1 teaspoon ground cumin**
- **½ teaspoon ground fennel**
- **2 teaspoons ground paprika**
- **1 teaspoon salt, Celtic or sea**
- **2 tablespoons (28 ml) apple cider vinegar**
- **2½ pounds (1.1 kg) chicken thighs, deboned, cut into chunks**
- **2 medium tomatoes, peeled and chopped**
- **5 cardamom pods**
- **1 stick cinnamon**
- **1 stalk lemongrass, minced**
- **1 cup (235 ml) coconut milk**

Heat the oil or ghee in a large frying pan or wok over medium heat. Add the onions, garlic, and ginger and cook until the onions are golden and tender, about 5 minutes. Add the turmeric, chile, coriander, cumin, fennel, paprika, salt, and vinegar and stir until well combined. Add the chicken and stir until it is thoroughly coated with the spices. Add the tomatoes, cardamom, cinnamon, and lemongrass and cover. Cook over medium heat for 45 minutes. Remove the lid and add the coconut milk. Stir and cook uncovered for 2 minutes.

Serve with Balancing Basmati Almond Rice (page 146), Antioxidant Ginger, Date, and Orange Chutney (page 155), and Restorative Cucumber-Yogurt Raita (page 157).

Yield: 4 servings

Note: Studies have shown that turmeric, one of the main spices in curry, almost completely prevented joint swelling in rats with arthritis.

[NUTRITIONAL ANALYSIS]

Per serving: 232.6 calories; 16.7 g fat; 7.7 g protein; 13.2 g carbs; 2.2 g fiber; 390.5 mg sodium.

TANTALIZING CHICKEN SATAY WITH POWERFUL PEANUT-COCONUT SAUCE

Succulent and full of flavor, this Thai-style chicken satay is marinated in a tasty, nutrient-dense peanut-coconut sauce, which is the perfect complement to chicken. Even more, this is simple and easy to make and will explode with flavor in your mouth.

1 pound (455 g) chicken breast

½ cup (120 ml) coconut milk

1 tablespoon (15 ml) fish sauce

2 teaspoons red curry paste

1 teaspoon ground turmeric

1 teaspoon organic honey

2 tablespoons (2 g) chopped fresh cilantro

½ teaspoon salt, Celtic or sea

¼ teaspoon black pepper

1 tablespoon (15 ml) coconut oil

Chop the chicken into 2-inch (5-cm) strips. Place the coconut milk, fish sauce, curry paste, turmeric, honey, cilantro, salt, and pepper in a large bowl and combine well. Add the chicken, cover, and let marinate in the refrigerator for at least 1 hour.

Thread the chicken strips onto 8 skewers. Heat the oil in a large frying pan over medium to high heat and cook the chicken for about 7 minutes, turning them halfway through. They should be lightly browned and cooked through. Top them with Punchy Peanut-Coconut Sauce (page 152) and serve over Balancing Basmati Almond Rice (page 146).

Yield: 4 servings

Note: These satays also make a great starter for your meal or may be served as finger food when you are expecting guests. You can make them a day in advance and reheat them in the oven for several minutes before serving.

[NUTRITIONAL ANALYSIS]
Per serving: 280.2 calories; 13.7 g fat; 34.9 g protein; 4.7 g carbs; 0.5 g fiber; 567.6 mg sodium.

SUPERCHARGED CHICKEN OR TURKEY MEATLOAF

This dish is a family favorite and supereasy to prepare. It provides plenty of protein and vitamin- and mineral-rich veggies. The turmeric and cumin give it a decidedly bold flavor and marry nicely with the raisins. The walnuts are loaded with omega-3s and add a delicious, crunchy texture. This meat loaf pairs nicely with steamed asparagus, broccoli, or cauliflower and tastes great with Spice-It-Up Sweet Chili Sauce (page 152) or Antioxidant BBQ Sauce (page 154) on top.

1 tablespoon (14 g) butter or coconut oil

1 pound (455 g) minced or ground chicken or turkey

2 cloves garlic, minced

1 teaspoon grated fresh ginger, peeled

1 teaspoon ground turmeric

1 teaspoon ground cumin

2 eggs

¾ cup (83 g) grated peeled carrots

1 cup (150 g) finely chopped red bell pepper

½ cup (75 g) raisins

½ cup (60 g) walnuts, roughly chopped

Preheat the oven to 350°F (180°C, gas mark 4). Grease a 4- by 8-inch (10- by 20-cm) loaf pan or casserole dish with butter or coconut oil.

Place the chicken or turkey, garlic, ginger, turmeric, cumin, and eggs in a large bowl and blend together using your hands or a large wooden spoon. Mix in the carrots and bell pepper. Add the raisins and walnuts and mix together. Pack the ingredients into the greased oven dish and bake in the oven for 40 minutes, until the loaf is cooked through and golden on top. Remove from the oven and let stand for 10 minutes. Cut into slices and serve.

Yield: 4 servings

Note: It's always best to choose certified organic ground turkey and chicken, as these are a source of other important nutrients, such as vitamin C, iron, magnesium, and phosphorus, based on the organic diet that was fed to the animals.

[NUTRITIONAL ANALYSIS]

Per serving: 506 calories; 30.4 g fat; 38 g protein; 21.5 g carbs; 3.4 g fiber; 197 mg sodium.

ANTI-INFLAMMATORY TURMERIC TURKEY BURGERS

Enjoy the delicious combination of herbs and spices in these flavorful burgers that pack a punch of powerful, nutrient-dense compounds. Turmeric has more positive qualities than any other spice, particularly when it comes to anti-inflammatory antioxidants. The active compound in turmeric is curcumin, which has been shown to prevent the oxidation of cholesterol and plaque buildup in the body that can lead to cardiovascular disease. Turmeric reduces fat in the liver, which in turn helps the liver metabolize other fats that have accumulated there, perhaps from excess sugars and refined carbohydrates.

1 pound (455 g) ground turkey, preferably organic

1 small onion, chopped

2 eggs, beaten

½ cup (75 g) raisins (optional)

2 tablespoons (14 g) ground turmeric

1 or 2 cloves garlic, minced

1 teaspoon chopped fresh ginger, peeled

1 teaspoon ground cumin

½ teaspoon salt, Celtic or sea

Pinch of black pepper

Dash of cayenne pepper (optional)

1 tablespoon (15 ml) extra-virgin olive or coconut oil

2 teaspoons tamari

These burgers can be grilled or baked. If baking, pre-heat the oven to 350°F (180°C, gas mark 4). Combine all the ingredients in a large bowl and mix well. Divide the mixture into 6 pieces, shape into burger patties, and place on an oiled baking sheet. Bake for 20 minutes, or until cooked through. The burgers should reach an internal temperature of 165°F. If grilling, place on the heat and cook for about 4 minutes, until browned on one side, then flip over and cook for about 2 to 3 minutes, or until cooked through.

Serve the burgers on buns or alone and with toppings of your choice. The Antioxidant BBQ Sauce (page 154) goes well and tastes delicious with these burgers!

Yield: 6 burgers

Note: Turmeric is the powder of a rhizome. It looks like yellow ginger and is part of curry powder, but it is not curry. For the most curcumin, use turmeric rather than curry powder. Try to select organically grown turmeric to ensure against irradiation. Store turmeric powder in a tightly sealed container in a cool, dark, and dry place.

——[**NUTRITIONAL ANALYSIS**]——

Per serving: 265.8 calories; 14 g fat; 23.7 g protein; 11.2 g carbs; 0.7 g fiber; 328.5 mg sodium.

GET-UP-AND-GO INDIAN CHICKPEA DELIGHT

Enjoy the buttery, nutlike taste of chickpeas (aka garbanzo beans) along with an aromatic blend of heart-healthy spices in this nourishing Middle Eastern dish. Chickpeas are an excellent source of fiber, manganese, and folate as well as providing ample amounts of protein. I often make this dish to nosh on as a snack or to accompany my raw salad at lunchtime.

1 tablespoon (14 g) ghee or coconut oil

½ medium red onion, chopped

2 cloves garlic, minced

2 teaspoons minced fresh ginger, peeled

1½ teaspoons each coriander, cumin, and chili powder

½ teaspoon each ground cardamom, cloves, and nutmeg

1 teaspoon ground cinnamon

1 teaspoon ground turmeric

2 cups (480 g) crushed tomatoes

½ teaspoon each salt, Celtic or sea, and black pepper

2 cups (328 g) cooked chickpeas, or use canned

1½ cups (355 ml) coconut milk

2 tablespoons (2 g) chopped fresh cilantro

Heat the ghee or oil in a sauté pan over medium-high heat. Add the onion, garlic, and ginger and cook until softened, about 5 minutes. Add the coriander, cumin, chili powder, cardamom, cloves, nutmeg, cinnamon, and turmeric and sauté for 1 minute. Reduce the heat to medium-low, add the tomatoes, salt, and pepper, and simmer gently for about 25 minutes.

Transfer the mixture to a blender and purée until smooth. Return the purée to the pan, add the chickpeas and coconut milk, and simmer until heated through, about 5 to 8 minutes. Garnish with cilantro. Serve immediately.

Yield: 4 servings

Note: Unlike most other canned vegetables, chickpeas lose very little nutrients when canned. Just be sure to rinse them well with filtered water after removing them from the can.

—————[NUTRITIONAL ANALYSIS]—————
Per serving: 400 calories; 19.3 g fat; 9.7 g protein; 44.6 g carbs; 7.9 g fiber; 887.7 mg sodium.

FRAGRANT CAULIFLOWER-QUINOA RISOTTO

This combination of nutritional superstars is a balanced meal all in itself. Quinoa contains all nine essential amino acids that are the building blocks of protein, fiber, and the minerals manganese and magnesium. Cauliflower is loaded with antioxidant nutrients C, K, and B complex to boost detoxification and support a healthy heart. The spices add a rich, pungent flavor and nutritional kick.

1 tablespoon (15 ml) coconut oil

1 medium leek, diced

1 clove garlic, minced

1 teaspoon minced fresh ginger, peeled

½ teaspoon ground cumin

¼ teaspoon ground nutmeg

4 cups (400 g) cauliflower, cut into small florets

1½ tablespoons (22 g) Bone-Strengthening Lemon Tahini (page 151)

1½ cups (355 ml) Digestive Vegetable Stock (page 104)

1½ cups (255 g) cooked quinoa

1 teaspoon lemon juice

½ teaspoon salt, Celtic or sea

Dash of black pepper

2 tablespoons (2 g) chopped fresh cilantro

Heat the oil in a large frying pan over medium heat. Add the leek and garlic and sauté for about 2 minutes, until they wilt. Add the ginger, cumin, and nutmeg and mix for about 1 minute. Stir in the cauliflower, then cook the mixture for about 5 minutes to remove some of the moisture and soften, stirring occasionally. While the cauliflower is cooking, whisk together the tahini and vegetable stock in a medium bowl.

When the cauliflower is cooked, add the quinoa to the pan and pour in the whisked vegetable broth mixture. Mix together well. Bring the risotto to a simmer and cook until all the excess liquid has evaporated, about 5 minutes. Remove from the heat and stir in the lemon juice, salt, and pepper. Sprinkle with cilantro and serve immediately.

Yield: 4 servings

Note: One cup of dry quinoa yields about 3 cups of cooked quinoa. Rinse quinoa well in a mesh strainer before cooking, as this removes the natural bitterness of its outer coating.

[NUTRITIONAL ANALYSIS]
Per serving: 239.7 calories; 8.1 g fat; 8.3 g protein; 37 g carbs; 7.6 g fiber; 241.9 mg sodium.

LUSCIOUS LIMA BEAN MASH

Make the most of the delicate, buttery flavor of fresh lima beans in this mellow, mouthwatering mash. Better than traditional mashed potatoes, this preparation provides more nutrients such as protein, fiber, magnesium, iron, and folate and works wonders on the digestive system. You'll love the flavorful spices in it and probably come back for seconds.

- **1 cup (156 g) dried lima beans**
- **1 cup (235 ml) Digestive Vegetable Stock (page 104)**
- **½ cup (120 ml) filtered water**
- **1 clove garlic, minced**
- **½ teaspoon salt, Celtic or sea**
- **½ teaspoon black pepper**
- **2 tablespoons (28 ml) extra-virgin olive oil**
- **1½ tablespoons (9 g) fennel seeds**
- **2 tablespoons (8 g) chopped fresh parsley**
- **½ lemon, juiced**
- **1 tablespoon grated lemon rind**

Soak the lima beans overnight in filtered water. Next morning, discard the water and rinse the beans well. Place the beans in a medium-size pot and cover with vegetable stock and filtered water. Bring to a boil and simmer for up to 2 hours, until the beans have softened. Drain and place into a food processor, adding the garlic, salt, pepper, oil, fennel, parsley, and lemon juice. Process until smooth. Serve with grated lemon zest sprinkled on top.

Yield: 4 servings

Note: Lima beans are excellent for energy and keeping blood sugar levels balanced. This is due mainly to their high fiber content, which prevents blood sugar levels from rising too fast and provides slow-burning energy.

Recipe Substitution

You can use fava beans, also known as broad beans, in place of the lima beans in this recipe. Fava beans provide adequate amounts of folate, selenium, manganese, potassium, and vitamin K, all of which support heart health.

[NUTRITIONAL ANALYSIS]

Per serving: 200.8 calories; 7.5 g fat; 10 g protein; 30.2 g carbs; 10.6 g fiber; 194 mg sodium.

ANTI-OX PUMPKIN AND CAULIFLOWER MASH

Smooth, sweet, and rich in phytonutrients and antioxidants, this succulent combination is the perfect addition to any meal. Butternut squash and pumpkins are abundant in nutrients known as carotenoids, which are amazingly beneficial for overall cardiovascular health. Cauliflower has a mild flavor and is an excellent source of vitamin C, K, folate, and fiber.

3 cups (420 g) diced butternut squash, peeled

2 cups (200 g) cauliflower, cut into large florets

3 tablespoons (42 g) butter or ghee

¼ cup (30 g) grated Cheddar cheese

1 teaspoon salt, Celtic or sea

1 teaspoon black pepper

2 tablespoons (18 g) pumpkin seeds

2 tablespoons (8 g) chopped fresh parsley

Place the butternut squash in a large saucepan, cover with water, and bring to a boil. Add the cauliflower and let simmer for about 5 minutes, or until both vegetables are soft. Transfer to a food processor, add the butter or ghee, cheese, salt, pepper, and pumpkin seeds and process until smooth. Garnish with fresh parsley and serve immediately.

Yield: 4 servings

Note: Add an Italian taste to this dish by using Parmesan cheese instead of Cheddar. You can also sprinkle a little over the top and place under the broiler for a minute or two to brown on top.

Pumpkin—the Potassium Heavyweight

Pumpkin is a nutritious but overlooked vegetable that is ridiculously low in calories while very high in potassium and vitamin A. Pumpkin is actually a potassium heavyweight, more so than even bananas. One 49-calorie cup of mashed pumpkin contains a whopping 564 mg of the stuff.

Why should you care? Let us count the ways! Several large epidemiological studies suggest that increased potassium intake is associated with a decreased risk of stroke. Four large studies have reported significant associations between dietary potassium and bone mineral density. And a number of studies have shown that people who eat a lot of potassium have lower blood pressure than people who don't.

──────── **[NUTRITIONAL ANALYSIS]** ────────

Per serving: 284.8 calories; 11.1 g fat; 2.9 g protein; 15.8 g carbs; 4.3 g fiber; 350.8 mg sodium.

SAUTÉED SHIITAKE MUSHROOMS WITH A KALE KICK

The rich, buttery, meaty flavor and chewy texture of shiitake mushrooms pair nicely with the earthy-flavored kale. Shiitakes are high in B-complex vitamins, protein, fiber, and numerous minerals, and are well known for their effective immune-strengthening qualities. Kale is considered to be one of the healthiest vegetables around because of its antioxidants and high mineral content. This is medicinal food at its best.

- **2 tablespoons (28 g) butter**
- **2 cloves garlic, minced**
- **2 cups (140 g) shiitake mushrooms, sliced**
- **1 teaspoon salt, Celtic or sea**
- **½ teaspoon black pepper**
- **2 cups (110 g) kale, chopped**
- **¼ cup (60 ml) dry red wine**

Melt the butter in a medium saucepan over medium heat. Add the garlic and cook for about 1 minute, or until soft. Add the mushrooms, salt, and pepper and sauté for about 5 minutes. Add the kale and red wine and cook for about 3 minutes longer. Serve immediately.

Yield: 4 servings

Note: This recipe can be served as a side dish or as a topping over chicken, fish, venison, or beef.

ZESTY BROCCOLI WITH GARLIC AND GINGER

Delicious, tender broccoli florets flavored with orange zest and garlic, served as a side dish and ready in a snap. High in antioxidant vitamins and minerals, broccoli is one vegetable you'll want to include in your diet on a regular basis.

- **2 tablespoons (28 g) butter or ghee**
- **1 clove garlic, minced**
- **1 teaspoon chopped fresh ginger, peeled**
- **3 cups (213 g) broccoli, cut into small florets**
- **½ teaspoon salt, Celtic or sea**
- **½ teaspoon black pepper**
- **1 teaspoon grated orange zest**

Melt the butter or ghee in a medium saucepan over medium heat. Add the garlic and ginger and cook for about 1 minute, or until soft. Add the broccoli, salt, and pepper and sauté for about 5 minutes, until the broccoli is softened. Add the orange zest at the end and mix in. Serve immediately.

Yield: 4 servings

Note: Broccoli is a good source of minerals such as manganese, magnesium, calcium, selenium, zinc, iron, and phosphorus.

[NUTRITIONAL ANALYSIS]

Per serving: 115.7 calories; 6.1 g fat; 2 g protein; 13.2 g carbs; 2.1 g fiber; 343.2 mg sodium.

[NUTRITIONAL ANALYSIS]

Per serving: 70.9 calories; 6 g fat; 2.1 g protein; 3.8 g carbs; 2 g fiber; 183.8 mg sodium.

BALANCING BASMATI ALMOND RICE

This fragrant and savory Indian-style rice dish flavored with spices and fresh vegetables is almost a meal in itself. It's easy to digest and is chock-full of fiber, B vitamins, and iron. It goes well with Indian curry or dal (lentils).

1 cup (180 g) brown basmati rice

¼ cup (48 g) brown rice

1 cup (235 ml) Digestive Vegetable Stock (page 104)

1 cup (235 ml) filtered water

½ cup each carrots (65 g), zucchini (62 g), and green bell peppers (75 g), all chopped

½ teaspoon salt, Celtic or sea

2 tablespoons (28 ml) extra-virgin olive oil

½ teaspoon cumin seeds

¼ teaspoon black pepper

Pinch each of ground nutmeg and cinnamon

½ cup (72 g) roasted almonds, chopped

¾ cup (45 g) chopped fresh parsley

Dash of cayenne pepper (optional)

Wash and drain the rice. In a medium-size pot, combine the rice, stock, water, carrots, zucchini, bell peppers, and salt and bring to a boil. Reduce to low heat and simmer, covered, for 20 minutes, or until the rice is soft and the liquids are absorbed.

In a small skillet, melt the olive oil over medium heat and sauté the cumin seeds for 30 seconds. Stir in the pepper, nutmeg, and cinnamon. Add the spice mixture to the cooked rice and vegetables and mix together with a fork. Stir in the almonds, parsley, and cayenne, if using. Serve immediately.

Yield: 4 servings

Note: Because basmati is refined white rice that has been stripped of its bran layer, mixing basmati rice with brown rice ensures that you get the benefits of more fiber in your diet.

───── **[NUTRITIONAL ANALYSIS]** ─────

Per serving: 327.5 calories; 13.9 g fat; 8.5 g protein; 45.1 g carbs; 4.6 g fiber; 206.1 mg sodium.

SUMPTUOUS SPINACH AND SWISS CHARD WITH PINE NUTS

A staple of the Mediterranean diet, Swiss chard and spinach are about as good as it gets when it comes to heart-healthy nutrients. They are loaded with antioxidants for strengthening your heart, nourishing your cells, and even reversing aging. The pine nuts add a nice crunch and help bring out the vegetable flavors. You'll enjoy every bite of this tasty dish that's oh-so easy to make!

2 tablespoons (28 ml) extra-virgin olive oil, coconut oil, or ghee

2 small shallots or 2 cloves garlic, minced

4 cups (210 g) Swiss chard, chopped

8 cups (240 g) baby spinach

¼ cup (35 g) toasted pine nuts

Dash salt, Celtic or sea

Heat the oil or ghee in a large frying pan over medium heat. Add the shallots or garlic and sauté for a minute or two, until translucent. Add the Swiss chard and sauté for 2 more minutes. Add the spinach and stir until wilted. Stir in the toasted pine nuts and salt. Serve immediately.

Yield: 4 servings

Note: Pine nuts are a great source of monounsaturated fats, as well as ample amounts of vitamins E and K and the minerals iron, copper, and manganese, all of which help support the cardiovascular system.

Swiss Chard: Low-Cal Superfood

Chard is a member of the goosefoot family of plants. It's a relative of beets, and it comes in both red and white varieties. The red kind is a standout in supermarkets. It's very quick cooking—like spinach—so for goodness sake don't overcook it, or you'll compromise its nutritional value.

Speaking of nutritional value, this vegetable is nothing short of a powerhouse. A cup of cooked chard gives you almost 4 grams of fiber (!), more than 100 mg of calcium, an almost unbelievable 961 mg of potassium, and more than 10,000 IUs of vitamin A. And all this for about 35 calories. Talk about a superfood!

[NUTRITIONAL ANALYSIS]

Per serving: 174.4 calories; 13 g fat; 6.5 g protein; 11.8 g carbs; 6 g fiber; 437 mg sodium.

CARDIOPROTECTIVE GREEN BEANS

These are crunchy, buttery, and lightly steamed to bring out their peak flavor. Green beans are loaded with heart-healthy minerals, potassium, and calcium.

- **4 cups (400 g) green beans, cut into 1-inch (2.5-cm) pieces**
- **1 teaspoon finely chopped fresh ginger, peeled**
- **½ teaspoon salt, Celtic or sea**
- **1 teaspoon butter or extra-virgin olive oil**
- **1 tablespoon (15 ml) fresh lemon or lime juice**
- **3 tablespoons (21 g) slivered, roasted almonds**
- **4 tablespoons finely chopped fresh parsley (16 g) or cilantro (4 g)**

Place the beans in a medium bowl, add the ginger and salt, and mix lightly. Place the beans in a steamer on medium to high heat and cook for 7 to 10 minutes, until bright green and still crisp. Remove from the heat and place in a serving dish. Add the butter or oil and let it melt into the beans. Toss with lemon or lime juice and sprinkle with almonds and parsley or cilantro.

Yield: 4 servings

Note: If you are unable to obtain fresh green beans, use frozen, because they will still retain at least 90 percent of their B vitamins.

SUSTAINING GINGER-SESAME CARROTS

Carrots are loaded with beta-carotene and vitamin C, both antioxidants that strengthen arterial walls and contribute to heart health. Sesame seeds are a good source of calcium to build strong bones and of B vitamins, which are essential to the health of red blood cells and support your body's ability to derive energy from food. The ginger adds not only a special flavor and zest, it also helps improve digestion.

- **1 tablespoon (15 ml) sesame oil**
- **4 medium carrots, peeled and cut diagonally**
- **1 tablespoon (6 g) finely chopped fresh ginger, peeled**
- **1½ teaspoons salt, Celtic or sea**
- **1 tablespoon (8 g) sesame seeds**

Heat the sesame oil in a medium pan, add the carrots, and sauté for 3 minutes. Add the ginger and salt and cook for about 15 minutes on low heat, or until tender. Transfer to a serving dish and sprinkle with sesame seeds.

Yield: 4 servings

Note: To add more variety and nutrition to this dish, include green beans along with carrots.

[NUTRITIONAL ANALYSIS]

Per serving: 84 calories; 4 g fat; 3.3 g protein; 9.7 g carbs; 4.8 g fiber; 205.1 mg sodium.

[NUTRITIONAL ANALYSIS]

Per serving: 69.3 calories; 4.5 g fat; 1.1 g protein; 6.6 g carbs; 2 g fiber; 207.4 mg sodium.

· NOURISHING ·
ACCOMPANIMENTS
AND MENU ENHANCEMENTS

- **CHOICE CONDIMENTS**..150

- **SUCCULENT SAUCES** 152

- **POWERFUL PRESERVES & FABULOUS FERMENTS** 155

Your heart-healthy menu would not be complete without a set of team-player foods and dishes that contribute a complementary blend of nutritional attributes and synergy in the form of condiments, sauces, preserves, and fermented foods. I included these dishes as much for their flavor as their nutrient-dense beneficial qualities. The recipes in this section comprise an extraordinary collection of culinary superstars you'll want to keep on hand to enhance your flavorful and nutritive experience. Enjoy the condiments alongside your favorite vegetables, smeared over crackers, wraps, and sandwiches, or added to salads, meats, and fish. Fermented foods provide a healthy dose of friendly bacteria known as probiotics to strengthen both your immunity and digestion. You'll find a pleasing array of antioxidant-laden sauces to enjoy with many of the other dishes in this book. Last but not least, I've included several of my favorite preserves that are simply scrumptious, irresistibly good for your health, and easy to make.

MEDITERRANEAN BLACK OLIVE TAPENADE

This bold, zesty, Mediterranean-inspired, and nutritious dip is loaded with essential fatty acids, vitamins E and C, as well as amino acids and protein, all of which support a healthy heart. It can be enjoyed as a delicious pasta sauce, too.

1 cup (100 g) pitted black kalamata olives

1 clove garlic, minced

1 teaspoon Dijon mustard

1 teaspoon fresh lemon or lime juice

2 tablespoons (6 g) dulse flakes

1 tablespoon (15 ml) extra-virgin olive oil

¼ cup (60 ml) filtered water

1 tablespoon (8 g) walnuts

½ teaspoon grated lemon zest

Place all the ingredients in a food processor and puree. Transfer to a small bowl and let stand for at least 20 minutes to allow the flavors to meld together and develop. Spread over Low-Carb Herbed Cheddar Crackers (page 109) and vegetables or use in sandwiches and wraps.

Yield: ⅔ cup

Note: Black olives help stimulate the production of hydrochloric acid in the stomach, which is vital for digestion and breaking down food.

SUPER-HEALTHFUL HUMMUS

This creamy, fiber-filled dip goes especially well with crackers and raw vegetables or can be used as a spread in sandwiches or wraps. Garbanzo beans, affectionately known as chickpeas, are high in folate, tryptophan, iron, and antioxidants and are a good source of plant protein.

2 cups (328 g) cooked garbanzo beans

2 cloves garlic, minced

2 tablespoons (18 g) sunflower seeds

2 tablespoons (30 g) Bone-Strengthening Lemon Tahini (page 151)

⅓ cup (80 ml) fresh lemon or lime juice

1 small celery stalk, chopped

½ teaspoon ground paprika

¾ teaspoon salt, Celtic or sea

1 tablespoon (15 ml) extra-virgin olive oil

Dash of cayenne pepper

Place all the ingredients in a food processor and blend until smooth and creamy. Transfer to a bowl and serve. This will keep in the refrigerator for up to 1 week.

Yield: About 2 cups

Note: Use a dollop of healthy hummus in place of mayonnaise—it will add more protein and fiber and keep you feeling satisfied longer, which can aid in weight loss.

--------[NUTRITIONAL ANALYSIS]--------
Per tablespoon: 13.8 calories; 1.2 g fat; 0.1 g protein; 0.2 g carbs; 0.1 g fiber; 34.2 mg sodium.

--------[NUTRITIONAL ANALYSIS]--------
Per tablespoon: 40.6 calories; 1.7 g fat; 1.3 g protein; 5.3 g carbs; 1.1 g fiber; 123.3 mg sodium.

BONE-STRENGTHENING LEMON TAHINI

As far as health foods go, there aren't many that are as versatile or that pack the same nutritional punch as this tasty tahini. It is loaded with heart-healthy nutrients such as calcium and almost a full profile of B-complex vitamins for helping you strengthen bones and reduce stress.

1 cup (240 g) raw tahini
¼ cup (60 ml) lemon juice
¼ cup (60 ml) extra-virgin olive oil
½ cup (120 ml) filtered water
½ teaspoon salt, Celtic or sea
1 clove garlic, minced
1 teaspoon chopped cilantro
Dash of cayenne pepper (optional)
½ cup (72 g) sesame seeds

in a quart-size jar, combine the tahini, lemon juice, olive oil, and water and thoroughly stir together. Stir in the salt, garlic, cilantro, and cayenne, if using. In a medium skillet over medium heat, toast the sesame seeds for 5 minutes, or until golden brown. Do not let them burn. Transfer the sesame seeds to a food processor and blend until coarsely ground. Stir the sesame seeds into the tahini mixture. Serve as a dip for veggies or with Low-Carb Herbed Cheddar Crackers (page 109). Store in the refrigerator.

Yield: About 2 cups (480 g)

Note: Turn this dip into a salad dressing by adding more water until you reach the desired consistency.

[NUTRITIONAL ANALYSIS]

Per tablespoon: 72.9 calories; 6.3 g fat; 1.8 g protein; 2.6 g carbs; 0.9 g fiber; 26.2g; sodium.

HEART-HEALTHY ALMOND MAYONNAISE

A healthy, delicious homemade mayonnaise recipe is something for every health-conscious person to have up their sleeve, or in their refrigerator! This one is loaded with vitamin E for your healthy heart, and numerous essential minerals. Plus, you won't believe how much better it tastes than the store-bought kind.

2 egg yolks
2 tablespoons (28 ml) fresh lemon juice
2 tablespoons (28 ml) filtered water
1 teaspoon raw organic honey
1 teaspoon mustard powder
½ teaspoon salt, Celtic or sea
½ teaspoon white pepper
1 cup (235 ml) grapeseed oil
2 tablespoons (12 g) ground almonds

Place 1 cup (235 ml) of water into a small pot and bring it to a simmer. Place a heatproof bowl in the pot. Add the egg yolks, lemon juice, water, honey, mustard, salt, and pepper and whisk until the mixture thickens. Remove from the heat and pour into a food processor. Add a small amount of oil to the mixture and blend together. Add the almonds and blend into the mixture. While blending, continue pouring small amounts of oil until it is all gone and the mixture has thickened. Pour the mayonnaise into a sealed jar and refrigerate. It will keep for up to 4 weeks in the refrigerator.

Yield: 1½ cups (340 g)

Note: Use this mayonnaise in egg and chicken salads and open-faced tuna sandwiches and wraps.

[NUTRITIONAL ANALYSIS]

Per tablespoon: 89 calories; 9.5 g fat; 0.2 g protein; 0.4 g carbs; 0 g fiber; 0.7 mg sodium.

PUNCHY PEANUT-COCONUT SAUCE

This spicy sauce has a delicious Thai taste and is perfect with chicken, shrimp, or beef dishes. Peanuts are rich in vitamins, minerals, and fiber that provide energy and contain monounsaturated fatty acids, especially oleic acid, which has been shown to be beneficial for heart health. Apart from its creamy, rich flavor, coconut milk contains magnesium, potassium, phosphorus, and iron, all of which support a healthy metabolism.

- **1 cup (235 ml) coconut milk**
- **1 tablespoon (15 g) red curry paste**
- **½ cup (130 g) crunchy, sugar-free peanut butter**
- **½ cup (120 ml) Nutritive Chicken Stock (page 103)**
- **2 tablespoons (40 g) organic honey**
- **2 tablespoons (28 ml) fresh lime juice**
- **½ teaspoon salt, Celtic or sea**

Pour the coconut milk into a small saucepan and bring to a boil. Whisk in the curry paste until dissolved. Add the peanut butter, stock, and honey. Reduce the heat and simmer until smooth, stirring constantly, about 5 minutes. Remove from the heat and add the lime juice and salt. Let cool to room temperature before refrigerating in an airtight container, where it will keep for up to 1 week.

Yield: About 2 cups

Note: Peanuts belong to the legume or bean family, which are the best sources of plant protein because of their high percentages of essential amino acids.

[NUTRITIONAL ANALYSIS]

Per tablespoon: 59.9 calories; 4.5 g fat; 1.9 g protein; 2.8 g carbs; .2 g fiber; 76.4 mg sodium.

SPICE-IT-UP SWEET CHILI SAUCE

This sweet chili sauce is simple to make and makes a superb condiment that goes with many dishes. It's great as a dip with finger foods and shrimp or as a glaze over chicken, beef, pork, and even grilled vegetables. Chiles are a good source of antioxidants, such as vitamins C and A, and contain a beneficial amount of heart-healthy minerals such as potassium, magnesium, manganese, calcium, and iron.

- **1 tablespoon (15 ml) coconut oil**
- **½ cup (80 g) chopped red onion**
- **8 cloves garlic, minced**
- **4 large red chile peppers, seeds removed, finely chopped**
- **2 red bell peppers, chopped**
- **3 tablespoons (24 g) grated fresh ginger, peeled**
- **6 kaffir lime leaves**
- **3 lemongrass stems, chopped**
- **1 bunch cilantro, chopped**
- **1 cup (340 g) organic honey**
- **4 tablespoons (60 ml) filtered water**
- **2 tablespoons (28 ml) apple cider vinegar**
- **1 tablespoon (16 g) tomato paste**
- **1 teaspoon fish sauce**
- **1 teaspoon salt, Celtic or sea**

Heat the oil in a medium saucepan over medium heat, add the onion and garlic, and cook until they turn a light golden brown and become slightly crispy. Remove from the pan and set aside.

In a food processor, combine the chiles, bell pepper, ginger, lime leaves, lemongrass, and cilantro and blend until finely chopped. Set aside.

[NUTRITIONAL ANALYSIS]

Per tablespoon: 26.2 calories; .3 g fat; .2 g protein; 6.8 g carbs; .2 g fiber; 46.9 mg sodium.

In the same saucepan, place the honey and water and heat until the honey starts to simmer. Add the chile paste mixture, vinegar, tomato paste, fish sauce, and salt and simmer for about 2 minutes. Return the onions and garlic to the pot and for cook an additional 1 minute. Adjust the taste, adding more fish sauce if you like it saltier, or more honey if you'd like it sweeter. Transfer the contents to an airtight jar and store in the refrigerator, where it will keep for up to 2 months.

Yield: About 3 cups (825 ml)

Note: Chile peppers are available year-round in either fresh, dried, or powdered form. Whenever possible, buy fresh chiles instead of powder, as these may contain adulterated spicy mixtures. Kaffir lime leaves and lemongrass are available in most Asian supermarkets.

HEALTH-GIVING HOLLANDAISE SAUCE

There's nothing better than homemade healthy hollandaise that's not only supersimple to make but packed full of goodness and fantastic flavor. This one is loaded with protein and healthy fats that most store-bought brands are devoid of and that usually contain inferior, genetically modified oils such as soybean or vegetable oil.

3 egg yolks

2 tablespoons (28 ml) filtered water

¾ cup (165 g) unsalted butter, cubed

2 tablespoons (28 ml) fresh lemon juice

¼ teaspoon salt, Celtic or sea

Dash of black pepper

Place a heatproof bowl over a medium-size saucepan filled a quarter of the way with hot, but not boiling, water and maintain the temperature at a simmer. Put the egg yolks and water into the bowl and whisk for about 3 minutes, or until the mixture thickens and has doubled in volume. Add the butter, one cube at a time, ensuring each cube has fully melted before adding the next one. This will take approximately 10 minutes. Whisk constantly until the sauce thickens and then remove from heat. Whisk in the lemon juice, salt, and pepper. Feel free to use an electric whisk to speed up the process and reduce time. Serve immediately. This sauce is best used soon after making it and does not keep well in the refrigerator.

Yield: About 1 cup

Note: Include this hollandaise over your favorite egg dishes, such eggs Benedict, or over fresh, steamed asparagus, spinach, kale, broccoli, or cauliflower.

[NUTRITIONAL ANALYSIS]
Per tablespoon: 87 calories; 9.5 g fat; .6 g protein; .2 g carbs; 0 g fiber; 31.8 mg sodium.

ANTIOXIDANT BBQ SAUCE

If you're a lover of livening up certain dishes with barbecue sauce like I am, then you'll love this healthy, homemade version that's overflowing with antioxidant nutrients and flavor. Most store-bought versions of barbecue sauce contain high-fructose corn syrup and lots of sugar. This one is naturally sweetened with raisins and honey, plus it's packed with antioxidant vitamins and minerals. You'll never go back to store-bought brands once you've tasted this delicious blend, which will give your body a healthy boost.

10 large tomatoes

3 tablespoons (45 ml) extra-virgin olive oil

1½ cups (240 g) diced onions

5 cloves garlic, minced

1 teaspoon minced fresh ginger, peeled, optional

1½ cups (180 g) diced celery

1 medium green bell pepper, diced

½ cup (75 g) raisins

½ cup (170 g) organic honey

¾ cup (175 ml) apple cider vinegar

2 teaspoons each dried mustard powder, ground paprika, and salt, Celtic or sea

1 teaspoon black pepper

½ teaspoon dried, whole chile pepper

½ teaspoon cayenne pepper

Place the whole tomatoes into a pot of boiling water for 1 to 2 minutes to loosen their skins and make them easier to remove. Remove and rinse under cold water. Set aside to cool and drain. Once the tomatoes are cool enough to handle, remove their skins and then dice them.

Add the oil to a large pot over medium heat. Add the onions and garlic and sauté until soft, about 3 to 5 minutes. Add the ginger, celery, and bell pepper and cook until soft, about 3 to 4 minutes. Add the raisins, honey, vinegar, mustard powder, paprika, salt, black pepper, chile, and cayenne and bring to a boil, stirring constantly. Turn the heat down and let simmer, stirring often, for about 1 hour, or until thickened to your liking. Remove from the heat and let cool. Pour into a food processor and process until smooth. Transfer to sealed glass containers and refrigerate for 2 or more hours to allow the flavors to meld. This can be frozen for later use.

Yield: 1 quart (946 ml)

Note: Liberally spread this sauce over your favorite meats, poultry, beans, grains, and other dishes that are sure to be enhanced by its superb taste and nutritional goodness.

[NUTRITIONAL ANALYSIS]

Per tablespoon: 25.3 calories; .8 g fat; .3 g protein; 5 g carbs; .5 g fiber; 62.9 mg sodium.

ANTIOXIDANT GINGER, DATE, AND ORANGE CHUTNEY

Who doesn't love the hot, sour, and sweet taste of tangy chutney, especially one that's loaded with antioxidant goodness to provide multiple health benefits? This condiment goes well with rice, quinoa, vegetables, and meats, and believe it or not, it's wonderfully delicious smeared over toast, sandwiches, and wraps accompanied with other fillings.

- 2 oranges, peeled, seeded, and chopped
- 1½ cups (240 g) chopped dates
- 1 tablespoon (8 g) grated fresh ginger, peeled
- ¼ cup (60 ml) fresh orange juice
- 1 tablespoon (6 g) finely grated orange zest
- 3 tablespoons (45 ml) apple cider vinegar
- 2 tablespoons (40 g) organic honey
- 3 tablespoons (45 ml) lemon or lime juice
- 1 teaspoon mustard seeds
- 1 tablespoon (7 g) ground cinnamon
- ¼ teaspoon salt, Celtic or sea
- Dash of cayenne pepper

Place all the ingredients in a nonstick saucepan and cook, covered, over medium-low heat for 30 minutes, stirring occasionally. Add more liquids if needed. Let cool before transferring the mixture to an airtight jar and store in the refrigerator. The chutney will keep for up to 3 or 4 weeks refrigerated.

Yield: 2 cups

Note: Experiment with the flavors of fruit and spices by switching some out for other favorites, such as mango, tamarind, tomatoes, peaches, or whatever is in season.

[NUTRITIONAL ANALYSIS]

Per tablespoon: 33.8 calories; 0.1 g fat; 0.3 g protein; 8.9 g carbs; 1 g fiber; 14.7 mg sodium.

BERRY-BUZZ JELLY

This delectable, sugar-free berry jam is simple to make and loaded with heart-healthy antioxidant nutrients. It contains vitamins C and E, minerals such as potassium and magnesium, and lots of fiber, too. It's a great choice for spreading over muffins, breads, bagels, scones, pancakes, yogurt, or ice cream.

- 1 cup (145 g) blueberries
- 1 cup (125 g) raspberries
- ½ cup (170 g) organic honey
- 3 tablespoons (45 ml) fresh orange juice
- ½ teaspoon salt, Celtic or sea

Place all the ingredients in a saucepan, cover, and bring to a boil over medium heat. Simmer for 1 hour, stirring occasionally. The jam should thicken with a small amount of juice left. Remove from the stove and let cool. Transfer to an airtight container and refrigerate for at least 3 hours before serving.

Yield: About 1 cup (320 g)

Note: Berries have been found to contain some of the highest antioxidant power of any fresh fruits, consistently scoring high on the ORAC test, which has been used by the U.S. Department of Agriculture and other agencies to measure the antioxidant power of foods. Antioxidants inhibit oxidation, which prevents damaging effects to cells and promotes longevity.

[NUTRITIONAL ANALYSIS]

Per tablespoon: 42.3 calories; 0.1 g fat; 0.2 g protein; 11.2 g carbs; 0.8 g fiber; 42.2 mg sodium.

IMMUNE-BUILDING LEMON-GINGER BUTTER

Enjoy the creamy texture and deliciously sweet and sour flavors of this healthy spread, which is super-quick and easy to make. The addition of ginger not only provides antioxidants and improves digestion, it adds pungent flavor. Lemons are an excellent source of vitamin C, which is well known for boosting the immune system and cleansing the liver by helping to produce more bile. In doing so, this speeds up the process of digestion.

½ cup (112 g) butter, melted

½ cup (170 g) organic honey

½ cup (115 g) Immune-Boosting Yogurt (page 158)

½ cup (120 ml) lemon juice

2 tablespoons grated lemon rind

½ teaspoon minced fresh ginger, peeled

¼ teaspoon salt, Celtic or sea

½ teaspoon vanilla extract

Place the butter and honey in a food processor and blend until fluffy. Add the yogurt, lemon juice, lemon rind, ginger, salt, and vanilla extract and whip until the butter becomes fluffy. Transfer the contents to an airtight container and refrigerate for at least 3 hours before using.

Yield: 2 cups

Note: Ginger has been used for centuries both for its culinary offerings and powerful medicinal benefits. Several health compounds in ginger, including gingerols and zingerone, are effective anti-inflammatory agents and have gastrointestinal soothing effects. Some research has shown ginger to be more effective against bacterial infections than antibiotics.

Sweet and Savory Sensations

Use Immune-Building Lemon and Ginger Butter as a creamy, delicious base for cakes and muffins. Or, for a tantalizing taste sensation, add a dollop over cooked pasta and seafood dishes such as seared or roasted salmon or grilled clams.

--------[NUTRITIONAL ANALYSIS]--------

Per tablespoon: 47.6 calories; 3.1 g fat; 0.3 g protein; 5.1 g carbs; 0 g fiber; 37.4 mg sodium.

BONE-BUILDING FRENCH CREAM

This highly versatile, European-style, sour-tasting cream is loaded with beneficial bacteria called pro-biotics that provide a wide array of health benefits. This will become an indispensable ingredient in your kitchen, and you'll probably never go back to store-bought sour cream again after trying this one.

2½ cups (570 ml) heavy whipping cream, preferably organic

½ cup (115 g) Immune-Boosting Yogurt (page 158), or use plain yogurt, preferably organic

Pour the cream into a saucepan over medium heat and bring to just before boiling. Do not let boil. Remove from the heat and transfer to a glass jar with a screw-top lid. Mix in the yogurt, let cool to room temperature, secure with the lid, and place inside a cupboard at room temperature for 24 hours. After 24 hours remove the jar gently from the cupboard and refrigerate for at least 8 hours. It will keep in the refrigerator for up to 2 weeks.

Yield: 3 cups

Note: Studies have shown that fermented dairy products alleviate symptoms of lactose intolerance and improve calcium absorption.

RESTORATIVE CUCUMBER-YOGURT RAITA

Raita is a very versatile and cooling side dish that goes well with curry and over the top of spicy foods or hot dishes such as beans or rice. Cucumbers are loaded with antioxidant nutrients, such as vitamin C, and contain the heart-healthy minerals potassium and magnesium. Increase the sweetness of this dish by adding a few grapes or some diced pineapple.

2 cups (460 g) Immune-Boosting Yogurt (page 158), or use unsweetened natural yogurt

1 cucumber, peeled and coarsely grated

2 fresh scallions, finely chopped

1 small green chile pepper, finely chopped

1 clove garlic, minced

1 teaspoon grated fresh ginger, peeled

Juice of 1 lemon or lime

1 tablespoon (6 g) chopped fresh mint

¼ teaspoon black peppercorns

1 teaspoon cumin seeds

Pour the yogurt and cucumber into a small bowl and combine well. Add the scallions, chile, garlic, ginger, lemon or lime juice, mint, and peppercorns and blend together. Heat the cumin seeds over medium heat in a dry pan until they smoke, about 30 seconds, then add to the raita. Leave at least 1 hour in the refrigerator before serving so that flavors meld.

Yield: 2 ½ cups

Note: Yogurt is a good source of bioavailable calcium and protein because of its live cultures.

[NUTRITIONAL ANALYSIS]

Per tablespoon: 46 calories; 4.8 g fat; 0.4 g protein; 0.6 g carbs; 0 g fiber; 7.3 mg sodium.

[NUTRITIONAL ANALYSIS]

Per tablespoon: 10.4 calories; 0.5 g fat; 0.5 g protein; 0.9 g carbs; 0.2 g fiber; 6.7 mg sodium.

IMMUNE-BOOSTING YOGURT

No healthy kitchen is complete without fermented foods such as yogurt, which are laden with enzymes and friendly bacteria that balance your "inner eco-system." The probiotics in yogurt have a powerful, beneficial effect on your gut's immune system, your first line of defense against pathogens. Flavor your yogurt using 3 tablespoons of a natural, all-fruit jam, such as our Berry-Buzz Jelly (page 155).

1 quart (946 ml) milk, preferably organic

¼ cup (60 g) natural yogurt or 1 package powdered yogurt starter such as Greek or Bulgarian

Scald the milk by bringing it to just below boiling in a medium pan. Do not boil. Allow it to cool to around 110°F (43°C). Whisk in the yogurt or starter culture and pour into a screw-top jar and attach lid. Store for 24 hours in a dark place at room temperature. Yogurt is finished culturing when the milk solids gently separate from the walls of the jar when tipped gently to one side. When the yogurt is finished culturing, reserve ¼ cup to be used to culture your next batch. Refrigerate in an airtight jar for up to 2 weeks.

Yield: 2 cups

Note: To make coconut milk yogurt, use 1 quart (946 ml) of coconut milk in place of the dairy milk. Coconut milk yogurts are not typically able to be recultured time and time again as are dairy-based yogurts.

─────[**NUTRITIONAL ANALYSIS**]─────

Per tablespoon: 19.4 calories; 1 g fat; 1 g protein; 1.5 g carbs; 0 g fiber; 15.6 mg sodium.

PROBIOTIC FRUIT CHUTNEY

Pineapple is rich in food enzymes, particularly bromelain, which helps to break down protein. It is also a good source of manganese. The fresh cilantro and serrano chiles give a nice kick to this dish, which goes well with grilled fish or meats or with a salad.

1 small, ripe pineapple, peeled, cored, and chopped

2 ripe pears, peeled, cored, and chopped

1 cup (16 g) finely minced cilantro leaves

1 tablespoon (10 g) finely minced ginger, peeled

2 serrano chile peppers, seeded if desired, and minced

½ teaspoon ground cloves

1 teaspoon ground cinnamon

¼ cup whey starter culture plus 2 additional tablespoons

In a food processor, place all the ingredients except the starter culture and process until finely chopped. Stir in ¼ cup of the starter culture. Spoon the chutney mixture in batches into a mason jar and mash with a wooden spoon until the pineapple and pear release their juices. Continue spooning the mixture into the jar and mashing it until the liquid covers the pineapple and pear solids. Spoon the additional 2 tablespoons starter culture over the chutney and cover it loosely, leaving 1 inch (2.5 cm) of headspace to allow for expansion. Place the chutney in a dark spot in your kitchen at room temperature and allow to ferment for 2 to 3 days before removing to cold storage. Secure the lid before refrigerating. It should keep for 6 to 8 weeks if refrigerated.

Yield: 1 quart

─────[**NUTRITIONAL ANALYSIS**]─────

Per tablespoon: 9.3 calories; 0.1 g fat; 0.2 g protein; 2.2 g carbs; 0.3 g fiber; 8.8 mg sodium.

SWEET ENDINGS
DESSERTS
AND OTHER DELIGHTS

- **COOKIES, CAKES, & BREADS** 160
- **PUDDINGS, PIES, & OTHER DESSERTS** 166

Few things are more rewarding in life than treating yourself to the occasional sweet treat, especially one that is packed with antioxidants, minerals, phytonutrients, and more! These simple and delectable pleasures are made entirely from nature's finest sweets, utilizing natural, high-quality ingredients and smart substitutions for notoriously no-no ingredients. Dried and fresh fruits, fruit juice and fruit juice concentrate, honey, molasses, and maple syrup are healthier choices compared to sugar and artificial sweeteners. I've also included whole grains, nuts, and even a few vegetables that come from whole food sources. They are nutrient dense to provide plenty of essential vitamins and minerals, and will not only satisfy your desire to indulge those sweet cravings, but actually enhance the flavors and improve the desserts. These are sweets to celebrate.

HEARTY HAZELNUT ROUNDS

Enjoy the sweet, nutty burst of flavor with these crispy cookies made from a combination of nut flours. Hazelnuts, also known as filberts, are packed full of heart-healthy nutrients, such as magnesium, calcium, protein, fiber, and vitamins E and B complex. Hazelnut is quite often added to coffee for a rich, delicious flavor, so enjoy one or two of these with your morning or afternoon brew.

2½ cups (338 g) hazelnuts

⅓ cup (75 g) butter, softened

⅔ cup (230 g) organic honey

3 eggs

2½ cups (288 g) almond flour

¼ teaspoon ground cardamom

¼ teaspoon ground cloves

½ teaspoon ground ginger

1 teaspoon ground cinnamon

1 teaspoon vanilla extract

1 teaspoon grated orange or lemon rind

Dash of salt, Celtic or sea

Preheat the oven to 300°F (150°C, gas mark 2). Line a baking sheet with parchment paper or grease with butter.

Place the hazelnuts in a food processor and grind into a meal. In a medium bowl, combine the butter, honey, and eggs until creamy. In another bowl, combine the almond flour, hazelnut meal, spices, vanilla extract, and lemon rind and mix together until smooth. Spread the dough onto the baking sheet about ¼ inch (6 mm) thick. Bake for 20 minutes. Remove from the oven and let cool for about 10 minutes. Using a round cookie cutter, cut out as many shapes as possible. Store them in an airtight container.

Yield: About 20 cookies

Note: Hazelnuts are one of the best sources of the antioxidant vitamin E, which is supportive of the heart muscle and all other muscles in the body.

[NUTRITIONAL ANALYSIS]

Per serving: 188 calories; 14.1 g fat; 4.7 g protein; 13.5 g carbs; 2.1 g fiber; 48 mg sodium.

LUSCIOUS LEMON-PINEAPPLE YOGURT CAKE

With its combination of sweet and sour tastes, this deliciously light and moist yogurt cake is a perfect after-dinner treat or something to enjoy with your morning tea on those special occasions. Pineapple and lemons are both rich in antioxidants, particularly vitamin C, to support a healthy heart, and are known for their anti-inflammatory qualities. This one is sure to be a hit with the whole family and your guests.

1 teaspoon butter or coconut oil

4 eggs, separated

½ cup (170 g) organic honey

2 teaspoons vanilla extract

½ teaspoon almond extract

2 cups (460 g) Immune-Building Yogurt (page 158)

Juice of 1 lemon

Rind of 1 lemon, finely grated

1 cup (155 g) pineapple, finely chopped

2 cups (230 g) almond flour

2 teaspoons baking soda

1 cup (125 g) raspberries

Preheat the oven to 350°F (180°C, gas mark 4). Grease an 8-inch (20-cm) square baking tin with the butter or coconut oil.

In a large mixing bowl, combine the egg yolks with the honey, vanilla and almond extracts, yogurt, lemon juice, and rind and mix well. Add the pineapple. In a separate bowl, combine the almond flour with the baking soda and add to the egg yolk mixture. Beat the egg whites until stiff, about 3 or 4 minutes, and gently fold into the mixture. Pour the mixture into the prepared cake tin and bake for 1 hour, or until the cake feels spongy. Let cool before removing from the tin. Serve with fresh raspberries and Bone-Building French Cream (page 157).

Yield: 8 servings

Note: Pineapple contains the enzyme bromelain, which helps regulate the secretions of the pancreas to aid in digestion.

[NUTRITIONAL ANALYSIS]

Per serving: 363.7 calories; 21 g fat; 13.5 g protein; 34.5 g carbs; 4.3 g fiber; 417.1 mg sodium.

HEALTH-GRATIFYING GRAPEFRUIT AND ORANGE CAKE

This lusciously light and fluffy cake is a family favorite that doesn't last long whenever I make it. It has just the right amount of tang and sweetness, which is enhanced when served with the sour taste of Bone-Building French Cream (page 157). Oranges and grapefruits are loaded with antioxidant nutrients that protect against heart disease and are effective in preventing and treating many others.

FOR THE CAKE:

1 tablespoon (14 g) coconut butter

2 medium oranges

1 lemon

1 teaspoon minced fresh ginger, peeled

¾ cup (255 g) organic honey

6 eggs

½ cup (58 g) coconut flour

1 ½ cups (173 g) almond flour

1 teaspoon baking soda

½ teaspoon salt, Celtic or sea

FOR THE SYRUP:

¾ cup (255 g) organic honey

½ cup (120 ml) fresh grapefruit juice

½ cup (120 ml) fresh orange juice

Rind from half of orange, thinly sliced

Rind from half of grapefruit, thinly sliced

To make the cake: Preheat the oven to 350°F (180°C, gas mark 4). Grease a 9-inch (23-cm) round cake pan with the coconut butter. Wash the orange and lemon and place them whole in a saucepan covered with cold water. Bring to a boil and simmer for 1 hour, or until the fruit becomes soft. Check the water level and add more if needed. Slice the fruit open, remove the seeds, place in a food processor, and puree. Add the ginger, honey, eggs, flours, baking soda, and salt and blend well. Add a tablespoon of filtered water if the mixture is too dry. Pour the mixture into the greased cake pan and bake for 1 hour, until a tooth-pick stuck in the center comes out clean. Cool in the pan for 2 hours before removing.

To make the syrup: Place the honey, grapefruit and orange juices, and rinds in a small saucepan. Bring to a boil. Simmer for about 10 minutes, until the rinds look translucent. Remove the rinds and decorate the top of the cake with them. Pour the syrup over the top and serve with Bone-Building French Cream.

Yield: 6 to 8 servings

Note: Grapefruit contains compounds that are known to increase circulating levels of certain drugs, including statins. If this is an issue for you, then you may want to eliminate the grapefruit and add more orange instead. In general, it's recommended that you avoid consuming grapefruit if you take any pharmaceutical medications.

[NUTRITIONAL ANALYSIS]

Per serving: 109.6 calories; 0.1 g fat; 0.3 g protein; 29.2 g carbs; 0.1 g fiber; 1.6 mg sodium.

ALMIGHTY ALMOND AND WALNUT PUMPERNICKEL BREAD

This dense, high-fiber bread has a wonderful flavor that goes well with sweet or savory toppings. The nuts and seeds give it extra nutrients, while the almond flour allows you to consume baked bread without any gluten.

1 cup (120 g) walnuts

¼ cup (36 g) sunflower seeds

¼ cup (35 g) pumpkin seeds

3 cups (345 g) almond flour

1 teaspoon baking soda

½ teaspoon ground nutmeg

1 teaspoon anise or caraway seeds (optional)

½ teaspoon salt, Celtic or sea

3 eggs

⅓ cup (75 g) butter or ghee

1 tablespoon (20 g) unsulphured molasses

1 teaspoon vanilla extract

Preheat the oven to 350°F (180°C, gas mark 4). Grease a 4- by 8-inch (10- by 20-cm) loaf pan. Place the walnuts, sunflower seeds, and pumpkin seeds into a food processor and blend for about 10 seconds. Remove the sharp blade from the processor and insert the mixing blade. Add the flour, baking soda, nutmeg, anise or caraway seeds, and salt and pulse the ingredients together. Add the eggs, butter or ghee, molasses, and vanilla extract and blend into the mixture. Pour the batter into the greased loaf pan and bake for 45 minutes, or until the top is browned and cracked. Remove from the oven and let cool before removing from the pan. Transfer to an airtight container and refrigerate. It will keep for up to 1 week.

Yield: 10 silces

Recipe Variation

You can add a banana, or 1 cup (145 g) of raisins or dates (160 g), to this bread to increase sweetness or add more flavor.

---[NUTRITIONAL ANALYSIS]---

Per serving: 382.5 calories; 34.6 g fat; 11.9 g protein; 12.3 g carbs; 4.8 g fiber; 59.1 mg sodium.

POWERHOUSE PUMPKIN, SPICE, AND ALMOND BREAD

This mouthwatering, nutritious pumpkin bread is a good source of dietary fiber and helps in regulating blood sugar levels. The combination of almond flour and coconut flour creates a more breadlike texture than using either one alone. This tastes great as is or with a smearing of butter or fruit jelly.

1 tablespoon (15 ml) coconut oil

3 cups (345 g) almond flour

½ cup (58 g) coconut flour

½ teaspoon salt, Celtic or sea

1 teaspoon baking soda

3 large eggs

¼ cup (55 g) butter or ghee

1 tablespoon (15 ml) apple cider vinegar

1 cup (240 g) pumpkin, peeled, cooked, and mashed

1 teaspoon minced fresh ginger, peeled

½ teaspoon cinnamon

½ teaspoon ground cloves (optional)

1 tablespoon (6 g) grated orange zest

1 cup (120 g) walnuts, chopped

½ cup (75 g) raisins (optional)

Preheat the oven to 350°F (180°C, gas mark 4). Grease an 8-inch (20-cm) loaf tin with the coconut oil. In a food processor, pulse the almond flour, coconut flour, salt, and baking soda together. Add the eggs, butter, and vinegar and mix together. Add the pumpkin, ginger, cinnamon, cloves, if using, and orange zest and blend together. Toss in the walnuts and raisins, if using. Transfer the contents to the prepared loaf tin and bake for 35 to 45 minutes, until the top of the loaf feels firm. Cool the bread in the pan for 2 hours before removing. Serve immediately or store in an airtight container in the refrigerator.

Yield: 10 slices

Note: This bread freezes well. Thaw at room temperature for 2 hours and reheat by placing in the oven for 10 minutes.

---[NUTRITIONAL ANALYSIS]---

Per serving: 368.6 calories; 30.1 g fat; 11.4 g protein; 17.6 g carbs; 5 g fiber; 215 mg sodium.

NOURISHING CRUSTY ONION AND PARMESAN ROLLS

These scrumptious rolls are always a hit and are snapped up quickly whenever I make them. I sometimes spice them up with a clove of fresh garlic, which goes nicely with Italian dishes, such as lasagna. The almond flour not only gives them a delicious, nutty taste compared with wheat flour but contains heart-healthy micronutrients such as vitamin E, potassium, and calcium.

4 tablespoons (56 g) butter or ghee, divided

1 large onion, finely chopped

2 tablespoons (40 g) organic honey

1 teaspoon finely chopped rosemary

1 teaspoon salt, Celtic or sea

1 teaspoon black pepper

2 large eggs

3 cups (345 g) almond flour

1 teaspoon baking soda

¾ cup (75 g) grated Parmesan or Cheddar cheese

1 tablespoon (4 g) finely chopped parsley

1 tablespoon (15 ml) olive oil

Preheat the oven to 350°F (180°C, gas mark 4). Grease a 9- by 13-inch (23- by 33-cm) baking sheet with 1 tablespoon (14 g) butter or ghee. Heat 1 tablespoon butter or ghee in a large skillet over medium-high heat. Add the onions, honey, rosemary, salt, and pepper and cook for about 5 to 7 minutes, until golden brown.

In a large bowl, whisk together the eggs and 2 tablespoons (28 g) butter or ghee, then add the flour, baking soda, cheese, and parsley and blend together. Add the cooked onion mixture and knead together until a sticky dough forms. Moisten your hands with water, form the dough into 8 balls, and place them onto the greased baking sheet, spacing evenly. With a sharp knife, trace a cross over the top of the buns and brush the tops with the olive oil. Bake until the rolls are golden, about 15 to 20 minutes. The rolls should feel firm. Remove from the oven and let cool for several minutes before serving.

Yield: 8 rolls

Note: The rolls can be made into biscuits by increasing the onion and cheese to 1 cup each. Form into drop biscuits on a parchment-lined sheet, and bake for 15 to 20 minutes, or until lightly browned on top and cooked through.

[NUTRITIONAL ANALYSIS]

Per serving: 390.5 calories; 32.5 g fat; 14.8 g protein; 15.5 g carbs; 4.9 g fiber; 440 mg sodium.

FORTIFYING FIG AND MINTY BLUEBERRY BRÛLÉE

Enjoy the creamy, sweet taste of these delicious fresh fruit and custard treats. Figs are loaded with potassium, a mineral that helps to control blood pressure. Blueberries contain a ton of antioxidants, especially vitamin C, and a tangy flavor that comes to life in this dish.

½ cup (85 g) ripe fresh figs, sliced

1 cup (145 g) fresh blueberries

1 tablespoon (6 g) finely chopped fresh mint

3 cups (705 ml) Bone-Building French Cream (page 157)

5 egg yolks

¼ cup (85 g) organic honey

1 teaspoon vanilla extract

3 fresh strawberries, halved

Preheat the oven to 350°F (180°C, gas mark 4). Set aside 6 small ramekins. Combine the figs, blueberries, and mint in a bowl. In a medium saucepan over medium heat, pour the cream, egg yolks, honey, and vanilla extract and whisk until well combined, about 1 minute. Do not boil. Remove from the heat and set aside.

Place the fruit into the bottom of the ramekins. Add the cream mixture over the top of the fruit. Place the ramekins into a deep baking dish with water that reaches halfway up the ramekins and bake for 35 minutes, until the custard has set but is still slightly jiggly. Remove from the water bath and let cool at room temperature before refrigerating. Refrigerate for at least 3 hours before serving. Garnish with half a strawberry on top.

Yield: 6 servings

Note: Switch up the flavors by changing the fruits you use. For example, add 1 tablespoon of orange zest when heating the cream and eggs, and line the bottom of the ramekins with fresh orange pieces.

[NUTRITIONAL ANALYSIS]

Per serving: 485.4 calories; 42.2 g fat; 5.8 g protein; 23.6 g carbs; 1.2 g fiber; 67.3 mg sodium.

ENERGY-GIVING COCONUT, ALMOND, AND RAISIN CUSTARD

This refreshing nondairy custard is delicious served for dessert or enjoyed at breakfast over granola. The coconut and almond milks contain more nutrients than dairy milk and provide your body with protein and healthy fats to boost your metabolism. Feel free to add a few dates with the raisins for added sweetness.

½ cup (75 g) raisins

1 cup (235 ml) almond milk

1 cup (235 ml) coconut milk

5 egg yolks, whisked

1 teaspoon vanilla extract

½ teaspoon ground nutmeg

1 teaspoon cinnamon

1 cup (145 g) strawberries, halved

Preheat the oven to 300°F (150°C, gas mark 2). Evenly sprinkle the raisins over the bottom of an 8-inch (20-cm) square oven dish. Have a larger-size oven dish at the ready that will house the smaller dish.

In a medium saucepan, combine the almond milk, coconut milk, and egg yolks over medium heat. Do not boil. Remove from the heat and stir in the vanilla extract. Pour the mixture over the raisins and sprinkle with nutmeg and cinnamon. Place the dish inside of the larger oven dish and fill the larger dish with hot water until it reaches halfway up the smaller dish. Gently place in the oven for 35 minutes, or until the top starts to feel firm but is still slightly jiggly.

Remove from the oven and water bath and let stand for 5 or 10 minutes before serving or refrigerating. Decorate with slices of strawberry before serving.

Yield: 6 servings

Note: Almond milk is high in heart-healthy vitamin E and is a good source of calcium.

---[NUTRITIONAL ANALYSIS]---

Per serving: 186.3 calories; 11 g fat; 3.7 g protein; 16.9 g carbs; 1.4 g fiber; 42.7 mg sodium.

BLUEBERRY AND APPLE CRUMBLE GONE NUTS

Blueberries and apples are a great combination for a wonderful, warm crisp that can be made in a snap. They are loaded with antioxidant vitamins C, A, and E and minerals such as selenium and zinc, all of which boost your immune system. Walnuts add a crunchy texture and are rich in essential ALA, the plant-based form of omega-3 fatty acids.

FOR THE FILLING:

4 large green apples, peeled, cored, and cut into thin wedges

Juice of ½ lemon (about 1 tablespoon [15 ml])

¼ cup (60 ml) filtered water

1 teaspoon grated lemon rind

2 tablespoons (40 g) organic honey, divided

2 cups (290 g) blueberries, fresh or frozen

½ teaspoon cinnamon

¼ teaspoon mace (optional)

FOR THE TOPPING:

⅔ cup (76 g) almond flour

½ cup (40 g) rolled oats

¼ cup (55 g) butter

1 teaspoon organic honey

1 cup (120 g) walnuts

Preheat the oven to 350°F (180°C, gas mark 4). Grease an 8-inch (20-cm) square baking dish with butter.

To make the filling: Toss the apples, lemon juice, water, lemon zest, and 1 tablespoon of the honey into a medium saucepan and cook, covered, for 5 minutes, over low heat. Remove the lid and simmer on high for another 5 minutes. Remove from the heat, add the blueberries, cinnamon, and mace to the pot, and let sit for about 10 minutes, until the blueberries soften and flavors meld. Drain the fruit of its juices in a sieve and set the fruit aside in a small bowl. Pour the juice back into the saucepan, adding the remaining tablespoon of honey, and simmer until reduced down by half. Retain this syrup for later. Cool the fruit in the refrigerator.

To make the topping: In a food processor, add the almond flour, rolled oats, butter, honey, and walnuts and blend until chunky crumbs are formed. Refrigerate the crumble for 10 minutes. When the fruit has cooled, place the fruit into a baking dish and top it with the crumble. Bake for 20 minutes. Serve warm topped with Bone-Building French Cream (page 158) or Immune-Boosting Yogurt (page 157).

Yield: 4 servings

Note: This nutritionally loaded dish is great served at breakfast or as an afternoon snack.

---[NUTRITIONAL ANALYSIS]---

Per serving: 659 calories; 41.7 g fat; 11.9 g protein; 69.1 g carbs; 12.1 g fiber; 87.3 mg sodium.

BERRY-BENEFICIAL BLUEBERRY AND PECAN PIE

This pecans in this classic pie are an excellent source of the antioxidant vitamin E, which is well known for improving heart health. Blueberries are packed with the antioxidant vitamin C and add a tangy flavor that comes to life when you add a hint of lemon.

FOR THE CRUST:

2½ cups (250 g) pecans

2 tablespoons (28 ml) coconut oil

¼ cup (85 g) organic honey

1 teaspoon vanilla extract

½ cup (58 g) coconut flour

1 egg

¼ teaspoon salt, Celtic or sea

½ teaspoon baking soda

FOR THE FILLING:

3 cups (465 g) frozen blueberries

2 green apples, peeled, cored, and cut into thin wedges

⅓ cup (80 ml) fresh lemon juice

1 teaspoon grated fresh lemon zest

¾ cup (255 g) organic honey

To make the crust: Soak the pecans in filtered water for 1 hour and then drain and dry with a paper towel. When dried, spread the nuts evenly over a baking sheet and place in an oven heated to 150°F for about 5 hours, or until crispy. Remove from the oven, transfer the crispy nuts to a food processor, and grind to a nut butter. Transfer to a large bowl. Turn the oven temperature up to 300°F (150°C, gas mark 2). Add the oil, honey, and vanilla extract to the processed nuts and blend. Add the coconut flour, egg, salt, and baking soda and blend together. If the batter is too soft, add more coconut flour, 1 teaspoon at a time, until it thickens into a ball. Press the crust batter into a greased 9-inch (23-cm) round pie dish and bake for 30 minutes, until the crust is golden brown. If the crust is getting too dark, cover with a piece of foil. Remove from the oven and let cool completely at room temperature.

To make the filling: Place the blueberries, apples, lemon juice, zest, and honey in a large pot and bring to a boil. Reduce to a simmer and cook uncovered for about 15 to 20 minutes, until the liquid has thickened. Remove from the heat, place in a covered bowl, and refrigerate for at least 3 to 4 hours, or overnight. Once set, fill the piecrust with the mixture. Serve warm or cold with Bone-Building French Cream (page 157).

Yield: 6 to 8 servings

Note: Research has shown that adding just a small handful of pecans to your diet each day can inhibit unwanted oxidation of blood lipids, thus helping prevent the oxidation of LDL cholesterol.

[NUTRITIONAL ANALYSIS]

Per serving: 589.3 calories; 33 g fat; 7.4 g protein; 75.9 g carbs; 11.9 g fiber; 169.3 mg sodium.

ANTI-OX ORANGE MOUSSE

Enjoy the tangy, sweet taste of oranges in this super-simple mousse. Oranges contain a high amount of antioxidants and more than 170 phytonutrients and 60 flavonoids, all of which have been shown to have anti-inflammatory, anticancer, and heart-healthy benefits and to promote optimum health. It's deliciously smooth and creamy.

½ cup (170 g) organic honey, divided

Grated rind from 1 orange

¼ cup (60 ml) + 2 tablespoons (28 ml) cold filtered water, divided

1 teaspoon gelatin

1½ cups (355 ml) Bone-Building French Cream (page 157)

⅔ cup (160 ml) fresh orange juice

2 tablespoons (28 ml) lemon juice

1 teaspoon vanilla extract

½ teaspoon ground nutmeg

1 teaspoon cinnamon

4 orange slices

In a small, nonstick saucepan, combine the honey, orange zest, and ¼ cup (60 ml) water and simmer for 1 minute. Turn the heat off. Soak the gelatin in 2 tablespoons (28 ml) cold water and add to the hot honey, stirring well. Transfer the contents to a ceramic bowl, refrigerate for about 20 minutes, and then remove.

In a medium bowl, whip the cream until quite thick. Add the orange and lemon juices, vanilla extract, and the thickened honey. Pour equal amounts of the mixture into 6 individual ramekins and refrigerate for at least 3 to 4 hours, until the mousse sets. Remove from the refrigerator and dip the ramekins into hot water for about 10 seconds. Using a knife, separate the edges of the mousse away from the ramekins and place upside down onto the center of a dessert plate. Decorate with nutmeg, cinnamon, and a slice of orange and serve.

Yield: 4 servings

Note: Apart from their delightful taste, oranges also contain vitamins A and B$_1$. One medium-size orange contains nearly 100 percent of the daily intake of vitamin C.

[NUTRITIONAL ANALYSIS]

Per serving: 472 calories; 29 g fat; 3.4 g protein; 53.5 g carbs; 0.3 g fiber; 47.2 mg sodium.

SOOTHING PEAR, DATE, AND ALMOND PUDDING WITH GRAPEFRUIT CREAM SAUCE

The soft, sweet, buttery flesh of pears studded with sticky dates makes for a comforting dessert fit for any occasion. Pears are packed with heart-healthy fiber, potassium, and vitamin C. Dates are loaded with essential minerals such as calcium, iron, potassium, magnesium, and phosphorus. Serve it with whipped cream or as-is—it's simply divine!

FOR THE PUDDING:

3 tablespoons (42 g) butter, room temperature

2 tablespoons (40 g) organic honey, divided

1½ cups (173 g) almond flour

½ teaspoon salt, Celtic or sea

1 teaspoon vanilla extract

1 teaspoon almond extract or 2 tablespoons (28 ml) amaretto liqueur

1 whole egg

3 eggs, separated

7 to 8 large dates, pitted and finely chopped

2 large pears, peeled, cored, and finely chopped

FOR THE SAUCE:

3 egg yolks

4 tablespoons (80 g) organic honey

1 teaspoon vanilla extract

1 cup (235 ml) Bone-Building French Cream (page 157)

½ cup (120 ml) fresh grapefruit juice

1 teaspoon grated orange zest

Preheat the oven to 370°F. Lightly butter 6 small ramekins.

To make the pudding: In a large bowl, add the butter and 1 tablespoon (20 g) honey and beat until creamy. Blend in the almond flour, salt, vanilla extract, almond extract or amaretto, whole egg, and 3 egg yolks. Fold the dates and pears into the mixture.

In a separate bowl, whisk the egg whites until they stiffen, about 2 to 3 minutes with a handheld whisk or 1 minute with an electric beater. Add the rest of the honey and whisk until thick and creamy. Fold this into the almond flour mixture. Spoon the mixture into the prepared ramekins and bake for 25 to 30 minutes, or until the puddings feel spongy. Remove from the oven and let cool for 10 minutes before turning them onto serving plates. Top with grapefruit cream sauce. Sprinkle with orange zest.

To make the sauce: In a small bowl, combine the egg yolks, honey, and vanilla extract and place in a pot of hot water that reaches a quarter of the way up the bowl. Simmer the water gently and do not let it boil. Remove from the heat after 2 minutes as it begins to thicken. Add the cream, grapefruit juice, and orange zest and whisk until smooth. Let cool and serve with the puddings.

Yield: 6 servings

Note: For a different taste sensation, try swapping the pears for pineapple or apple or a combination of these with the pears.

[NUTRITIONAL ANALYSIS]

Per serving: 531.8 calories; 36.7 g fat; 12.8 g protein; 44.3 g carbs; 5.1 g fiber; 232 mg sodium.

SWEET BROWN RICE PUDDING WITH AN ANTIOXIDANT TWIST

Because of its high fiber content, this delicious pudding is especially helpful in maintaining a healthy digestive system. The eggs and cream combine well to give a fluffy texture, and the nuts provide crunch as well as nutrient density. Enjoy this tasty, hearty dish for dessert, breakfast, or as an anytime snack.

3 eggs

1 cup (235 ml) Bone-Building French Cream (page 157) or use heavy cream, preferably organic

⅓ cup (80 ml) maple syrup

1 teaspoon vanilla extract

1 teaspoon ground cinnamon

½ teaspoon ground nutmeg

1 cup (160 g) whole grain brown rice, rinsed, drained, and cooked

1 tablespoon (8 g) finely grated fresh ginger, peeled

1 cup (145 g) raisins

1 cup (110 g) pecans or walnuts (120 g), chopped

1 mashed banana (optional)

Preheat the oven to 325°F (170°C, gas mark 3). Beat the eggs with the cream, maple syrup, vanilla extract, cinnamon, and nutmeg. Stir in the rice, ginger, raisins, nuts, and banana. Pour the contents into a 9-inch (23-cm) baking dish and bake for approximately 45 minutes, or until the eggs have set. Remove from the oven and let cool or serve hot with Bone-Building French Cream (page 157). This will stay fresh refrigerated for up to 1 week.

Yield: 4 servings

Note: Ginger contains several medicinal compounds, including gingerol, which is especially effective for supporting heart health.

[NUTRITIONAL ANALYSIS]

Per serving: 531.5 calories; 29.7 g fat; 10.9 g protein; 62.8 g carbs; 4 g fiber; 60.3 mg sodium.

NO-BAKE SUPERFOOD FUDGE BROWNIES

Enjoy the fruity, nutty, and chocolate flavor of this nutritionally superb dessert that lies somewhere between a brownie and fudge square. Cacao is a well-known superfood because of its high content of antioxidants and other important nutrients such as protein, healthy fat, magnesium, calcium, zinc, fiber, and iron. And best of all, you can make these in about 5 minutes!

1 cup (100 g) raw walnut pieces

1 cup (160 g) packed, soft Medjool dates, (about 10 or 11), pits removed

½ cup (50 g) cacao powder

¾ cup (60 g) shredded coconut, divided

½ teaspoon salt, Celtic or sea

1 to 2 tablespoons (15 to 28 ml) filtered water

½ cup (85 g) cacao nibs

Place the walnuts in a food processor and pulse for a few seconds to form a coarse meal. While the machine is still running, add the dates, cacao powder, ½ cup shredded coconut, salt, and 1 tablespoon (15 ml) of the filtered water, processing until a moist, crumblike dough forms. Depending on the natural moisture of the dates, you may need to add a touch more water to get the crumbs to stick when pinched together.

Spread the mixture into an 8- by 8-inch (20- by 20-cm) pan and sprinkle with the cacao nibs and remaining shredded coconut. Press the mixture firmly into a solid brownie layer. Refrigerate for about 2 hours. Cut into bite-size squares and serve.

Yield: 24 small squares

Note: Cacao is a type of tropical tree that produces the world's chocolate in raw form, before sugar, fat, and other ingredients are added. Several hundred years ago, cacao beans were so valuable that they were used as a form of currency.

[NUTRITIONAL ANALYSIS]

Per serving: 85.7 calories; 5.8 g fat; 1.7 g protein; 9.1 g carbs; 2 g fiber; 29.7 mg sodium.

A MONTH OF
• MENU PLANS •
FOR HEART HEALTH

WEEK 1 EATING PLAN SUGGESTIONS

Sunday

BREAKFAST
Brain-Boosting Salmon Eggs Benedict (page 85), or Hearty Mediterranean Frittata (page 87)

LUNCH
Feel-Good Turkey or Salmon Tomato Panini (page 102), or Energizing Thai Spice Chicken Salad (page 95) with Energizing Thai Spice Salad Dressing (page 98)

SNACK (OPTIONAL)
Spiced Honey-Glazed Nuts (page 113), or Blood Sugar–Balancing Butternut and Leek Pies (page 110)

DINNER
Protein-Packed Vegetarian Shepherd's Pie (page 119), or Soul-Warming Tuna Lasagna (page 133) with Cardioprotective Green Beans (page 148)

Monday

BREAKFAST
Get-Up-and-Go Banana Berry Quinoa Porridge (page 81), or Melt-in-Your Mouth Baked Granola (page 82)

LUNCH
Cardioprotective Salmon Caesar Salad (page 94) with Cardioprotective Caesar Salad Dressing (page 97), or Stress-Less Turkey, Avocado, and Veggie Nori Wrap (page 99)

SNACK (OPTIONAL)
2 to 3 Low-Carb Herbed Cheddar Crackers (page 109), or High-Energy Chicken and Cauliflower Croquettes (page 111)

DINNER
Revitalizing Vegetable Biryani (page 122), or Anti-Inflammatory Turmeric Turkey Burgers (page 140) with Anti-Ox Pumpkin and Cauliflower Mash (page 144)

Tuesday

BREAKFAST
Regenerating Herb Scrambled Eggs (page 83), or Melt-in-Your Mouth Baked Granola (page 82)

LUNCH
Almighty Avocado and Black Bean Salad (page 91), or Feel-Good Turkey or Salmon Tomato Panini (page 102)

SNACK (OPTIONAL)
High-Energy Chicken and Cauliflower Croquettes (page 111), or Spiced Honey-Glazed Nuts (page 113)

DINNER
Spicy Moroccan Tempeh with Lentils (page 117), or Favorite Sweet, Spicy, and Crunchy Meatloaf (page 128) with Zesty Broccoli with Garlic and Ginger (page 145)

DESSERT
Blueberry and Apple Crumble Gone Nuts (page 168), or Soothing Pear, Date, and Almond Pudding with Grapefruit Cream Sauce (page 171)

Wednesday

BREAKFAST

Protein-Powered Muesli with Coconut and Raisins (page 83), or Melt-in-Your Mouth Baked Granola (page 82)

LUNCH

Pumping Jumping Bean Salad (page 96), or Feel-Good Turkey or Salmon Tomato Panini (page 102)

SNACK (OPTIONAL)

Spiced Honey-Glazed Nuts (page 113), or Calming Coconut-Date Balls (page 114)

DINNER

Strengthening Spinach, Feta, and Rice Casserole (page 124), or Metabolism-Boosting Chicken Curry Feast (page 137) with Sustaining Ginger-Sesame Carrots (page 149)

Thursday

BREAKFAST

Melt-in-Your Mouth Baked Granola (page 82), or Protein-Powered Muesli with Coconut and Raisins (page 83)

LUNCH

Energizing Thai Spice Chicken Salad (page 95) with Energizing Thai Spice Salad Dressing (page 98), or Feel-Good Turkey or Salmon Tomato Panini (page 102)

SNACK (OPTIONAL)

High-Energy Chicken and Cauliflower Croquettes (page 111), or Spiced Honey-Glazed Nuts (page 113)

DINNER

Nutrient-Rich Roasted Quinoa with Mushrooms, Cumin, and Coriander (page 120), or Healing Baked Halibut or Salmon and Shiitake (page 134) with Luscious Lima Bean Mash (page 143)

Friday

BREAKFAST

Fortifying Flourless Chicken Flapjacks (page 84), or Regenerating Herb Scrambled Eggs (page 83)

LUNCH

2 slices of Gluten-Free Mediterranean Veggie Pizza (pages 99-100) or Feel-Good Turkey or Salmon Tomato Panini (page 102)

SNACK (OPTIONAL)

Turkey, Lamb, or Beef Koftas with a Heart-Healthy Kick (page 112), or Spiced Honey-Glazed Nuts (page 113)

DINNER

Stress-Less Shiitake and Asparagus Risotto (page 126), or Supercharged Chicken or Turkey Meat Loaf (page 139) with Sautéed Shiitake Mushrooms with a Kale Kick (page 145)

DESSERT

Blueberry and Apple Crumble Gone Nuts (page 168), or Berry-Beneficial Blueberry and Pecan Pie (page 169)

Saturday

BREAKFAST

Super-Energizing Baked Beans (page 88), or Strengthening Sun-Dried Tomato and Feta-Chive Omelet (page 86)

LUNCH

Build-Me-Up Butternut and Macadamia Nut Bisque (page 108), or 2 slices of Gluten-Free Mediterranean Veggie Pizza (pages 99-100)

SNACK (OPTIONAL)

High-Energy Chicken and Cauliflower Croquettes (page 111), or Detoxifying Lima Bean Blinis with Artichoke Herbed Dip (pages 114-115)

DINNER

Immune-Boosting Thai Tempeh Cakes with Sweet Spicy Dipping Sauce (page 125), or Nice and Spiced Beef or Chicken Stir-Fry (page 129) with Balancing Basmati Almond Rice (page 146)

DESSERT

Energy-Giving Coconut, Almond, and Raisin Custard (page 167), or Blueberry and Apple Crumble Gone Nuts (page 168)

WEEK 2 EATING PLAN SUGGESTIONS

Sunday

BREAKFAST

Get-Up-and-Go Banana Berry Quinoa Porridge (page 81), or Melt-in-Your Mouth Baked Granola (page 82)

LUNCH

Almighty Avocado and Black Bean Salad (page 91), or Love-Your-Heart Red Lentil Soup (page 106)

SNACK (OPTIONAL)

Blood-Sugar-Balancing Butternut and Leek Pies (page 110), or High-Energy Chicken and Cauliflower Croquettes (page 111)

DINNER

High-Fiber Butternut Gnocchi with Herbed Cream Sauce (page 121), or Metabolism-Boosting Chicken Curry Feast (page 137) with Sumptuous Spinach and Swiss Chard with Pine Nuts (page 147)

Monday

BREAKFAST

Regenerating Herb Scrambled Eggs (page 83), or Fortifying Flourless Chicken Flapjacks (page 84)

LUNCH

Vitalizing Broccoli and Cauliflower Salad (page 97) with Simply Nourishing Salad Dressing (page 93), or Stress-Less Turkey, Avocado, and Veggie Nori Wrap (page 99)

SNACK (OPTIONAL)

Detoxifying Lima Bean Blinis with Artichoke Herbed Dip (pages 114–115), or Spiced Honey-Glazed Nuts (page 113)

DINNER

Protein-Packed Vegetarian Shepherd's Pie (page 119), or Favorite Sweet, Spicy, and Crunchy Meat Loaf (page 128) with Zesty Broccoli with Garlic and Ginger (page 145)

Tuesday

BREAKFAST

Melt-in-Your Mouth Baked Granola (page 82), or Protein-Powered Nut Muesli with Coconut and Raisins (page 83)

LUNCH

Mood-Boosting Chicken and Pineapple Coleslaw with Coconut-Lime Dressing (page 92), or Pumping Jumping Bean Salad (page 96)

SNACK (OPTIONAL)

Turkey, Lamb, or Beef Koftas with a Heart-Healthy Kick (page 112), or Spiced Honey-Glazed Nuts (page 113)

DINNER

Hi-Fibe Red Bean Burgers (page 118), or Nice and Spiced Beef or Chicken Stir-Fry (page 129) with Cardioprotective Green Beans (page 148)

DESSERT

Sweet Brown Rice Pudding with an Antioxidant Twist (page 172), or Fortifying Fig and Minty Blueberry Brûlée (page 166)

Wednesday

BREAKFAST

Regenerating Herb Scrambled Eggs (page 83), or Fortifying Flourless Chicken Flapjacks (page 84)

LUNCH

Feel-Good Turkey or Salmon Tomato Panini (page 102), or Vibrant Avocado and Veggie Salsa Collard Wrap (page 101)

SNACK (OPTIONAL)

1 slice of Almighty Almond and Walnut Pumpernickel Bread (page 163) with Immune-Building Lemon-Ginger Butter (page 156), or Spiced Honey-Glazed Nuts (page 113)

DINNER

Stress-Less Shiitake and Asparagus Risotto (page 126), or Fisherman's Omega-3 Fish Fingers (page 130) with Fragrant Cauliflower-Quinoa Risotto (page 142)

Thursday

BREAKFAST

Get-Up-and-Go Banana Berry Quinoa Porridge (page 81), or Melt-in-Your Mouth Baked Granola (page 82)

LUNCH

Love-Your-Heart Red Lentil Soup (page 106), or Cardioprotective Salmon Caesar Salad (page 94) with Cardioprotective Caesar Salad Dressing (page 97) and 1 Nourishing Crusty Onion and Parmesan Roll (page 165)

SNACK (OPTIONAL)

1 slice of Almighty Almond and Walnut Pumpernickel Bread (page 163) with Super-Healthful Hummus (page 150)

DINNER

Revitalizing Vegetable Biryani (page 122), or Healing Baked Halibut or Salmon and Shiitake (page 139) with Cardioprotective Green Beans (page 148)

Friday

BREAKFAST

Melt-in-Your Mouth Baked Granola (page 82), or Protein-Powered Muesli with Coconut and Raisins (page 83)

LUNCH

2 slices Gluten-Free Mediterranean Veggie Pizza (pages 99-100), or Feel-Good Turkey or Salmon Tomato Panini (page 102)

SNACK (OPTIONAL)

Blood-Sugar-Balancing Butternut and Leek Pies (page 110), or 2 Calming Coconut-Date Balls (page 114)

DINNER

Spicy Moroccan Tempeh with Lentils (page 117), or Mega-Omega Spice Crusted Salmon (page 131) with Sumptuous Spinach and Swiss Chard with Pine Nuts (page 147)

DESSERT

Hearty Hazelnut Rounds (page 160), or Luscious Lemon-Pineapple Yogurt Cake (page 161)

Saturday

BREAKFAST

Super-Energizing Baked Beans (page 88), or Strengthening Sun-Dried Tomato and Feta-Chive Omelet (page 86) with 1 Zesty Digestive Herb and Cheddar Breakfast Muffin (page 89)

LUNCH

Almighty Avocado and Black Bean Salad (page 91), or Immune-Boosting Basque Bean and Cabbage Soup (page 107)

SNACK (OPTIONAL)

Detoxifying Lima Bean Blinis with Artichoke Herbed Dip (pages 114-115) with 2 to 3 Low-Carb Herbed Cheddar Crackers (page 109), or High-Energy Chicken and Cauliflower Croquettes (page 111)

DINNER

Comforting Cheddar and Broccoli Quiche with Quinoa Crust (page 123), or Spicy Shrimp and Tomato Kebabs with Herbed Lima Beans (page 135) with Sustaining Ginger-Sesame Carrots (page 149)

DESSERT

Berry-Beneficial Blueberry and Pecan Pie (page 169), or Sweet Brown Rice Pudding with an Antioxidant Twist (page 172)

WEEK 3 EATING PLAN SUGGESTIONS

Sunday

BREAKFAST

Strengthening Sun-Dried Tomato and Feta-Chive Omelet (page 186)

LUNCH

1 cup Build-Me-Up Butternut and Macadamia Nut Bisque (page 108) with 2 Low-Carb Herbed Cheddar Crackers (page 109), or 1 Feel-Good Turkey or Salmon Tomato Panini (page 102)

SNACK (OPTIONAL)

1 to 2 Blood-Sugar-Balancing Butternut and Leek Pies (page 110), or a handful of Spiced Honey-Glazed Nuts (page 113)

DINNER

Protein-Packed Vegetarian Shepherd's Pie (page 119), or Soul-Warming Tuna Lasagna (page 133) with Cardioprotective Green Beans (page 148)

Monday

BREAKFAST

Protein-Powered Muesli with Coconut and Raisins (page 83), or Regenerating Herb Scrambled Eggs (page 83)

LUNCH

Energizing Thai Spice Chicken Salad (page 95), or Vibrant Avocado and Veggie Salsa Collard Wrap (page 101)

SNACK (OPTIONAL)

1 to 2 High-Energy Chicken and Cauliflower Croquettes (page 111), or 1 to 2 Turkey, Lamb, or Beef Koftas with a Heart-Healthy Kick (page 112)

DINNER

Strengthening Spinach, Feta, and Rice Casserole (page 124), or Mega-Omega Spice-Crusted Salmon (page 131) with Zesty Broccoli with Garlic and Ginger (page 145)

Tuesday

BREAKFAST

Fortifying Flourless Chicken Flapjacks (page 84), or Melt-in-Your Mouth Baked Granola (page 82)

LUNCH

Stress-Less Turkey, Avocado, and Veggie Nori Wrap (page 99), or Cardioprotective Salmon Caesar Salad (page 94) with Cardioprotective Caesar Salad Dressing (page 97)

SNACK (OPTIONAL)

1 to 2 slices of Powerhouse Pumpkin, Spice, and Almond Bread (page 164), or handful of Spiced Honey-Glazed Nuts (page 113)

DINNER

Revitalizing Vegetable Biryani (page 122), or Spicy Shrimp and Tomato Kebabs with Herbed Lima Beans (page 135) with Luscious Lima Bean Mash (page 143)

DESSERT

Sweet Brown Rice Pudding with an Antioxidant Twist (page 172), or 1 to 2 Hearty Hazelnut Rounds (page 160)

Wednesday

BREAKFAST

Regenerating Herb Scrambled Eggs (page 83), or Get-Up-and-Go Banana Berry Quinoa Porridge (page 81)

LUNCH

Mood-Boosting Chicken and Pineapple Coleslaw with Coconut-Lime Dressing (page 92), or Pumping Jumping Bean Salad (page 96)

SNACK (OPTIONAL)

1 to 2 Calming Coconut-Date Balls (page 114), or a handful of Spiced Honey-Glazed Nuts (page 113)

DINNER

Favorite Sweet, Spicy, and Crunchy Meat Loaf (page 128) with Anti-Ox Pumpkin and Cauliflower Mash (page 144), or High-Fiber Butternut Gnocchi with Herbed Cream Sauce (page 121)

Thursday

BREAKFAST

Protein-Powered Muesli with Coconut and Raisins (page 83), or Regenerating Herb Scrambled Eggs (page 83)

LUNCH

Stress-Less Turkey, Avocado, and Veggie Nori Wrap (page 99), or Love-Your-Heart Red Lentil Soup (page 106)

SNACK (OPTIONAL)

A handful of Spiced Honey-Glazed Nuts (page 113), or 1 to 2 Calming Coconut-Date Balls (page 114)

DINNER

Stress-Less Shiitake and Asparagus Risotto (page 126), or Mighty Moroccan Chicken Tagine (page 136) with Sustaining Ginger-Sesame Carrots (page 149)

Friday

BREAKFAST

Regenerating Herb Scrambled Eggs page 83), or Fortifying Flourless Chicken Flapjacks (page 84)

LUNCH

Almighty Avocado and Black Bean Salad (page 91), or Mood-Boosting Chicken and Pineapple Coleslaw with Coconut-Lime Dressing (page 92)

SNACK (OPTIONAL)

1 to 2 Turkey, Lamb, or Beef Koftas with a Heart-Healthy Kick (page 112), or a handful of Spiced Honey-Glazed Nuts (page 113)

DINNER

Protein-Packed Vegetarian Shepherd's Pie (page 119), or Nice and Spiced Beef or Chicken Stir-Fry (page 129) with Zesty Broccoli with Garlic and Ginger (page 145)

DESSERT

Blueberry and Apple Crumble Gone Nuts (page 168), or Berry-Beneficial Blueberry and Pecan Pie (page 169)

Saturday

BREAKFAST

Super-Energizing Baked Beans (page 88), or Strengthening Sun-Dried Tomato and Feta-Chive Omelet (page 86)

LUNCH

Pumping Jumping Bean Salad (page 96), or Feel-Good Turkey or Salmon Tomato Panini (page 102)

SNACK (OPTIONAL)

Cup of Build-Me-Up Butternut and Macadamia Nut Bisque (page 108), or 1 to 2 Detoxifying Lima Bean Blinis with Artichoke Herbed Dip (pages 114–115)

DINNER

Comforting Cheddar and Broccoli Quiche with Quinoa Crust (page 123), or Metabolism-Boosting Chicken Curry Feast (page 137) with Cardioprotective Green Beans (page 148)

DESSERT

Slice of Health-Gratifying Grapefruit and Orange Cake (page 162), or 1 to 2 Hearty Hazelnut Rounds (page 160)

WEEK 4 EATING PLAN SUGGESTIONS

Sunday

BREAKFAST

Brain-Boosting Salmon Eggs Benedict (page 85), or Strengthening Sun-Dried Tomato and Feta Chive Omelet (page 86)

LUNCH

Almighty Avocado and Black Bean Salad (page 91), or Stress-Less Turkey, Avocado, and Veggie Nori Wrap (page 99)

SNACK (OPTIONAL)

Blood-Sugar-Balancing Butternut and Leek Pies (page 110), or Detoxifying Lima Bean Blinis with Artichoke Herbed Dip (pages 114–115)

DINNER

Immune-Boosting Thai Tempeh Cakes with Sweet Spicy Dipping Sauce (page 125), or Soul-Warming Tuna Lasagna (page 133) with Vitalizing Broccoli and Cauliflower Salad (page 93)

Monday

BREAKFAST

Melt-in-Your Mouth Baked Granola (page 82), or Sweet Brown Rice Pudding with an Antioxidant Twist (page 172)

LUNCH

Love-Your-Heart Red Lentil Soup (page 106), or Feel-Good Turkey or Salmon Tomato Panini (page 102)

SNACK (OPTIONAL)

Spiced Honey-Glazed Nuts (page 113), or Calming Coconut-Date Balls (page 114)

DINNER

Strengthening Spinach, Feta and Rice Casserole (page 124), or Fisherman's Omega-3 Fish Fingers (page 130) with Zesty Broccoli with Garlic and Ginger (page 145)

Tuesday

BREAKFAST

Melt-in-Your Mouth Baked Granola (page 82), or Protein-Powered Muesli with Coconut and Raisins (page 83)

LUNCH

Cardioprotective Salmon Caesar Salad (page 94) with Cardioprotective Caesar Salad Dressing (page 97), or Vibrant Avocado and Veggie Salsa Collard Wrap (page 101)

SNACK (OPTIONAL)

Spiced Honey-Glazed Nuts (page 113), or Calming Coconut-Date Balls (page 114)

DINNER

Strengthening Spinach, Feta, and Rice Casserole (page 124), or Anti-Inflammatory Turmeric Turkey Burgers (page 140) with Sustaining Ginger-Sesame Carrots (page 149)

DESSERT

No-Bake Superfood Fudge Brownies (page 173), or Fortifying Fig and Minty Blueberry Brûlée (page 166)

Wednesday

BREAKFAST

Regenerating Herb Scrambled Eggs (page 83), or Fortifying Flourless Chicken Flapjacks (page 84)

LUNCH

Pumping Jumping Bean Salad (page 96), or Feel-Good Turkey or Salmon Tomato Panini (page 102)

SNACK (OPTIONAL)

Slice of Almighty Almond and Walnut Pumpernickel Bread (page 163), or a handful of Spiced Honey-Glazed Nuts (page 113)

DINNER

Stress-Less Shiitake and Asparagus Risotto (page 126), or Favorite Sweet, Spicy, and Crunchy Meat Loaf (page 128) and Zesty Broccoli with Garlic and Ginger (page 145)

Thursday

BREAKFAST

Fortifying Flourless Chicken Flapjacks (page 84), or Regenerating Herb Scrambled Eggs (page 83)

LUNCH

Pumping Jumping Bean Salad (page 96), or Feel-Good Turkey or Salmon Tomato Panini (page 102)

SNACK (OPTIONAL)

Super-Healthful Hummus (page 150) with 2 Low-Carb Herbed Cheddar Crackers (page 109)

DINNER

Comforting Cheddar and Broccoli Quiche with Quinoa Crust (page 123), or Tantalizing Thai Fish Cakes (page 132) with Anti-Ox Pumpkin and Cauliflower Mash (page 114)

Friday

BREAKFAST

Regenerating Herb Scrambled Eggs (page 83), or Protein-Powered Muesli with Coconut and Raisins (page 83)

LUNCH

Vitalizing Broccoli and Cauliflower Salad (page 93), or Gluten-Free Mediterranean Veggie Pizza (pages 99–100)

SNACK (OPTIONAL)

Bone-Strengthening Lemon Tahini (page 151) with 2 Low-Carb Herbed Cheddar Crackers (page 109), or a handful of Spiced Honey-Glazed Nuts (page 113)

DINNER

Nutrient-Rich Roasted Quinoa with Mushrooms, Cumin, and Coriander (page 120), or Mighty Moroccan Chicken Tagine (page 136) with Balancing Basmati Almond Rice (page 146) and Zesty Broccoli with Garlic and Ginger (page 145)

DESSERT

Sweet Brown Rice Pudding with an Antioxidant Twist (page 172)

Saturday

BREAKFAST

Strengthening Sun-Dried Tomato and Feta-Chive Omelet (page 86), or Hearty Mediterranean Frittata (page 87)

LUNCH

Cardioprotective Salmon Caesar Salad (page 94) with Cardioprotective Caeser Salad Dressing (page 97), or Vibrant Avocado and Veggie Salsa Collard Wrap (page 101)

SNACK (OPTIONAL)

Blood-Sugar-Balancing Butternut and Leek Pies (page 110), or a handful of Spiced Honey-Glazed Nuts (page 113)

DINNER

Spicy Moroccan Tempeh with Lentils (page 117), or Soul-Warming Tuna Lasagna (page 133) with Sumptuous Spinach and Swiss Chard with Pine Nuts (page 147)

DESSERT

Berry-Beneficial Blueberry and Pecan Pie (page 169)

ENDNOTES

INTRODUCTION

Walker, Ross, M.D., presentation on metabolic syndrome, University of California, Los Angeles, May 30, 2013.

CHAPTER 1: THE WRONGFUL DEMONIZATION OF SATURATED FAT

Emken, E. A., Adlof, R. O., and Gulley, R. M. "Dietary linoleic acid influences desaturation and acylation of deuterium-labeled linoleic and linolenic acids in young adult males." *Biochimica et Biophysica Acta–Molecular and Cell Biology of Lipids*, August 4, 1994; 1213(3): 277-88.

Hoenselaar, R. "Saturated fat and cardiovascular disease: The discrepancy between the scientific literature and dietary advice." *Nutrition*, February 2012; 28(2): 118-23.

Mozaffarian, D., Rimm, E. B., and Herrington, D. M. "Dietary fats, carbohydrate, and progression of coronary atherosclerosis in postmenopausal women." *American Journal of Clinical Nutrition*, November 2004; 80(5): 1175-84. www.ncbi.nlm.nih.gov/pubmed/15531663.

Siri-Arino, P. W., Sun, Q., Hu, F. B., et al. "Meta-analysis of prospective cohort studies evaluating the association of saturated fat with cardiovascular disease." *American Journal of Clinical Nutrition*, March 2010; 91(3): 535-46. Epub, January 13, 2010.

CHAPTER 2: HORMONES 101

American Diabetes Association, American Diabetes Association website, "Living with diabetes: Complications." www.diabetes.org/living-with-diabetes/complications/, accessed June 12, 2013.

Ford, E. S., Giles, W. H., and Dietz, W. H. "Prevalence of the metabolic syndrome among U.S. adults: Findings from the third National Health and Nutrition Examination Survey." *JAMA*, January 16, 2002; 287(3): 356-9.

Gaziano, J. M., Hennekens, C. H., O'Donnell, C. J., et al. "Fasting triglycerides, high-density lipoprotein, and risk of myocardial infarction." *Circulation*, 1997; 96: 2520-25.

Miller, M. "What is the association between the triglyceride-to-high-density-lipoprotein cholesterol ratio and insulin resistance?" *Medscape Education*, Medscape website, www.medscape.org/viewarticle/588474. Accessed June 12, 2013.

O'Connell, Jeff. *Sugar Nation* (Hyperion, 2010).

Rabbani, N., Godfrey, L., Xue, M., et al. "Glycation of LDL by methylglyoxal increases arterial atherogenicity: A possible contributor to increased risk of cardiovascular disease in diabetes." *Diabetes*, July 2011; 60(7): 1973-80.

Song, F., and Schmidt, A. M. "Glycation and insulin resistance: Novel mechanisms and unique targets?" *Arteriosclerosis, Thrombosis, and Vascular Biology*, August 2012; 32(8): 1760-5.

Urbina, E. M., et al. "Triglyceride to HDL-C ratio and increased arterial stiffness in children, adolescents, and young adults." *Pediatrics,* April 2013; 131(4): e1082-90.

Volek, J., and Phinney, S. "The art and science of low-carb living." *Beyond Obesity, LLC*, 2011.

CHAPTER 3: THE CASE AGAINST SUGAR

Casey, J. "The hidden ingredient that can sabotage your diet." *WebMD Weight Loss Clinic*, www.medicineNet.com, accessed June 7, 2013. www.sciencedaily.com/releases/2013/01/130101182010.htm.

Page, K., Chan, O., Arora, J., et al. "Effects of fructose vs glucose on regional cerebral blood flow in brain regions involved with appetite and reward pathways." *JAMA*, 2013; 309(1): 63-70. doi: 10. 1001/jama.2012.116975.

Rutledge, A. C., and Adeli, K. "Fructose and the metabolic syndrome: Pathophysiology and molecular mechanisms." *Nutrition Reviews*, June 2007; 65(6): S13-23.

Tappy, L., Lê, K. A. "Metabolic effects of fructose and the worldwide increase in obesity." *Physiological Reviews*, January 2010; 90(1): 23-46. doi: 10.1152/physrev.00019.2009. www.ncbi.nlm.nih.gov/pubmed/20086073.

CHAPTER 4: THE TRUTH ABOUT GRAINS

Fasano, A., Berti, I., Gerarduzzi, T., et al. "Prevalence of celiac disease in at-risk and not-at-risk groups in the United States." *Archives of Internal Medicine*, 2003; 163(3): 268-92.

Jenkins, D. J., Wolever, T. M., Taylor, R. H., et al. "Glycemic index of foods: A physiological basis for carbohydrate exchange." *American Journal of Clinical Nutrition*, March 1981; 34(3): 362-6.

Lieberman, Shari. *The Gluten Connection*. Rodale Press, 2007.

Liu, S., Manson, J. E., Buring, J. E., et al. "Relation between a diet with a high glycemic load and plasma concentrations of high-sensitivity C-reactive protein in middle-aged women." *American Journal of Clinical Nutrition*, March 2002; 75(3): 492-8. www.ncbi.nlm.nih.gov/pubmed/11864854.

Ludvigsson, J. F., Montgomery, S. M., Ekbom, A., et al. "Small-intestinal histopathology and mortality risk in celiac disease." *JAMA*, September 16, 2009; 302(11): 1171-8. http://jama.jamanetwork.com/article.aspx?articleid=184586.

Roeder, A. "'Whole grain' not always healthy." *Harvard University Gazette*. Accessed June 11, 2013. http://news.harvard.edu/gazette/story/2013/01/whole-grain-not-always-healthy/.

Sieri, S., Krogh, V., Berrino, F., et al. "Dietary glycemic load and index and risk of coronary heart disease in a large Italian cohort: the EPICOR study." *Archives of Internal Medicine*, April 12, 2010; 170(7): 640-7. www.ncbi.nlm.nih.gov/pubmed/20386010.

Tel Aviv University. "How high carbohydrate foods can raise risk for heart problems." *ScienceDaily*, June 27, 2009. Accessed June 11, 2013, www.sciencedaily.com/releases/2009/06/090625133215.htm.

CHAPTER 5: FOODS FOR A HEALTHY HEART

Bes-Rastrollo, M., Wedick, N. M., Martinez-Gonzalez, M. A., et al. "Prospective study of nut consumption, long-term weight change, and obesity risk in women."

American Journal of Clinical Nutrition, June 2009; 89(6): 1913–9. http://ajcn.nutrition.org/content/89/6/1913.full.

Griffin, R. M. "How fiber protects your heart." WebMD feature, www.webmd.com/diet/fiber-health-benefits-11/fiber-heart, accessed June 11, 2013.

Lund University. "Fibre protects against cardiovascular disease, especially in women." *ScienceDaily,* April 16, 2012. Retrieved June 11, 2013, from www.sciencedaily.com/releases/2012/04/120416112920.htm.

Ratliff C., Mutungi, G., Puglisi, M. J., et al. "Eggs modulate the inflammatory response to carbohydrate restricted diets in overweight men." *Nutrition & Metabolism,* February 20, 2008; 5:6. doi: 10.1186/1743-7075-5-6. www.ncbi.nlm.nih.gov/pubmed/18289377.

Sano, J., Inami, S., Seimiya, K., et al. "Effects of green tea Intake on the development of coronary artery disease." *Circulation Journal*, 2004; 68(7): 665–70. www.ncbi.nlm.nih.gov/pubmed/15226633.

CHAPTER 6: SUPPLEMENTS FOR A HEALTHY HEART

Jänicke, C., Grünwald, J., and Brendler, T. *Handbuch Phytotherapie*. Stuttgart, Germany: Wissenschaftliche Verlagsgesellschaft; 2003.

Michos, E. D., and Melamed, M. L. "Vitamin D and cardiovascular disease risk." *Current Opinion in Clinical Nutrition and Metabolic Care*, January 2008; 11(1): 7–12. www.ncbi.nlm.nih.gov/pubmed/18090651.

Perrinjaquet-Moccetti, T., Busjahn, A., Schmidlin, C., et al. "Food supplementation with an olive (Olea europaea L.) leaf extract reduces blood pressure in borderline hypertensive monozygotic twins." *Phytotherapy Research*, 2008; 22: 1239–42.

Pfister, R., Sharp, S. J., Luben, R., et al. "Plasma vitamin C predicts incident heart failure in men and women in European prospective investigation into cancer and nutrition–Norfolk Prospective Study." *American Heart Journal*, August 2011; 162(2): 246–53. doi: 10.1016/j.ahj.2011.05.007. Epub July 7, 2011. www.ncbi.nlm.nih.gov/pubmed/21835284.

Pilz, S., Kienreich, K., Tomaschitz, A., et al. "Vitamin D and cardiovascular disease: Update and outlook." *Scandinavian Journal of Clinical and Laboratory Investigation*, suppl., April 2012; 243: 83–91, www.ncbi.nlm.nih.gov/pubmed/22536768.

Rasmussen, H. S., McNair, P., Gøransson, L., et al. "Magnesium deficiency in patients with ischemic heart disease with and without acute myocardial infarction uncovered by an intravenous loading test." *Archives of Internal Medicine*, February 1988; 148(2): 329–32. www.ncbi.nlm.nih.gov/pubmed/3341837.

Ried, K., Sullivan, T. R., Fakler, P., et al. "Effect of cocoa on blood pressure." *Cochrane Database of Systematic Reviews*, August 15, 2012; 8. www.ncbi.nlm.nih.gov/pubmed/22895979.

Spencer, A., and, Saul, A. W. "Vitamin C and cardiovascular disease: A personal viewpoint." *Orthomolecular Medicine News Service*, June 22, 2010. http://orthomolecular.org/resources/omns/v06n20.shtml, accessed June 18, 2013.

Wang, N. P., Wang, Z. F., Tootle, S., et al. "Curcumin promotes cardiac repair and ameliorates cardiac dysfunction following myocardial infarction." *British Journal of Pharmacology*, December 2012; 167(7): 1550–62. doi: 10.1111/j.1476-5381.2012.02109.x. www.ncbi.nlm.nih.gov/pubmed/22823335.

ACKNOWLEDGMENTS

Jonny Bowden: "You didn't build that."

That quote, taken out of context, was widely thought to mean that one's own hard work and determination don't count for anything.

But that's not what it means at all.

Every one of our accomplishments happens in a context. Even the most brilliant innovators didn't spring from the head of Zeus. They had mentors, and teachers, and coaches. They had friends. They had family. They went to schools. They learned from the people in their field. They played on teams. They *built* teams.

That's what "You didn't build that" *really* means. You don't really build anything *alone*.

I can't think of a single success I've had in my career that would have been possible had I not had an incredible team—affectionately known as "Team Jonny"—to support me professionally or to just generally enrich my life so that when I do write professionally I have something to say! So this book is a perfect time to say thanks to all of them.

First and foremost, my amazing co-author on both *The Great Cholesterol Myth* and this book, cardiologist Stephen Sinatra, a leader in the field of integrative medicine whom I am honored to call a friend and colleague. And Deirdre Rawlings, whose recipes and wisdom made this book possible.

My Los Angeles family—Sky, Doug, Bootsie, Zack, Sage, and Luke.

My friends—Jeannette Bessinger, Peter Breger, Scott Ellis, Liz Neporent, Lauree Dash, Oz Garcia, Gina Lombardi, Kevin Sizemore and Gunnar, Susan Wood, Christopher Duncan, Charlie Ann, Miles, and Brock, Diana Lederman, and Ketura Whitman. Lauren Trotter. Marianna Riccio. I love you all.

My assistant, Amber Linder, who makes everything in my professional life work. Anja Christy, best friend and spiritual advisor-in-residence. My lawyer, Jeannette Boudreau. Robert Kernochan and Laura Hunt. Scott Nelson. Chad Ellingwood. My business partner in Rockwell Nutrition, Marc Stockman. Gabriella Periera. Dr. Richard Lewis. The entire team at Natural Health Sherpa—Marc, Jeff Radich, Spencer Smith, Alison Held, and the incomparable Jason Boehm. Mike Danielson and Heather Stetler at Media Relations. Christopher Loch. Anita Waxman and the team at SelfHealth. My indefatigable agent, Coleen O'Shea of the Allen O'Shea Literary Agency and my intrepid, beloved editor, Cara Connors. My nephews Pace and Jared and my niece Cadence. My professional pals—JJ Virgin (my sister from another mother), Daniel Amen, Prudence Hall, Glen Depke, Susanne Bennett, Sara Gottfried. My tennis buddies, even Jack. Ramon Osa. Zack Kleinman. Oliver and Roxy. Jade and Zoe. Luna. Emily. Bubba. Lucy.

And, of course, the leader of the pack—my beloved Michelle.

Deirdre Rawlings: It was such an honor and a privilege to work on this project for a number of reasons. Designing and creating the recipes for this audience was a heartfelt joy as I personally have been touched by this condition and wanted to ensure all of the ingredients will nourish your heart and feed your spirit.

Working with these two amazing doctors, Stephen Sinatra and Jonny Bowden, was a thrill and a sublime experience. I have admired and respected their work in the nutrition and integrative health field for many years.

Thank you to my fabulous and fun editor, Cara Connors, whose attention to detail and sharp editor's eyes transformed the work into something extraordinary. Many thanks to Jill Alexander, senior acquisitions editor, for believing in me and supporting my work. Your wisdom, kind words, and support mean the world to me. Special thanks to John Gettings. Your guidance and expertise on every project I have had the pleasure of working on with you has added tremendous value for our readers, and you are always up for going that extra mile.

Thank you Coleen O'Shea, my literary agent, who has a wealth of expertise when it comes to knowing how to streamline a project and simply give our audience what they want and need.

Many thanks to all the wonderful people at Fair Winds Press who contributed to this project and who always strive to produce a top-notch publication from start to finish.

ABOUT THE AUTHORS

Jonny Bowden, Ph.D., C.N.S., is a nationally known expert on weight loss, nutrition, and health. He is a board-certified nutritionist with a master's degree in psychology and the author of twelve books on health, healing, food, and longevity, including three best-sellers, *The Great Cholesterol Myth* (coauthored with Stephen T. Sinatra), *The 150 Healthiest Foods on Earth,* and *Living Low Carb.* A frequent guest on television and radio, he has appeared on CNN, MSNBC, Fox News, ABC, NBC, and CBS as an expert on nutrition, weight loss, and longevity. He is the nutrition editor for *Pilates Style* and is a regular contributor to *Clean Eating, Better Nutrition,* and *Total Health Online.*

He has contributed to articles for dozens of print and online publications, including *The New York Times, The Wall Street Journal, Forbes, O (The Oprah Magazine), The Daily Beast, The Huffington Post, Vanity Fair Online, Time, Oxygen, Marie Claire, Diabetes Focus, GQ, US Weekly, Cosmopolitan, Self, Fitness, Family Circle, Allure, Men's Heath, Prevention, InStyle,* and *Natural Health.* He appears regularly as an expert on ABC-TV Los Angeles. He is a member of the American College of Nutrition and the American Society for Nutrition. He lives in the Topanga Canyon section of Southern California with his dogs, Lucy and Emily. Follow him at www.jonnybowden.com and @ jonnybowden.

Stephen T. Sinatra, M.D., F.A.C.C., F.A.C.N., C.N.S., C.B.T., is a board-certified cardiologist and assistant clinical professor of medicine at the University of Connecticut School of Medicine. He is the author of many books, including *The Great Cholesterol Myth* (coauthored with Jonny Bowden), *The Sinatra Solution: Metabolic Cardiology, Earthing: The Most Important Health Discovery Ever, Reverse Heart Disease Now,* and *Lower Your Blood Pressure in Eight Weeks.* Certified as a bioenergetic psychotherapist and nutrition and antiaging specialist, Dr. Sinatra integrates psychological, nutraceutical, and electroceutical therapies in the matrix of healing. He is the founder of www.heartmdinstitute.com, an informational website dedicated to promoting public awareness of integrative medicine. He is a fellow in the American College of Cardiology and the American College of Nutrition. His websites include www.drsinatra.com.

Deirdre Rawlings holds a Ph.D. in holistic nutrition, a master's degree in herbal medicine, and is a naturopathic doctor. She is the founder of Nutri-Living, is a healthy cooking coach, and designs condition-specific meal plans and recipes. She is the author of *Foods That Fight Fibromyalgia, Fermented Foods for Health,* and coauthor of *Beat Sugar Addiction Now! Cookbook.* She lives in Atlanta.

INDEX

A

agave, 38
Almighty Almond and Walnut Pumpernickel Bread, 163
Almighty Avocado and Black Bean Salad, 91
almonds, 113, 146, 151, 164, 171
anchovies, 97
Anti-Inflammatory Turmeric Turkey Burgers, 140
Anti-Ox Orange Mousse, 170
Anti-Ox Pumpkin and Cauliflower Mash, 144
Antioxidant BBQ sauce, 154
Antioxidant Ginger, Date, and Orange Chutney, 155
apples, 168, 169
Artichoke Herb Dip, 114-115
artichokes, 114-115
asparagus, 126
avocados, 91, 98, 99, 101

B

Balancing Basmati Almond Rice, 146
bananas, 81
BBQ sauce, 154
beans, 58-59, 88, 91, 96, 107, 118, 119, 143, 148. see also specific beans
beef, 112, 127, 128, 129
    grass-fed, 54-55
bell peppers, 99-100
berries, 81, 155, 169. see also specific berries
Berry-Beneficial Blueberry and Pecan Pie, 169
Berry-Buzz Jelly, 155
black beans, 91, 119
blinis, 114-115
Blood Sugar-Balancing Butternut & Leek Pies, 110
blueberries, 155, 166, 168, 169
Blueberry and Apple Crumble Gone Nuts, 168
Bone-Building French Cream, 157
Bone-Strengthening Lemon Tahini, 151
Brain-Boosting Salmon Eggs Benedict, 85
breads
    Almighty Almond and Walnut Pumpernickel Bread, 163
    Nourishing Crusty Onion and Parmesan Rolls, 165
    Powerhouse Pumpkin, Spice, and Almond Bread, 164
breakfast
    Brain-Boosting Salmon Eggs Benedict, 85
    Cheddar cheese, 89
    Fortifying Flourless Chicken Flapjacks, 84
    Get-Up-and-Go Banana Berry Quinoa Porridge, 81
    Hearty Mediterranean Frittata, 87
    leisurely weekend, 85-89
    Melt-in-Your-Mouth Baked Granola, 82

Protein-Powered Muesli with Coconut and Raisins, 83
quick weekday, 81-84
Regenerating Herb Scrambled Eggs, 83
Strengthening Sun-Dried Tomato and Feta-Chie Omelet, 86
Super-Energizing Baked Beans, 88
broccoli, 93, 123, 145
broths
    Digestive Vegetable Stock, 104
    Nutritive Chicken Stock, 103
brown rice, 172
brownies, 173
browning, 129
brûlée, 166
Build-Me-Up Butternut and Macadamia Nut Bisque, 108
burgers, 118, 140
butternut squash, 108, 110, 121
butters, 156

C

cabbage, 95, 107
cacao nibs, 173
cacao powder, 173
caesar salad, 94
cakes
    Health-Gratifying Grapefruit and Orange Cake, 162
    Luscious Lemon-Pineapple Yogurt Cake, 161
Calming Coconut-Date Balls, 114
carbohydrates, 34-35, 37
Cardioprotective Green Beans, 148
Cardioprotective Salmon Caesar Salad, 94
Cardioprotective Salmon Caesar Salad Dressing, 97
carrots, 104, 105, 122, 149
casseroles, 124
cauliflower, 93, 111, 142, 144
celery, 104
chard, 147
Cheddar cheese, 89, 109, 123
chicken, 84, 95, 103, 111, 129, 136, 137, 138, 139
    Mood-Boosting Chicken and Pineapple Coleslaw with Coconut-Lime Dressing, 92
chickpeas, 141
chile peppers, 153-154, 158
chili sauce, 153-154
chives, 86, 105
chocolate, 173
    dark, 59
cholesterol, 5-9, 14-16, 28-29, 30, 32-33
chutneys, 155, 158
cilantro, 95, 98
citrus bergamot extract, 72, 74

CLA (conjugated linoleic acid), 19
cocoa flavanols, 75
coconut, 83, 114, 152, 173
    Mood-Boosting Chicken and Pineapple Coleslaw with Coconut-
    Lime Dressing, 92
coconut milk, 138
Coconut-Lime Dressing, 92
coleslaw, Mood-Boosting Chicken and Pineapple Coleslaw with
  Coconut-Lime Dressing, 92
collard greens, 101
Comforting Cheddar and Broccoli Quiche with Quinoa Crust, 123
condiments
    Antioxidant Ginger, Date, and Orange Chutney, 155
    Artichoke Herb Dip, 114-115
    Berry-Buzz Jelly, 155
    Bone-Building French Cream, 157
    Bone-Strengthening Lemon Tahini, 151
    Heart-Healthy Almond Mayonnaise, 151
    Immune-Building Lemon-Ginger Butter, 156
    Mediterranean Black Olive Tapenade, 150
    Probiotic Fruit Chutney, 158
    Restorative Cucumber-Yogurt Raita, 157
    Super-Healthful Hummus, 150
conjugated linoleic acid (CLA), 19
cookies, Hearty Hazelnut Rounds, 160
cooking oils, 20-21, 22, 61
CoQ$_{10}$, 64-65, 74
coriander, 120
crackers, 109
cream, 157, 170, 171, 172
crumbles, 168
cumin, 120
curcumin, 73, 74
curries, 137
custards, 167

D
dark chocolate, 59
dates, 114, 155, 171, 173
desserts
    Anti-Ox Orange Mousse, 170
    Berry-Beneficial Blueberry and Pecan Pie, 169
    Blueberry and Apple Crumble Gone Nuts, 168
    Energy-Giving Coconut, Almond, and Raisin Custard, 167
    Fortifying Fig and Minty Blueberry Brûlée, 166
    Health-Gratifying Grapefruit and Orange Cake, 162
    Hearty Hazelnut Rounds, 160
    Luscious Lemon-Pineapple Yogurt Cake, 161
    No-Bake Superfood Fudge Brownies, 173
    Soothing Pear, Date, and Almond Pudding with Grapefruit
    Cream Sauce, 171
    Sweet Brown Rice Pudding with an Antioxidant Twist, 172
Detoxifying Lima Bean Blinis with Artichoke Herbed Dip, 114-115
Digestive Vegetable Stock, 104
dinners
    Anti-Inflammatory Turmeric Turkey Burgers, 140
    Comforting Cheddar and Broccoli Quiche with Quinoa Crust,
    123
    Easy Beef Sauté with Fresh Herbs, 127

    Favorite Sweet, Spicy, and Crunchy Meatloaf, 128
    Fisherman's Omega-3 Fish Fingers, 130
    Healing Baked Halibut or Salmon and Shiitake, 134
    Hi-Fibe Red Bean Burgers, 118
    High-Fiber Butternut Gnocchi with Herbed Cream Sauce, 121
    Immune-Boosting Thai Tempeh Cakes with Sweet Spicy
    Dipping Sauce, 125
    Mega-Omega Spice-Crusted Salmon, 131
    Metabolism-Boosting Chicken Curry Feast, 137
    Mighty Moroccan Chicken Tagine, 136
    Nice and Spiced Beef or Chicken Stir-Fry, 129
    Nutrient-Rich Roasted Quinoa with Mushrooms, Cumin, and
    Coriander, 120
    Protein-Packed Vegetarian Shepherd's Pie, 119
    Revitalizing Vegetable Biryani, 122
    Soul-Warming Tuna Lasagna, 133
    Spicy Moroccan Tempeh with Lentils, 117
    Spicy Shrimp and Tomato Kebabs with Herbed Lima Beans, 135
    Strengthening Spinach, Feta, and Rice Casserole, 124
    Stress-Less Shiitake and Asparagus Risotto, 126
    Supercharged Chicken or Turkey Meatloaf, 139
    Tantalizing Chicken Satay with Powerful Peanut-Coconut
    Sauce, 138
    Tantalizing Thai Fish Cakes, 132
dressings
    Cardioprotective Salmon Caesar Salad Dressing, 97
    Coconut-Lime Dressing, 92
    Energizing Thai Spice Salad Dressing, 98
    Holy-Moly Guacamole Dressing, 98
    Simply Nourishing Salad Dressing, 97
d-ribose, 66-67, 74

E
Easy Beef Sauté with Fresh Herbs, 127
eggs, 56, 83, 84, 85, 86, 87, 94, 97
Energizing Thai Spice Chicken Salad, 95
Energizing Thai Spice Salad Dressing, 98
Energy-Giving Coconut, Almond, and Raisin Custard, 167

F
fats, 13-23
    cooking oils, 20-21, 22
    fatty acids, 13
    monounsaturated, 13
    omega-3s, 13, 14, 16-17, 18-19, 68-70, 74
    omega-6s, 13, 14, 18-19
    omega-9s, 11, 16-17
    polyunsaturated, 14, 18-19
    saturated, 10-18
    trans fats, 17-18, 19, 53
fatty acids, 13, 68-70, 74. see also specific fatty acids
fava beans, 143
Favorite Sweet, Spicy, and Crunchy Meatloaf, 128
Feel-Good Turkey or Salmon Tomato Panini, 102
ferments. see also yogurt
    Antioxidant Ginger, Date, and Orange Chutney, 155
    Immune-Boosting Yogurt, 158
    Probiotic Fruit Chutney, 158
feta cheese, 86, 124

figs, 166
fish, 130, 132, 134. *see also specific kinds of fish*
    wild-caught, 55
fish oil, 68-70, 74
fish sauce, 98
fish stock, 132
Fisherman's Omega-3 Fish Fingers, 130
foods, heart-healthy, 52-62
Fortifying Fig and Minty Blueberry Brûlée, 166
Fortifying Flourless Chicken Flapjacks, 84
Fragrant Cauliflower-Quinoa Risotto, 142
frittatas, 87
fructose, 37, 38-41
fruits, 57. *see also specific fruits*

G
garbanzo beans, 96, 141
garlic, 61, 72-73, 74, 145
Get-Up-and-Go Banana Berry Quinoa Porridge, 81
Get-Up-and-Go Indian Chickpea Delight, 141
ginger, 105, 145, 149, 155, 156, 158
glucose, 37
gluten, 46-48
gluten-free diets, 48-49
Gluten-Free Mediterranean Veggie Pizza, 99-100
glycation, 30, 32-33
glycemic index, 50-51
gnocchi, 121
grains, 42-51
granola, 82
grapefruit, 162, 171
green beans, 148
green tea, 60

H
halibut, 130, 132, 134
hazelnuts, 160
HDL cholesterol, 15-16, 28-29
Healing Baked Halibut or Salmon and Shiitake, 134
Health-Giving Hollandaise Sauce, 153
Health-Gratifying Grapefruit and Orange Cake, 162
heart disease, 6, 30, 32-33
Heart-Healthy Almond Mayonnaise, 151
heart-healthy foods, 52-62
heart-healthy supplements, 63-75
Heart-Protective Carrot-Ginger Soup with Chives, 105
Hearty Hazelnut Rounds, 160
Hearty Mediterranean Frittata, 87
herbs, 83, 89, 114-115, 121, 127, 135. *see also specific herbs*
Hi-Fibe Red Bean Burgers, 118
High-Energy Chicken & Cauliflower Croquettes, 111
High-Fiber Butternut Gnocchi with Herbed Cream Sauce, 121
high-fructose corn syrup, 35-36, 37
Hollandaise sauce, 153
Holy-Moly Guacamole Dressing, 98
honey, 113, 160, 161
hormones, 23-33
hot sauce, 153-154

hummus, 150
hypertension, 29

I
Immune-Boosting Basque Bean and Cabbage Soup, 107
Immune-Boosting Thai Tempeh Cakes with Sweet Spicy Dipping Sauce, 125
Immune-Boosting Yogurt, 158
Immune-Building Lemon-Ginger Butter, 156
inflammation, 18-19, 30, 31-32, 48
insulin, 23-33
insulin resistance, 25-33, 40

J
jellies, 155

K
kale, 145
kebabs, 135

L
lamb, 112
lasagna, 133
L-carnitine, 65-66, 74
LDL cholesterol, 15-16, 33
leeks, 104, 110
lemon, 156, 161
lemon juice, 151
lemongrass, 98
lentils, 106, 117, 119
lettuce, 94
lima beans, 114-115, 135, 143
lime, Mood-Boosting Chicken and Pineapple Coleslaw with Coconut-Lime Dressing, 92
Love-Your-Heart Red Lentil Soup, 106
low-carb diets, 16-17
Low-Carb Herbed Cheddar Crackers, 109
low-fat diets, 13
Luscious Lemon-Pineapple Yogurt Cake, 161
Luscious Lima Bean Mash, 143

M
macadamia nuts, 108
mackerel, 130, 132
magnesium, 68, 74
meatless main dishes
    Comforting Cheddar and Broccoli Quiche with Quinoa Crust, 123
    Hi-Fibe Red Bean Burgers, 118
    High-Fiber Butternut Gnocchi with Herbed Cream Sauce, 121
    Immune-Boosting Thai Tempeh Cakes with Sweet Spicy Dipping Sauce, 125
    Nutrient-Rich Roasted Quinoa with Mushrooms, Cumin, and Coriander, 120
    Protein-Packed Vegetarian Shepherd's Pie, 119
    Revitalizing Vegetable Biryani, 122
    Spicy Moroccan Tempeh with Lentils, 117
    Strengthening Spinach, Feta, and Rice Casserole, 124